The World Food Programme in Global Politics

The World Food Programme in Global Politics

Sandy Ross

Viva Books
New Delhi | Mumbai | Chennai | Kolkata
Bengaluru | Hyderabad | Kochi | Guwahati

First Indian Edition 2011

VIVA BOOKS PRIVATE LIMITED

- 4737/23 Ansari Road, Daryaganj, New Delhi 110 002
  E-mail: vivadelhi@vivagroupindia.net, Tel. 42242200
- 76, Service Industries, Shirvane, Sector 1, Nerul, Navi Mumbai 400 706
  E-mail: vivamumbai@vivagroupindia.net, Tel. 27721273, 27721274
- Jamals Fazal Chambers, 26 Greams Road, Chennai 600 006
  E-mail: vivachennai@vivagroupindia.net, Tel. 28290304, 28294241
- B-103, Jindal Towers, 21/1A/3 Darga Road, Kolkata 700 017
  E-mail: vivakolkata@vivagroupindia.net, Tel. 22836381, 22816713
- 7, Sovereign Park Apartments, 56-58, K. R. Road, Basavanagudi, Bengaluru 560 004
  E-mail: vivabangalore@vivagroupindia.net, Tel. 26607409, 26607410
- 101-102 Mughal Marc Aptt., 3-4-637 to 641, Narayanguda, Hyderabad 500 029
  E-mail: vivahyderabad@vivagroupindia.net, Tel. 27564481, 27564482
- First Floor, Beevi Towers, SRM Road, Kaloor, Kochi 682 018, Kerala
  E-mail: vivakochi@vivagroupindia.net, Tel: 0484-2403055, 2403056
- 232, GNB Road, Beside UCO Bank, Silpukhuri, Guwahati 781 003
  E-mail: vivaguwahati@vivagroupindia.net, Tel: 0361-2666386

Published by arrangement with

Lynne Rienner Publishers, Inc.
1800 30th Street, Boulder
Colorado 80301

ISBN : 978-81-309-1857-0

Published by Vinod Vasishtha for Viva Books Private Limited, 4737/23, Ansari Road, Daryaganj New Delhi - 110 002. Printed and bound by Anand Sons, Delhi.

For Helen Moffat Ross (1933-2000)

Contents

Tables and Charts

Tables

Charts

Acknowledgments

A book has many origins, but in this case it is important to acknowledge the role of Nancy Viviani, who first suggested the World Food Programme might be a good research project. At the University of Melbourne, Derek McDougall was unstinting in his support, and I must also thank Robyn Eckersley, who gave me crucial feedback and went beyond the call of duty to help me clarify my thinking about legitimacy.

Jim Ingram and Catherine Bertini were remarkably open and generous with their time and their knowledge.

The research I undertook would not have been possible without considerable assistance from the WFP—both as an organization and from individuals within it. The WFP gave me generous and open access to its workings as an observer to its Executive Board meeting in June 2005, along with a month at its Rome headquarters for interviewing and archival research. For assistance with my research at the WFP I owe particular thanks to Brian Gray, Allan Jury, Andreas Psoroulas, Sonnali Wickrama, Marianne Ward, Evelyn Togbe, and Anthony Beattie. Also in Rome, Nick Bredholt of Caritas International and Sylvie Mancini of Médicins Sans Frontières were very helpful. Joanne di Natale helped enormously with accommodations.

In Geneva, Katharina Samara, Ed Schenkenberg of the International Council of Volunteer Agencies, and Martin Loftus and Ioli Kimyaci at the UNHCR provided me with valuable assistance. In the United States, Lauren Landis, Margaret Zeigler, and Rick Leach were particularly generous with their time and advice. Simon Chesterman gave me valuable access to some of his extensive networks. In Australia, I am grateful to Alan Wilkinson and John Langmore for their help. Several AUSAID staff, who requested anonymity, were also of assistance.

As the book developed, the list of people I wish to thank for their help grew. Ray Hopkins and Jan Aart Scholte were generous with their feedback and encouragement, and acute with their comments. Thanks to Lynne Rienner for her interest and encouragement, and to Claire Vlcek for enthusiastic and professional assistance with the process of publication. Two anonymous reviewers also provided helpful feedback on the manuscript. A special thanks is due to my friend and colleague at the University of Melbourne Siobhan O'Sullivan, who provided useful comments for me on draft chapters.

My sister, Alison Ross, and brother-in-law, Amir Ahmadi, my father, Colin Ross, and his wife, Gay, all gave emotional and intellectual support—as well as helped with the more important things like child care—that make book writing possible.

Saving the most important for last, thanks are due to my partner, Cath Harmer, and our children, Alexandra and Joshua. They have borne with patience the occasional hint that this project might displace them from their centrality to my life.

Sandy Ross

1
The World Food Programme in the International System

We live in a world in which transnational problems, from existential threats such as climate change to various types of economic and humanitarian crises, have come to shape the lives of everyone on the planet. The problem of global hunger is one such crisis that threatens to intensify as food prices rise. The significance of this particular issue was brought home by the 2007-2008 global food crisis, which by late 2009 had left the numbers of malnourished people at over 1 billion, according to the Food and Agriculture Organization of the United Nations (FAO).

So far none of these crises seem to have been addressed convincingly by existing political structures or current political leaders, and there is a large question mark over whether the architecture of global governance is capable of responding adequately to them in its current forms. This raises some important questions: can we say that credible and successful global governance exists at all? If it does exist, what are its political characteristics, and do we have any prospect of fostering and developing organizations, alliances and relationships with those characteristics? This book seeks to start answering these questions with an examination of what is arguably the most successful and politically legitimate of the agencies in the United Nations (UN) system – the World Food Programme (WFP).

International relations since 1945 has been dominated by the evolution of a surprisingly robust international institutional architecture centered on the United Nations (UN) system, in which almost all nations, big and small, participate. These levels of participation implicitly accord that system some degree of legitimacy. Yet at the center of this system lies a paradox. The United States of America (US) has been the pre-eminent power amongst nations since 1945, a position reflected both in its role in the founding and viability of the UN system, and in its capacity to operate beyond the bounds of that, purportedly universal, system. In this, the US has both built the legitimacy of the system, and, at times, undermined that legitimacy.

The US/UN relationship involves many tensions between, on the one hand, the universality of the UN system, and on the other hand, the key role of the US in establishing the UN system and its ongoing material importance to that system. The failure of the 2009 Copenhagen summit on climate change highlighted these tensions, although the 2008 Global Financial Crisis and serious economic downturn have also suggested a decline in US power and underlined the rise of China as a potential rival to the US. Nevertheless, it is important that an examination of the WFP, an agency within the UN system, grasp the political centrality of the US as a 'hegemonic' actor – in the sense of not only material dominance, but of its ideological role in leading the construction of the rules of the system (Ikenberry and Kupchan 1990, 299-307).

The WFP is an international organization in which the US has a dominant role, traditionally explained with reference to the use of food aid to serve its national agricultural interests, in effect subsidising US agriculture at the expense of poorer countries. Given this, the WFP might appear to be a strong case for an analysis that depicts international cooperation as a by-product of states acting in pursuit of their interests, but this study shows there are more than just narrowly conceived state economic interests at play in the processes of global governance.

While neoliberal literature assumes the central role of interests in explaining the behaviour of states and non-state actors, the 'constructivist turn' (Checkel 1998) in international relations (IR) scholarship has highlighted the centrality of norms to the construction of identities and interests. The constructivist critique of the neoliberal assumption that interests are pre-eminent requires a deeper consideration of where interests come from and how they are constructed or perceived.

However, constructivist approaches themselves risk paralleling the problem of an *a priori* construction of interests by doing the same thing with norms – assuming that norms sit somehow behind interests in a linear relationship. As this study of the WFP shows, the significance of norms and interests lies in their *interrelationship*. Norms and interests are in a mutually constitutive relationship: each influence the other.

Norms, as shared understandings of what ought to be, are a social phenomenon, occurring as much outside as within organizational boundaries. That is, norms are often significant for their creation of a social context within which organizations operate. Thus, the interplay of norms and interests in international relations is often best understood as occurring in an institutional, or regime context, rather than a purely organizational context. The first part of this chapter introduces the basic concept of regimes as sub-systemic social institutions in IR scholarship, before examining the specific provenance of the concept of the international food aid regime. It is this regime that provides the key institutional setting for the WFP as an organization.

Having outlined the basic concept of the international food aid regime, the next section of the chapter briefly outlines the WFP's basic organizational structure within the context of the wider UN system. This then leads to a consideration of an appropriate analytical framework to deploy in examining the governance processes of the WFP as the central organization within the food aid regime. Here, in the last section of the chapter, a framework for legitimacy as an evaluative concept linking norms, interests and power is proposed. The framework is based on two groups of distinctions. The first relates to mainly procedural elements of governance – proposed here as inclusion and accountability. The second two relate more to the outcome end of the spectrum, defined in terms of relative effectiveness and absolute effectiveness.

Later chapters will apply these concepts of an institutional context and legitimacy to develop a contextualised analysis of the WFP and the international food aid regime. Chapter Two proposes the concept of a 'feed-the-hungry' norm, and considers its significance in terms of soft normative power, as opposed to the more common hard normative power derived from the framework of international law. This norm plays a central role in framing US support for and leadership within the international food aid regime. The norm is based on three sets of moral claims – of the hungry; of agricultural producers; and of food surplus states and appears in two variant forms. The first variant is the US domestic form in which the US farm sector attracts the producer moral claim. This form underpinned the founding of the international food aid regime. The second form, divergent from the first, is the international version of the feed-the-hungry norm in which developing country farmers attract the moral claim of producers; this latter variant has begun influencing some changes in the US domestic policy settings and implicitly in the US domestic version of the norm.

Chapter Three details the historical evolution of the regime from 1945, through the establishment of the WFP in 1961, until the cusp of the WFP's key transition from development agency to relief agency in the 1980s. Chapter Four follows with the evolution of the regime and the WFP under its two key Executive Directors, Ingram and Bertini, from 1982 up to the early years of the twenty-first century. This historical depiction emphasizes the interaction of norms and interests in US policy, in the context of evolving agricultural production and policy, as well as the context of wider changes in the UN system.

Chapter Five then considers the legitimacy of the WFP in terms of inclusion and accountability by analysing the roles and involvement of member states, NGOs, beneficiaries and the secretariat. While historically the distinction between recipient states and donor states has been central to the politics of the WFP, in recent years a new category of transitional state –former or current recipient states who also donate food aid – has highlighted the importance of the third moral claim. Overall, it is argued that the WFP is reasonably inclusive and accountable inasmuch as intergovernmental organizations can be.

Chapter Six argues that the WFP should be considered relatively effective as a competent and well-regarded humanitarian relief agency that works to maximise effective use of food aid, and to feed people suffering from malnutrition, albeit more in acute than chronic forms, and considers the main factors lying behind this effectiveness, as well as its limitations.

These limitations are articulated through a wider concept of absolute effectiveness. When looked at through the brutal metric of the dimensions of global hunger, the WFP can scarcely be considered effective in its stated mission of reducing hunger. Even before the 2007-08 food crisis, the raw numbers of people subject to malnutrition and food insecurity around the world had barely shifted. At best, given increases in population, there had been a small decline in the proportion of the world population subject to food insecurity. Since 2008 these gains have been wiped out. Nevertheless, such problems are well beyond the scope of an organization like the WFP to change, and it is likely more vigorous attempts to work on wider political issues to do with the production and distribution of food would have diminished the relative effectiveness and legitimacy of the organization. To some degree the price for relative effectiveness has been to limit the capacity to work on the bigger canvas of global hunger.

When put together, the fifth and sixth chapters establish the WFP as a highly legitimate node of global governance activity. The final Chapter considers the implications of the most recent global food crisis and the future prospects of the WFP and the international food aid regime. While legitimacy can wax and wane with the evolution of institutions and organizations, there is sufficient political stability in the international food aid regime, and sufficient call on its operation to meet both political and humanitarian needs to leave room for optimism that the WFP can continue as a relatively effective and legitimate part of the UN system. However, the specific circumstances that have constructed this legitimacy are not so easy to duplicate, and the complex and powerful forces maintaining high global levels of malnutrition and food insecurity look unlikely to change for the better in the near future. Reflecting this, and other pressures for change, the WFP has begun rebadging itself as a 'food assistance' rather than food aid organization, implying a potential evolution of the concept of an international food aid regime into an international food assistance regime.

Overall, this book's examination of the WFP shows a distinctive and unusual set of circumstances that have enabled it to evolve into an international organization with both strong American involvement and high levels of legitimacy, all without the usual emphasis on a normative framework defined in terms of international law. At the same time, it is the normative context that is the key to understanding how American dominance and high levels of legitimacy, so often in tension in international politics, can co-exist in the WFP.

Norms are best understood as operating in an institutional environment, and it is to the concept of institutions, defined as international regimes, that we now turn.

International regimes

Since John Ruggie (Ruggie 1975, 568ff) first used the term 'regime' to describe international institutions, the argument for approaching IR scholarship through regime theory has strengthened due to a range of changes. These include the end of the Cold War, the shifts in world politics fuelled by and feeding into processes of globalization, the continued development and institutionalization of the UN system, and the increasing significance of global, transnational crises such as terrorism or climate change.

One consequence of these changes has been a shift from presuming the centrality of the state in international relations, with more attention to non-state actors and their interactions with states in complex transnational political processes. As Held points out (Held 2004), an important debate about globalization concerns the extent to which it presages the end of the role of the sovereign state as the dominant political actor in international affairs. The exponential growth in international organizations, both governmental and nongovernmental, in recent decades is well established (Archer 2001; Bennett and Oliver 2002; Diehl 2001; Held, McGrew et al. 1999; Jacobson 1984). Putting this together with technological, economic and regulatory change, globalists such as Rosenau (2002) and Cerny (1995) argue new kinds of political relationships are emerging which do not require states as actors at their center.

In order to articulate the apparently growing importance of non-state actors in global politics, a range of approaches have emerged. There is the 'world polity' approach (see Boli and Thomas 1999), which generally emphasises the role of social movements and activists. Many scholars use the concept of a 'global civil society' (Keane 2003; Lipschutz 1992; Ruggie 2003; Wapner 1995) as a means of making sense of the role non-state actors – NGOs in particular – play or could play in global governance. Networks are also proving a popular global governance concept, (e.g. Keck and Sikkink 1998; Slaughter 2004a). All emphasise a pluralist view of global polity.

This pluralism suggests the need for analysis of international politics below the systemic level. As the array of actors and their interactions expands and intensifies, the 'institutional density' of international politics has increased (Reus-Smit 2004, Ch3) together with the political significance of international institutions (Diehl 2001; Karns and Mingst 2004), making such institutions themselves a natural focus for inquiry.

While international regimes are international institutions, not all such institutions are regimes. Some institutions are posited at the systemic level as providing 'deep constitutional values' such as the principle of sovereignty (Reus-Smit 2004, 62), or establishing the 'constitutive' rules of the game (Klotz 1995, 22-5; Ruggie 1998, 28-9; Vogler 2003, 16-8), such as the institutions of international law and multilateralism (Reus-Smit 2004, 62). The subset of international institutions comprising international regimes is, in contrast, best defined as *subsystemic*. That is, regimes are interantional institutions bounded by an 'issue area', such as trade, environment, the Antarctic, or financial regulation. They are based on an interacting combination of rules and norms.

The international institutions referred to as regimes are posited as mid-level concepts to capture the notion that social structures exist beyond the formal extent of intergovernmental organizations, but below the system level (Kratochwil and Ruggie 1986, 760). Indeed, the concept of regimes was developed, in particular, to distinguish international institutions from international organizations (Kratochwil and Ruggie 1986, 754-9).

Krasner's well known and widely accepted definition states that regimes exist where actors' expectations 'converge in a given issue-area' constituted by 'principles, norms, rules and decision-making procedures,' (Krasner 1983, 1). Similarly, Reus-Smit suggests regimes involve 'the realm of substantive international rules, rules that define rights and obligations, lay down standards of behaviour, and specify decision-making procedures and modes of enforcement in distinct domains of international life.' (Reus-Smit 2004, 63; see also Evans and Wilson 1992, 336).

These definitions suggest two problems with which regime theory as sub-systemic theory must contend: the concept of regime is notoriously imprecise (Strange 1983, 342-4), and tends also to favor a state-centric mode of analysis. These problems point to the need for a balanced approach in two areas. First, achieving an analytical balance between the formal rules and organizational elements on the one hand, and their relationship with the less concrete, more ideational aspects of the food aid regime on the other. This is done by placing due emphasis on the normative aspects of the regime and how they relate to the WFP and its governance processes. Second, acknowledging the roles of both state and non-state actors within the regime by analysing both regime and organization within a framework of legitimacy that includes assessing the involvement of both state and non-state actors. However, the weight of this analysis also leans towards a view that states remain by far the most significant actors in the international realm.

The International Food Aid Regime (IFAR)

The concept of an IFAR only emerged in the late 1980s, and is closely linked to the central role of the WFP in global food aid. However, it also comprehends a range of actions, policy debates, norms and principles not all of which are bounded by that organization, despite its centrality to the regime. In fact, as I will show in Chapter Three, while the *concept* of the regime dates from around 1990, the regime itself, now it has been conceptualized, can be traced back at least to the early 1950s.

Early theorizing about the IFAR was influenced by the development focus of the WFP; thus, there was a tendency to view the IFAR normative architecture in terms of principles of development and multilateralism. Over the last 20 years or so, however, change in the WFP focus from development to emergency relief, and renewed American leadership in the regime suggest two different characteristics provide a more appropriate framework for analyzing the regime. These are US hegemony, and the operation of an international feed-the-hungry norm.

Constructing an international regime – from food to food aid

Early regime literature in the late 1970s and early 1980s suggested a global food regime either existed or was at least in the process of formation (Hopkins 1977; Hopkins and Puchala 1979; Puchala and Hopkins 1983, 75-85). Following the 1960s 'Green Revolution' in which agricultural production became transformed (Fore 2007; George 1979; Gilpin 1987; Patel 2007; Sen 1981), the food crisis of 1972–74, and the associated UN World Food Conference in November 1974, there seemed to be a coherence to the idea of an international issue area around 'food'. At this time, the WFP was a minor player, largely seen almost as a division of the Food and Agriculture Organization of the United Nations (FAO).

Thompson, on the other hand, critiqued the idea of the food-related international organizations demonstrating the existence of an international food regime (Thompson 1981). He argued that the various international organizations had only a marginal impact on state sovereignty and food distribution, and therefore could not be said to be engaged in 'governance'. He did conclude, however, that the organizations were worth maintaining as an arena for dialogue, information and intelligence sharing, and suggested that their influence may increase in importance in the future. Thompson's critique of the concept of a food regime had little discernible impact, with the concept seeming to last, if only implicitly, as late as 1990 in Talbot (1990). However, the concept of an international food regime lost viability during the latter half of the 1980s due to the interaction of two factors: the concept's relative lack of analytical clarity, given its extremely broad dimensions; and shifts in the political economy of food and agriculture.

The notional international food regime incorporated elements of agricultural production and trade, scientific and technological research, food aid, and agricultural and rural development involving a number of international organizations, though the FAO was the most significant of these. The problems such breadth created for a coherent concept of a food regime were heightened by changes in the global political economy of agriculture.

The structure of agricultural economics in developed countries went through major changes in the post-war period. Industrialization, vertical integration, the decline in the family farm and the rise of intensive production and agribusiness all occurred increasingly during the 1970s (though these processes had started earlier – see e.g. Coleman, Grant et al. 2004; George 1979). These changes to the economics of agriculture met with other political shifts in the early 1980s, resulting in the agricultural trade regime shifting from a 'dependent paradigm' in which agricultural sectors were characterised as depending on state subsidies, to a neoliberal 'competitive paradigm' during the 1980s (Coleman, Grant et al. 2004, Ch4-5).

Thus Coleman, Grant and Josling argue that in the 1980s domestic economy-based traditional supply, control, and surplus disposal policies 'became increasingly problematic in a more open world economy and a less regulated domestic market.' Increasingly, policy-makers asked questions about spending on the farm sector as opposed to other economic policy objectives in the context of fiscal restraint and a wider shift to neo-liberal policies (Coleman, Grant et al. 2004, 90).

These changes led to the ending of exemptions for agricultural commodities from international trade regimes that dated back to the commencement of the General Agreement on Tariffs and Trade (GATT) in the late 1940s (Coleman, Grant et al. 2004, 113ff). In the competitive paradigm, agricultural produce was, at least theoretically, to become just one more lot of trade commodities. It was formally brought into the international trade regime at the conclusion of the Uruguay Round of the GATT with the 1994 Agreement on Agriculture (Clapp 2004; FAO 2006a).

Agricultural trade has remained the most significant obstacle to the completion of the Doha Round of international trade negotiations, and there seems little doubt that, despite the Agreement on Agriculture being within the ambit of the World Trade Organization, agricultural trade remains in a separate political category from other international trade to some degree. However, the connection of agricultural trade to a food regime is no longer tenable. Agricultural trade had always involved more products than just food – for example, cotton, jute, rubber, and inputs to food such as seed. Therefore, it had never been an entirely easy fit into a food regime. This fact, along with the shift to the competitive paradigm in the 1980s, effectively ended agricultural trade tenure as an element within a notional international food regime.

Without trading elements, the concept of an international food regime lost a significant plank. At least since the FAO had proposed a World Food Bank in 1946 (Hambidge 1955, 59), a goal of international coordination or governance in food had been present in the minds of many liberal internationalists. In turn this implied that a specialist integration of agricultural production processes, trade, and distribution (including food aid) would be required. Such notions had enjoyed an Indian summer in the context of the food crisis in the early 1970s (see Chapter Three for detailed discussion of the crisis), but by the 1980s they were off the table. Without agricultural trade as the issue area linking production and distribution of food, intergovernmental organizations in what had been the food issue-area were left to work on food aid and agricultural development. Even then, in the latter area their role during the 1980s became increasingly technical and secondary to the World Bank's domination of aid and development financing (Bird 2001; Woods 2006).

Food aid refers to the deployment of food resources as aid. Until the 1980s, multilateral food aid had been largely secondary to bilateral food aid and used principally for development projects. However, during the 1980s, multilateral food aid (95% of which goes through the WFP) grew significantly as a proportion of overall food aid (see Table 1.1)[1], and changed its emphasis to emergency relief (Chapter Five discusses this in more detail). This increasingly delinked it from the other, agricultural development, elements of the putative international food regime.

Table 1.1: Multilateral food aid (via WFP) as share of global food aid

Year	% of food aid through the WFP
1959	0%
1971	4%
1979	5%
1989	23%
2007	53%

Sources: (Charlton 1992, 8; INTERFAIS/WFP 2008, xi; WFP 2000, 12). WFP food aid constitutes 95% of multilateral food aid.

Thus the concept of a specific international food aid regime became increasingly relevant during the 1980s and early 1990s in the context of the removal of trade from the purview of food related global governance, and the growth in importance of the WFP and multilateralism in food aid, linked to the growth of emergency relief as the focus for food aid. The prominent mid-1980s famine crises in Africa were one factor in this; food aid to the former Eastern bloc nations in the early 1990s was another. A further relevant factor was the existence of an 'epistemic community' (Haas 1992) in the food aid area, formed by a group of technical specialists with shared understandings of a range of technical issues related to the operation of food aid programs and projects (Hopkins 1992). By the early 1990s, both Hopkins and Uvin were positing an international food aid regime (Hopkins 1992; Uvin 1992).[2]

Linked in part to the resilience and effectiveness of the WFP (Clay 2003), which has given the food aid regime an organizational core, but also to its analytical clarity, the concept of an international food aid regime has lasted since then as a useful tool for IR scholars (see, for example, Clapp 2005).

Characteristics of the IFAR

As noted above, Hopkins and Uvin have been the main sources of explicit regime analysis in relation to the food aid regime. Their analyses give weight to the constitutive role of ideas and norms with both arguing that analysing the food aid regime in terms of narrow ideas of state self-interest is inadequate, though such analysis was relevant in its early years (Hopkins 1992, 229; Uvin 1992, 301).

Hopkins argued the regime had come to reflect incremental change led by an epistemic community of agricultural economists, development experts and food aid policy experts (Hopkins 1992, 264). Due to the work of this epistemic community, new principles became 'embedded in the institutional practices of multilateral agencies, particularly the WFP, and of bilateral agencies as well' (Hopkins 1992, 246). These principles concern the optimal functioning of food aid in order to achieve development. Hopkins' argument can be seen as implicitly assuming the regime functions in accordance with a norm of supporting development through multilateralism rather than unilateral state actions.

Uvin, like Hopkins, implicitly linked increasing multilateralism in the regime with a normative shift away from the realist paradigm of states pursuing their material interests. He emphasized the inadequacy of the standard arguments explaining the regime in terms of economic interests (getting rid of surplus produce to advantage), strategic interests (using aid to further strategic interests) and, to a lesser extent, humanitarian preferences (desire to act on humanitarian need) (Uvin 1992, 297). Rather, in Uvin's analysis, the international food aid regime is described as a 'developmental' regime, meaning a regime 'which is predominantly non-self-interested in nature', and influences state behavior (Uvin 1992, 300). In this account, the classical realist framework is inadequate as it relegates humanitarian motivations to 'a background role, creating conditions that render food aid "popular" ' while assuming that food aid fundamentally serves economic and strategic self-interests (Uvin 1992, 297).

Economic state-level interests in the realist analysis were served by food aid being given to build markets and to offload surpluses (Uvin 1992, 296). American food aid has long been linked to domestic rhetoric and arguments, on display in the very title of its founding legislation, Public Law 480 (*The Agriculture Trade Development and Assistance Act, 1954*), that food aid would build a taste for, or even dependence on, American grains, and hence export markets. However there is little empirical evidence that it has such trade impacts (Uvin 1992, 298; see also Barrett and Maxwell 2005, 78, 181-2).[3] The use of such arguments prominently in the US Congress (see e.g. Rothschild 1993, 87-8) can be ascribed to their propensity to garner domestic support for food aid policies rather than as telling evidence of its actual contribution to economic interests of the US (Uvin 1992, 299). Also, after the 1960s, surplus disposal became a significantly smaller economic issue for the US (Ruttan 1993a; Uvin 1992). Barrett and Maxwell demonstrate that the operation of self-interest in US food aid policy benefits a very small group of well-organized domestic interests, and benefits to American farmers or a more generic economic 'national interest' are largely illusory (Barrett and Maxwell 2005).

Strategic (or what Uvin describes as 'political') interests refer to the idea that food aid 'serves both as carrot and stick in inducing recipient countries to comply with the foreign policy objectives of the donor.' (Uvin 1992, 297). However, Uvin found little evidence that food aid policy actually worked as a tool for inducing strategic cooperation, and much evidence to the contrary (Uvin 1992, 299ff). There is a surprisingly long list of states that have received US food aid with little or no change to their strategic relationship to the US, including Ethiopia in the 1970s and 1980s, and North Korea from 1995 (Barrett and Maxwell 2005, 39-42; Uvin 1992, 309). Uvin found one case of attempted use of emergency aid as a tool or lever of foreign policy, when in 1974, '[d]espite obvious famine, the U.S. delayed food aid shipments in order to force Bangladesh to end its export of jute to Cuba'. However it is not even clear that this proved successful (Uvin 1992, 300; see also Sen 1981, 135-6; McHenry and Bird 1977, 82).

In the absence of food aid actually serving donor interests, Uvin argued, an international food aid regime can provide an explanation of the observed outcomes. It is through the creation of institutional constraints that the regime influences the definition of state interests, helping to explain why states do things that do not make sense when analyzed in terms of economic or strategic interests. Thus Uvin posited the existence of 'a generally shared international norm against famine and acute starvation' compelling countries to donate and constraining their use of emergency food aid for furthering their strategic interests (Uvin 1992, 300).

Hopkins proposed a more technical set of norms in operation in the food aid regime, as follows:

> Today a set of widely shared norms exist for the appropriate use of food aid. According to these norms, resource transfers should take into account the effects of the aid on the food system and the economy of the recipient country...food aid without sound management can have negative effects but that food aid with 'appropriate' design can be extremely useful. (Hopkins 1992, 263).

However, food aid can only be described as 'extremely useful' if it is useful *for* something – this is where the multilateral development norm emerged in Hopkins' argument. In other words, food aid is useful for international development (that is, deployment as a resource to underpin development projects), which should result in poorer people and nations becoming healthier and wealthier. Both Uvin and Hopkins showed that analysis of the food aid regime needs to be historical to explain how the regime has evolved from an early emphasis on state self-interest to something driven by a multilateral norm. This shift is illustrated at a practical level by changes in donor practices and policies, which in turn both have contributed to and reflected shifts in regime norms. The evolving regime and the multilateral norm are mutually constitutive, feeding into each other.

As Chart 1.1 shows, in the period since Hopkins and Uvin published their analyses of the international food aid regime, the use of food aid for development in the WFP has been largely displaced by its use in emergency relief and recovery operations (see Chapter Four for a more detailed discussion of this). Under influence of this trend and the views of the epistemic food aid community on best practice use of food aid, the wider regime, including bilateral food aid arrangements, has trended in the same direction, (see Chapter Six).

This shift away from a development focus for the WFP means a development ethos integrated with a multilateral norm is no longer an adequate normative script for framing the IFAR. A different normative script provides a more productive understanding of the relationship between the regime and the United States as the hegemonic state actor in it, as well as accounting for the shift to an emergency relief focus. This central regime norm I am terming the feed-the-hungry norm. The two defining characteristics of the IFAR are this norm and the hegemonic role of the US within the regime – ideas that are explored in more detail in the next chapter.

Chart 1.1: WFP food assistance by category, 1982-2007 (thousand tons)

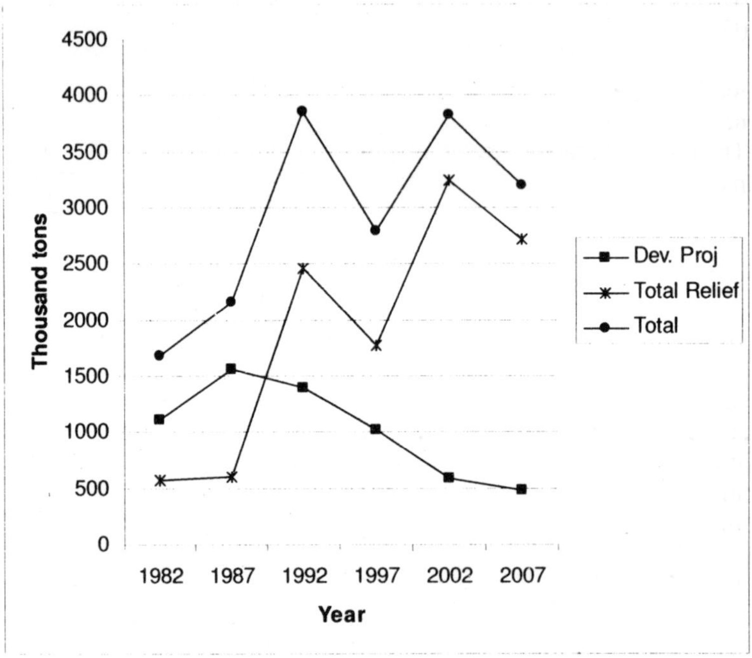

Data Sources: (Ingram 2006, 356[4]; INTERFAIS/WFP 2008, ix, 22). Dev. Proj - Development Projects. The category of Total Relief incorporates Emergency Operations and Protracted Relief and Rehabilitation Operations.

It is important to note that the IFAR has many dimensions to it apart from the WFP. While the WFP dominates multilateral food aid, it has played a marginal (though arguably increasing) role as a service provider in relation to bilateral food aid. Clapp (2004) demonstrates the way in which events in agricultural trade negotiations are connected to food aid; this connection has also been an explicit source of tension between the US and the European Union at the WFP Executive Board. Yet the WFP itself has remained at most peripheral to these debates. Moreover, the WFP has lacked sufficient resources to develop the capacity to have a significant impact on food aid policy by itself

(Interview #16 2005; Bertini 2005b; Ingram 2005a). Significant policy inputs on food aid come from governmental agencies in the development field,[5] NGOs such as Oxfam, CARE or Bread for the World Institute, or other multilateral actors such as the European Union (EU), the Organisation for Economic Cooperation and Development (OECD), or the World Bank.

Nevertheless, the WFP is central to the operation of international food aid politics. It is the venue within which the key elites meet, negotiate, coordinate, and attempt to generate and define good practice. The principal practitioners in food relief almost all have worked for or in partnership with WFP at some stage; all policy players regard it as central to capability, practice and reform in the sector.

The UN system and the WFP

Beyond the General Assembly of member states, and the UN Security Council, the UN system is a sort of 'confederation of...essentially autonomous inter-governmental organisations' (Ingram 2006, 8). These global intergovernmental organizations comprise, in the first instance, the various UN specialized agencies, established like the UN itself by intergovernmental treaty. These organizations differ from other international intergovernmental organizations such as the (EU) or Asia Pacific Economic Cooperation (APEC) which can more accurately be termed regional rather than global and are not part of the UN system, and include organizations such as the FAO, the International Monetary Fund (IMF), the World Bank, and the World Health Organization (WHO).[6]

Held et al. define the UN specialized agencies as follows:

> Legally separate organizations, many of which predate the UN, with their own membership, budgets, and programmes. Nominally, the specialized agencies are subject to coordination by the UN via its Economic and Social Council, and an annual heads of agencies meeting... (Held, McGrew et al. 1999, 66).

The *specialized* agencies are legally separate organizations because they have been established in their own right by intergovernmental treaties in parallel to the UN. This distinguishes them from the UN *operational* agencies, which are Programs or Funds created by resolution of the General Assembly, such as the WFP, the UN Development Programme (UNDP), the UN Children's Fund (UNICEF), and the UN Environment Programme (UNEP). Consequently, UN operational agencies have intergovernmental governing councils, but cannot change their own constitutions. The heads of these organizations are formally appointed by the UN Secretary-General, so have lower status than the heads of specialized agencies who are elected directly by governments.

While the UN and the specialized agencies are funded by compulsory 'assessed' member-state contributions, the UN operational agencies, apart from UN resources they may be allocated, are funded by voluntary contributions from member states and publicly solicited donations (Ingram 2006, 9). Nevertheless, many of the operational agencies have larger budgets and higher public profiles than the specialized agencies (Ingram 2006, 9).

The World Food Programme is unlike the other UN operational agencies in two respects. The WFP was created by joint resolutions of the UN General Assembly and of the Conference of a specialized agency, the FAO, and is, formally, jointly governed by FAO and the UN. Its intergovernmental executive board is elected half by the FAO Conference and half by the UN Economic and Social Council (ECOSOC); the WFP Executive Director is formally appointed jointly by the UN Secretary-General and the FAO Director-General. As a consequence of this joint parentage and its initial 'trial' establishment, unlike other UN operational agencies, the WFP receives no funding from the UN budget, but relies wholly on voluntary contributions. (Chapters Three and Four consider the historical background to this parentage and Chapter Five discusses contemporary WFP governance arrangements in more detail). However, while having some historical significance, these differences have not created a contemporarily significant difference in structure. Indeed, all of the UN operational agencies have complex histories, involving complex foundational politics, and considerable variations in leadership, structure and function over time (see e.g. Barnett and Finnemore 2004; Murphy 2006). In the context of that variability, WFP does not stand out as structurally unique in any significant way.

Like all other UN operational agencies, the WFP is established by resolution of the UN General Assembly (Appendix 1), albeit its establishment was not by the General Assembly alone, but by joint resolutions of the General Assembly and the FAO Conference. The WFP is structurally typical in that it is subject to the tensions between the behaviour of member states, member state representatives, and wider system politics, through its governance structures and position within the UN system. Following a UN General Assembly resolution in 1993 (UN General Assembly 1993), the WFP has had an Executive Board structure identical to that of the UN Development Program (UNDP), UN International Children's Fund (UNICEF), and the UN Fund for Population Activities (UNFPA). In effect, despite the formal role for the FAO, the processes by which the WFP participates in the UN system are little different from other operational agencies. The formal power distribution on the WFP Board is also, in structural terms, typical of UN agencies. Notwithstanding a numerical majority of developing countries, the US undoubtedly plays a dominant role, with other developed countries also contributing actively to governance and resources. NGOs based in developed countries also play an at times influential role, along with a secretariat staffed by many nationalities, albeit with strong western and especially American representation at senior levels. There is movement of staff from and to other UN agencies, and engagement with UN coordination activities along with other agencies such as the Joint UN Programme on HIV/AIDS (UNAIDS) and the UN High Commissioner for Refugees (UNHCR).

Yet, while the WFP may be structurally typical within the UN system, the resources it controls and deploys are far from typical. WFP has become the largest and most significant of the UN operational agencies (Barrett and Maxwell 2005, 220) in terms of the resources it deploys. It has emerged as the second largest global source of development funds after the World Bank (Barrett and Maxwell 2005, 15). In 2004, WFP had a staff of 8,829 and operational expenditures of $US3.1 billion (WFP 2006d). In 2008, in the context of the global food crisis, WFP received record levels of resources from donors, in excess of $US5 billion (WFP 2009).

This material significance is closely linked to two interrelated factors. First, the WFP is also currently widely regarded as one of the most successful and respected of the UN agencies (Clay 2003) – the reasons for which will be discussed further in Chapter Six. Without such strongly positive perceptions it is doubtful that a voluntarily funded agency would be able to command the level of resources at the WFP's disposal. Secondly, easily the most significant donor to the WFP is the US, which has historically never provided less than a third of its resources, and on average provided half of the donations to it in the decade to 2006 (Hanrahan and Canada 2006). This strong support from the US can be traced in part to the US role in its founding, and the use of food aid to pursue US interests; however, its continuation and evolution can only be understood with reference to the unique norm that underpins the WFP and the international food aid regime – the feed-the-hungry norm. In turn, these factors play an important role in constituting the WFP's high levels of legitimacy.

Legitimacy: An evaluative framework

Assessing or evaluating international regimes can be done using a range of overlapping concepts: robustness, strength, effectiveness, coherence and legitimacy are all terms used in regime theory literature relating to some notion of evaluation. Of these, legitimacy has come to the fore in contemporary constructivist IR (Clark 2005), perhaps because, more than the others, it is capable of comprehending the range of normative, political and ideational issues involved in institutional and organizational functioning.

Analysis of legitimacy is not always straightforward. It can often appear to conflate causes and effects by confusing evidence of the presence of legitimacy with the source or cause of that legitimacy. However, to see such a conflation as a problem underestimates the reflexive nature of causality in complex social phenomena. That is, a perception of legitimacy demonstrated in an indicator measure, such as an evaluation of efficiency, or poll results expressing support for a regime, in itself can contribute to further gains in legitimacy. Indicators of legitimacy themselves often, at least partially, constitute causal factors.

In response to these points, it might be argued that, nevertheless, the indicators are not the whole story and must themselves have originated out of some prior development of legitimacy. This prior development of legitimacy is best understood as occurring through the process of institutionalisation – that is, the evolution of relevant social institutions as a framework for legitimizing relevant actors, organizations and authorities. This points to the importance of an historically contextualised understanding of the IFAR and the WFP for developing a fully nuanced grasp of their legitimacy, and hence the importance of tracing their evolution as I do in Chapters Three and Four.

In the context of tracing the evolution of a regime and organization, an empirical assessment of their legitimacy implicitly involves considering the processes by which their legitimacy increases and/or decreases. Legitimacy is neither a zero-sum game, nor a fixed, all or nothing category. It exists to varying degrees and over time can be expected to vary as a barometer of the political fortunes of a given institution. The framework for assessing legitimacy in the WFP proposed below functions more to give a snapshot of its legitimacy in the first decade of the twenty-first century than to trace in detail its general gaining of legitimacy over earlier decades, albeit with historical context provided by earlier chapters. The concluding Chapter will consider this longer term process of gaining/losing legitimacy as it considers the political trajectory of the IFAR and the WFP and their prospects for the future.

The contemporary legitimacy of the international food aid regime can be most readily analysed through an examination of the governance processes of the World Food Programme – in particular its *inclusion, accountability* and *effectiveness*. These three concepts reflect various constitutive, procedural, and substantive aspects of institutional politics; they are not stand alone notions, but overlap in their content; put together they cover most of the significant political aspects of legitimacy *qua* governance. However, it is analytically useful to examine them separately. Before expanding on these three elements of legitimacy, it is worth noting two other aspects of legitimacy not comprehended by them.

First, a further important element of legitimacy in the international food aid regime, as I have implicitly argued above, is the interaction of the regime with US power. Reflecting the significance of the role of the US within the regime, consideration of this issue runs as a constant thread through the application of the analytical framework provided by inclusion, accountability and effectiveness.

Second, the moral nature of the work of the WFP arguably accords it greater legitimacy – that is, legitimacy in the IFAR arguably has a further source in morality. As with US power, the issue of morality runs as an implicit constant through my analysis, in particular through my emphasis on the feed-the-hungry norm in the IFAR, rather than as a separate empirical category for analysing WFP's governance.

Inclusion

Inclusion is concerned with membership of the polity in which the institution functions. In the case of the international food aid regime, this functioning can be understood most directly through the form of the WFP's governance structures.

Polity membership has two facets – that of *governing* and that of *being governed.* While the latter suggests that those subject to governance are thereby part of the polity, the former suggests that the polity is made up of those participating in decision-making, whether directly or through representative processes. There is a long normative tradition linking these two senses of polity membership. That is, those affected by decision-making *should* be represented in the decision-making process. This normative agenda, for example, is an important part of Held's arguments concerning the need for democratic reforms to global governance, based on the 'principle of inclusiveness and subsidiarity' which should aim to maximize 'each person's opportunity to influence the social conditions that shape his or her life' (Held 2004, 375).

Apart from the normative perspective, in empirical approaches more generally, who is included (or excluded) from participation and representation in governance and how such inclusion and exclusion operates in turn have a direct bearing on organizational and institutional political legitimacy. As Scharpf argues in relation to input-oriented legitimacy,

> under modern conditions, the legitimacy of political systems has come to depend entirely on the belief in, and the practice of, democratic self-determination which must assure that government of the people must also be government by the people and for the people. (Scharpf 1999, 1)

The campaign for reform of the UN Security Council, for example, is partly linked to inclusion-related legitimacy problems deriving from the small, non-representative group of nations constituting its permanent membership (Knight 2002).

In global-level politics, concerns with inclusion operate broadly at two levels – inter- and intra- state.

At the inter-state level, the significant differences in wealth and power between nation-states lead to concerns about differing capacities for involvement. For example, as Chapter Five shows, the relative sizes of delegations to the World Food Programme Executive Board at least partly reflect different levels of state wealth and power, and have some impact on the capacity to participate.[7]

At the intra-state level, inclusion concerns the problem of formal state representation sufficing to represent the views of large groups of people within that state. Sometimes this is framed as a particularist issue because of the effective exclusion from international decision making of domestically disenfranchised ethnic groups. At other times, it can be set more as a majoritarian issue due to the exclusion of the views of the citizenry who voted for different candidates and policies to the elected government, or as a democratic issue, where the state's authority is based on repression and itself lacks democratic legitimacy.

The inter- and intra-state levels are not independent from each other, but frequently interact in international institutions. Domestic groups excluded from equitable participation in the state (for example, non-whites in Apartheid South Africa; democracy activists in Burma) see their state's exclusion from international fora as an important means of delegitimizing that (non-legitimate) state. Conversely, acceptance of despotic regimes in international fora is perceived as granting them (unwarranted) legitimacy. The criticisms, and eventual dissolution of the UN Human Rights Commission exemplified the extent to which the two levels of inter- and intra-state legitimacy interact in international politics (Economist 2008).

Non-state actors become important in relation to inclusion primarily as a means to compensate for inter- and intra-state shortcomings. That is, the role of groups, from Armed Non-State Actors (Glaser 2005) to humanitarian NGOs is often depicted as at least partly compensating for these exclusions. In this context, NGOs are seen as making up for the deficiencies of state representation in international fora, or giving a voice to the unrepresented; as Keck and Sikkink put it, they 'multiply the channels of access' (Keck and Sikkink 1998, 1).

If important actors, whether state or, increasingly, non-state, are not included in governance processes, there is likely to be an impact on the legitimacy of that institution, and issues of inclusion are often, if not always, problematic in global intergovernmental organizations. However, the mere fact of inclusion, even if married to some basic assurance of capacity to contribute to decision making, is only the first part of building legitimacy.

Accountability

Where a process of governance is perceived to be insufficiently inclusive it begins to confront problems with legitimacy in two senses. First, as argued above, problems with inclusion diminish legitimacy directly. Secondly, problems with inclusion lead to problems with accountability, and hence diminish legitimacy, a problem conjured up by the critique of international bodies having a 'democratic deficit' (Held 2004; Moravcsik 2004).

In other words, accountability and inclusion overlap; however, inclusion is only tangentially part of the legitimacy issues invoked by accountability. That is because accountability specifically relates to the constraint of power and hence its legitimation. Following on from Hindess' distinction (Hindess 1996) between power as capacity and power as right (based on the consent of the governed), accountability creates 'power as right through establishing (the appearance of) legitimizing constraints on power as capacity. Accountability implies power as right; (because) it constrains power as capacity' (Ross 2000, 7).

There are three conceptions of accountability: accountability as *sanction*, as *judgement*, and as *participation* (Ross 2000, 70ff), which suggests a broader range of political issues invoked by accountability than just those related to inclusion.

Accountability as *sanction* relates to the notion of accountability as something that should occur after something bad happens, and tends to be bottom-up in perspective. It is articulated in statements in the form of:

> S1: 'Action X resulted in bad outcomes for certain people (us or fellow persons). Actor Y who was responsible for this should be held accountable.'

Accountability as sanction is bottom-up in the sense that S1 is typically made by those actually (or potentially) subject to the exercise of power by Actor Y. It generally refers to some form of abuse of power recognised after the fact, though it is also implicitly about then demonstrating that sanctions will occur in such events, and thereby reducing the likelihood of their recurrence. In contrast to this, accountability as *judgement* is linked more to a managerial perspective, connoting potential reward as well as punishment, and suggests more of a top down perspective. It is articulated in statements in the form of:

> S2: 'You will be held accountable for your performance in this role.'

Accountability as judgement tends to be top-down in the sense that S2 presumes the capacity to judge (hold the actor accountable) in a manner suggesting the actor is subject to the power of the person making the statement.

In both the case of sanction and judgement, the accountability lies as much in the *knowledge* that x will happen if an actor does/fails to do y, as in the actual doing of it. In contrast with these conceptions that separate actions and outcomes, accountability as *participation* is procedural, not outcome-based. That is, it is based on the idea that accountability can be constructed *through* a more inclusive process of power by involving potentially affected people in decision making at the outset, for example, through consultation or other more explicitly deliberative processes. Accountability as participation implies inclusion but does not equate to it, as it also concerns the forms which inclusion takes in relation to the constraint and exercise of authority, as opposed to a simple in or out test.

In liberal-democratic states these concepts are connected to an array of accountability mechanisms. The more formal ones include laws and regulation, institutional checks and balances, processes of inquiry and oversight, and the electoral process. Less formally, professional norms, social expectations, public approbation and so on are also important.

In the international realm, these conceptions of accountability relate back to structural and procedural constraints on state, intergovernmental, or non-state actors (Keohane 2003). For example, the Global Compact (GC) can be seen as an attempt by then UN Secretary-General Kofi Annan to move the regulatory debate about constraining the power of transnational corporations away from the notion of accountability as sanction based on strong regulation and effective sanctions for breaching regulations (Ruggie 2003). Rather, the GC sets out to propose 'softer' constraining mechanisms based on rewarding good performance at least as much as punishing bad (accountability as judgement), and engaging the corporations themselves in the creation of standards of behaviour (accountability as participation).

However, intergovernmental organizations are not analogous to government in a state when it comes to these issues (Nye, International Monetary Fund et al. 2003; Steffek 2003). Probably the most significant long standing concern with the concept of a world government has been with the difficulty of constructing meaningful constraints on such a body analogous to domestic level constraints on government. This concern is reflected in the literature on lack of UN accountability (Coultan 2006; Hancock 1989), and has played a part in entrenching what are arguably dysfunctional levels of state control and intervention in UN administration (Alger 2001; Evans 2006; Kennedy and Russett 1995; Urquhart 2006).

Also, the distress about American unilateralism undermining the UN system (Judt 2007) at least partly derives from its confronting demonstration of the incapacity of that system to constrain (i.e. render accountable) the most powerful state actor. There is also an increasing level of concern about accountability in relation to nongovernment organizations as they get larger, and their political capacities get more institutionalised (Mallaby 2004; Maren 1997; Townsend and Townsend 2004).

If inclusion relates to membership of the polity defined by the capacity to participate in governance, accountability relates to the modes and means of constraining the operation of governance power structures themselves. Inclusion and accountability clearly overlap as issues, but the distinction is important. Inclusion implies accountability and legitimization, but there are other processes and mechanisms potentially involved in accountability. Similarly, inclusion raises many more issues than just accountability and legitimization, for example, about how it can be broadened, or why it should be limited. In both cases, the specific nature of the issues derives from the organizational and institutional context, but both are crucial components of organizational and institutional legitimacy. Chapter Five considers these issues as they apply to governance in the WFP.

Effectiveness

Legitimacy and effectiveness can be approached in two different ways. In one take, effectiveness is, at least partly, a result of legitimacy. In this version, a legitimate organization is, if not axiomatically effective, thereby given the chance to be effective; legitimacy is the means and effectiveness the end. For example, some advocates of Security Council reform believe that a lack of legitimacy (as a result of failures of inclusion and accountability due to restricted membership and the use of veto power) compromises its effectiveness (Malone 2007, 280).

In the second approach, rather than being outside of and separate from legitimacy, effectiveness is an element of legitimacy – sometimes termed 'output legitimacy' (Scharpf 1999), or substantive legitimacy (Barnett and Finnemore 2004, 166). In this version, legitimacy is a result, in part, of the effectiveness of an institution or organization. This latter approach is being used here because an expansive and comprehensive version of legitimacy is being used as the basis for evaluation of an international regime. In the context of intergovernmental organizations having their legitimacy questioned or placed on a crisis footing (Clark and Reus-Smit 2007; Reus-Smit 2007) due in part to queries over effectiveness, it seems appropriate to render effectiveness as a subordinate element of legitimacy, rather than the other way around.

Effectiveness can be assessed in absolute (strong) or relative (weak) terms, depending on the criteria by which it is judged.

Effectiveness in relative terms suggests an assessment based on comparison with parallel or similar forms of governance. In the case of the WFP, as it is part of the UN system, it implies a rating of it against other organizations and agencies in the UN system in terms of effectiveness – that is in terms of its capacity to achieve its mandate. This type of effectiveness is political in as much as it derives from perceptions and credibility. In other words, an argument that WFP is relatively effective might refer more to perception than substantive fact, but when considering effectiveness in relative terms such perceptions in themselves *are* a substantive (political) fact.

Absolute effectiveness refers to a desirable impact on the global problems in a given issue area. Since 2000, the Millennium Development Goals (MDGs) (UN General Assembly 2000) have provided a reasonable approximation of what can be regarded as constituting absolute effectiveness – basically in the context of the international food aid regime this amounts to a goal of halving global hunger and poverty by the year 2015. While in a complex global system it is impossible to construct a linear relationship between such aggregate measures and the effectiveness of a specific organization, it is possible to consider the extent to which WFP contributes to such goals and can thence be seen as effective in the absolute sense.

What makes for effectiveness in global governance – and what does not – are important political questions which are linked to inclusion and accountability (who decides on aims and goals, who judges whether they are being met and how), as well as related operational and managerial factors. Chapter Six considers the effectiveness of WFP in both the relative and absolute senses, and how this relates to the other aspects of the legitimacy of the international food aid regime.

Conclusion

This book aims to consider the implications for improving global governance through an institutional examination of the World Food Programme's legitimacy. The approach taken is based on the assumption that the international realm is a complex social arena in which social institutions, or international regimes, play an important sub-systemic role involving the interaction of norms and interests. This occurs predominantly through the actions of state actors, though non-state actors are of some importance. The international food aid regime provides the institutional context for the WFP, which is the organizational center of the regime.

The WFP is part of the UN system, and is structurally comparable to other parts of that system. Consequently, its merits and successes as the basis of its legitimacy are potentially useful pointers as to how other parts of the system can evolve in ways that result in improved global governance. WFP's material significance, on the other hand, suggests its importance to the UN system, to the states involved with it, and to the hungry poor it serves. What it does, and how well it does it, do matter, beyond simply providing lessons for the wider system of international organizations.

Evaluating the legitimacy of the WFP requires the application of an analytical framework made up of three elements – inclusion, accountability and effectiveness. However, before undertaking this analysis it is important to establish a contextualized understanding of the WFP and the international food aid regime through tracing the evolution of the international food aid regime.

This contextualized analysis will illustrate a central theme of legitimacy within the regime: the crucial role of US power. There is no better starting place for understanding the significance of the relationship between the US and the international food aid regime than the norm underpinning that relationship. It is to the feed-the-hungry norm we now turn.

Endnotes

[1] Though it is important to note this was linked to a significant decline in the significance of food aid as a proportion of Official Development Assistance (ODA). That is, multilateral food aid became a larger part of a smaller whole.

[2] Though Uvin also argued the food aid regime is connected with the international hunger regime (Uvin 1994).

[3] Another form of trade development from food aid could be said to derive from its tied nature; that is, the benefits of many of the significant expenditures go directly to donor nation companies and interests, e.g. shipping and freight businesses; NGOs and field experts. Uvin notes there is some evidence to suggest attempts by certain companies to manipulate access to counterpart funds generated from the sale of food aid (Uvin 1992, 299). Tying of aid is a well-known problem with most types of aid (OECD 2006), though in the case of food aid, the benefits go to relatively small vested interest groups and are difficult to demonstrate empirically as benefits to the donor state (Barrett and Maxwell 2005).

[4] The data in Ingram (2006) for Table 1 on p355 has been transposed with the data for Table 2 on p356. The data used here appears on p356, but is labelled as Table 2, concerning staff employment.

[5] The most significant include the United Kingdom Department for International Development (DFID), the Canadian International Development Agency (CIDA), and the US Agency for International Development (USAID). Two significant evaluations of WFP have been undertaken under the direction of loose consortia of various such Western government agencies (Chr. Michelsen Institute 1994; Russo, Luzot et al. 2005).

[6] Note that all intergovernmental organizations are not purely and solely governmental in character. The International Labor Organization (ILO), for example, has representatives of employer and labor organizations as well as governments in its governing structure.

[7] Slaughter, following Chayes and Chayes (Chayes and Chayes 1998), argues for a 'new sovereignty' based on "the capacity to participate in cooperative regimes in the collective interest of all states" (Slaughter 2004b, 327). Slaughter's new sovereignty here echoes T.H. Marshall's proposition of an expanded concept of citizenship, based on the capacity to participate in

society (Marshall 1965; see also Sen 1999, 10 on the centrality of political participation to the intrinsic value of democracy).

2
The Feed-the-Hungry Norm

The international food aid regime is defined by a single constitutive norm, which I am terming the feed-the-hungry norm. This norm is reflected in, and modified by, the governance processes of the World Food Programme as the organizational core of the IFAR.

The feed-the-hungry norm has two distinctive characteristics. Firstly, the norm is not based on a contractual or rule-based logic, but on the humanitarian impulse connected to the moral claim of the hungry. In this it provides an example of what I term 'soft' normative power, in contrast to the 'hard' normative power of international regime norms that call upon international law to underpin them. Secondly, the international regime norm is congruent with an equivalent domestic norm in the United States, reflecting the historical development of the regime, and helping to generate the hegemonic relationship of the US to the WFP in a distinctively constructive form.

Before explaining these propositions in more detail through an examination of the normative foundations of food aid in both the US and the international regime, it is first important to define what I mean by the concept of 'norm'. This goes beyond simple definition, to typologies of norms, and propositions about how norms relate to interests.

Regime norms and actor interests

As I argued in Chapter One, I am taking norms to be the ideational core of regimes, underlying the formal rules and processes in international affairs, but this is not meant to attribute a simple causal relationship between the two levels. To say norms underlie formal rules and processes is not to imply that they cause or produce them, rather they can be conceived of as a deeper structure in sociological terms. Norms are often formalised in rules and processes; but also derive from and evolve through the operation of rules and procedures in a social context involving ideas, discourse and agent actions.

Finnemore and Sikkink suggest a basic, generally agreed 'definition of a norm as a standard of appropriate behavior for actors with a given identity' (Finnemore and Sikkink 1998, 891). That is, norms are shared or collective understandings of appropriate behaviour (Eckersley 2007, 14; Legro 1997, 33; Florini 1996, 364; Checkel 1999, 83). This consensus definition needs to be interpreted carefully, though, to avoid an implicit bias toward assessing norms in terms of behaviour. As Kratochwil points out, norms go beyond being 'guidance mechanisms'; they are also 'the means which allow people to pursue goals, share meanings, communicate with each other, criticize assertions, and justify actions.' (Kratochwil 1989, 11; Steffek 2003).

The existence of a social institution connotes the existence of one or more norms which create the intersubjective social understandings necessary to render that institution coherent and meaningful. Indeed, the very process of institutionalisation can be taken as referring to the embedding of shared understandings within a web of rules and processes.

Given the diversity of international institutions, and within that category, of regimes, it is only to be expected that norms are themselves highly diverse and difficult to generalise about, leading to various attempts to typologize them. Finnemore and Sikkink note that various categories for norms have been developed, most commonly with a distinction between 'regulative norms, which order and constrain behavior, and constitutive norms, which create new actors, interests, or categories of action' (Finnemore and Sikkink 1998, 891). However, such a distinction makes more sense to apply to rules than to norms (Ruggie 1998, 22-5). This is because, unlike at least some rules, all norms within their institutional context play a wider, discursive and, fundamentally, constitutive social role. In other words, norms are part of a set of social understandings which play a central role in constructing identities and interests, while at the same time themselves developing from social interactions around identities and interests. Rules may attempt to codify and reflect norms, but they should not be conflated with them, a point I will elaborate further on below in relation to the contrast between hard and soft normative power.

Another way of typologizing norms is via their institutional setting. For example, Reus-Smit's distinctions between constitutive institutions (sovereignty), fundamental institutions (international law and multilateralism), and regimes (Reus-Smit 2007, 159) imply different types of norms behind those institutions, in a way suggestive of the constitutive/regulative distinction. The deeper, more fundamental the institution is, the more diffuse – that is, embedded and implicit in social practices – its norms are. Regimes as sub-systemic institutions with narrower scope arguably tend to be more regulative (within an issue area) than broadly constitutive in the way systemic institutions are. However, this distinction is more accurately described as systemic/sub-systemic than constitutive/regulative.

Such a differentiation between systemic and sub-systemic institutions/norms is called up by Puchala and Hopkins' identification of a regime superstructure (Puchala and Hopkins 1983, 64-5), referring 'to general and diffuse principles and norms that condition the principles and norms operative in a specific issue-area' (Krasner 1983, 17). Another example is Elliott's distinction between regime norms deriving from the institution of sovereignty ('sovereignty norms') and regime norms deriving from the institution of multilateralism ('interdependence norms'), which suggests various regime norms differ depending on their derivation from deeper institutions and hence more fundamental or systemic-level norms (Elliott 1994, 11-2).

These distinctions point to regime norms, in part, developing from other pre-existing systemic level norms. But this relationship is constitutive rather than causal – systemic norms do not 'cause' regime norms, they help to constitute them given a particular context of issues and actors with identities and interests.[1]

This is not the only inter-norm relationship of interest, though. A growing literature is concerned with the relationship between international (mainly regime level) norms and domestic level norms (Checkel 1997; 1999; Cortell and Davis 1996; 2005; Klotz 1995; Risse 1999). The focus is on how one affects the other, from providing an originating source, to enhancing the 'transmission' (Checkel 1997), 'diffusion' (Cortell and Davis 2005) or adoption of the less established of the two.

The evolution of the international food aid regime demonstrates the complexity of the interrelationships between the international feed-the-hungry norm and the domestic US feed-the-hungry norm, but also points to the importance of the interrelationship between these norms and US power and interests (in both material and idealist senses). The complex nature of international social institutions requires an approach to their analysis that is cautious about abstracting individual elements such as norms from their institutional context. In turn, this suggests the importance of the long running debate about the nature of the relationship between norms and interests.

Norms and interests

Two schools of thought dominate the norms/interests debate. Neoliberal institutionalists argue from the premises of a rationalist model assuming the pursuit of interests by atomised egoist state actors (Hay 2002; Reus-Smit 2001). When norms are introduced to this model, they appear as intervening variables analytically independent from and caused by the prior structure of interests which is assumed as lying beneath the functioning of the international realm (Keohane 1984; Klotz 1995; Stein 1983, 14).

Constructivism evolved in part out of a dissatisfaction with the rationalist materialism implied in this approach (Ruggie 1998, 3-4). Constructivists such as Wendt point out that it is important to ask where interests come from, rather than simply assume them to be the basis for all actions (Wendt 1999, 33ff). In answering this question it becomes necessary to abandon the rationalist model of atomistic actors and adopt a social (Wendt 1999) or relational (Ruggie 1998) ontology which sees actors in a social context. Actor identities and ultimately actor perceptions of their interests derive from this context in which norms operate as significant ideational structures. However, this approach tends to result in an inversion of the neoliberal paradigm by suggesting that as norms are constitutive of identity and interests derive from identity, ultimately interests derive from norms: an emphasis on norms can lead to attributing to them a prior, causal relationship to interests. Thus Checkel notes that constructivists can fall into the trap of giving norms a structural role and struggle with the agency of actors vis-à-vis norms (Checkel 1999).

Rather than seeing interests as prior to and the cause of norms, or conversely, norms as preceding and constructing interests, interests and norms must be seen as mutually constituted (Klotz 1995, 27). The evolution of the international food aid regime demonstrates the interrelationships between material/ideational interests and the norms that they help construct – at both international and domestic US levels. These norms help generate actor perceptions of their interests, even as those interests contribute to the construction and evolution of the norms.

The constitutive nature of norms suggests it is very difficult if not unwise to attempt to analyse norms apart from their institutional settings. This problem requires empirical examination of the relationship between norms and regimes *in situ*, as it were, in order to tease out the significance of the interrelationships between a given norm and its institutional context, given they are mutually constituting concepts. Such empirical work can then help guide judgements of the extent to which norms may be amenable to causal theorising without reification in terms that gut them of their constitutive meanings.

In this context, it is useful to note that what follows about the feed-the-hungry norm is substantively consistent with Keck and Sikkink's (1998) empirically based argument implicitly concerning transnationally resonant norms. Keck and Sikkink propose that transnational advocacy networks have been particularly effective around 'issue characteristics' concerning bodily integrity and the prevention of bodily harm to vulnerable or innocent groups involving a short causal chain (Keck and Sikkink 1998, 27). As Finnemore and Sikkink point out, this amounts to an argument that norms based on such criteria have a particular 'transnational resonance' leading to their successful diffusion (Finnemore and Sikkink 1998, 907).

In arguing this, Keck and Sikkink distinguish the bodily harm issue characteristic with its 'normative logic' from the 'juridical and institutional logic' of issues characterised by arguments concerning legal equality of opportunity (Keck and Sikkink 1998, 27). This argument echoes the distinction I propose below between the 'soft normative' power of the feed-the-hungry norm and the 'hard normative' power associated with other norms based more explicitly on international law.

The Feed-the-Hungry Norm and the WFP

The 'feed-the-hungry' norm is a powerful 'interdependence norm' (Elliott 1994, 11), providing important motivational coherence, and a shared paradigm through which different interests can be conceived, defined and acted on within the international food aid regime.

This norm is both a belief in the rectitude of feeding hungry people, and an implicit statement of rights and obligations – that hungry people have a right to be fed, and those with food have an obligation to feed them.[2] Precisely what this norm means or implies is complex and subject to change, but it has generated important political stability for the WFP by providing a unifying logic with quite powerful expression in forums such as the WFP Executive Board.

In other words, the WFP is embedded within an international food aid regime which has a distinctive normative base – the feed-the-hungry norm. This results in the regime being characterised by two interrelated factors – soft normative power, and congruence with a domestic US version of the norm.

'Soft normative power'

Most international norms are ultimately defined in legal terms, categorizing obligations in terms of rights and responsibilities codified by international law, conventions and treaties. The feed-the-hungry norm, in contrast involves minimal use of such legal frameworks, and even avoids reliance on a discourse of rights.[3] Instead, the norm is based on moral claims (primarily of the hungry) rather than rights or obligations. It might be argued that moral claims and rights amount to the same thing, but this argument suffers from a similar problem to the conflation of norms and rules – a conflation of two quite different forms of normative power. This is because moral claims connote humanitarian (soft) rather than legal (hard) normative power.

One responds to a moral claim out of a moral sense of rightness – to refer to this as humanitarian means such a sense of rightness is based on a common bond of humanity. In contrast, response to a rights claim could be said to come as much from a sense of legal obligation implied by the existence of a 'right', as from a substantive sense of rightness. The sense of rightness in the case of a rights claim brings to bear an important procedural norm – that a set of rules ought to be commonly adopted and applied consistently as a basis for collective security – as well as relying on a common bond of humanity.

The development of the UN system has been largely modelled on a modernising liberal democratic state, one of the most significant effects of which has been a culture of articulating the work of the system largely in terms of the formulation and application of consistent sets of rules, governed principally through the concept of international law. These processes are referred to by Boli and Thomas as demonstrating the cultural principles of 'rationalizing progress', and of 'world citizenship' which is 'codified' in UN instruments (Boli and Thomas 1999, 38-40).

The norms and principles underpinning much of the regime and organizational structure in the UN system draw from assumptions about the centrality of laws and rules as a code for rights – whether state or human (Evans 1996). Many of the norms in international regimes ultimately call up the sense of being part of a system of rules or contracts linked to the notion that the rule of law is what can overcome a Hobbesian state of nature, acquiring legitimacy through its consistent, fair application. The treaties, agreements and protocols formally defining the terrain of much of the system are legal documents, and often the language of international regime norms is the language of law. Many of these rules are reflections of underlying norms pertaining to such things as fair treatment, respect for autonomy, protection from abuse or torture, for example. The codifying signals the shared acceptance and legitimacy of those norms, but it also creates a normative procedural overlay on top of those substantive norms. As a result of this overlay, conforming to the rules could mean respect for the underlying norm, but this is entwined with a signal of respect for the norm of following the rules (or fear of sanctions or loss of reputation for breaching the rules).

In making this argument, I am positing a difference between a norm and the legal mechanisms that claim to express the norm. The difference is analogous to the distinction between an international regime and an international organization. In both cases, the latter may be important, even central to the former, but it does not cover all aspects of it. Norms (regimes) do not constitute laws (organizations), but frame their establishment, and in turn are influenced by their operation (Kratochwil 1989).

Fundamental to rule-based codification of norms is the notion of sanctions for breaching the law/norm, linked to the notion that the threat of sanctions will help compel adherence, especially where compliance is viewed as against the short-run interest of a state. For example, US refusal to ratify the Kyoto Protocol on carbon emissions, or to be party to the International Criminal Court, is often portrayed as a problem in terms of the incapacity of the system to compel the most powerful state to adhere to important norms (Newman, Thakur et al. 2006). Conversely, from the perspective of US policy makers, the problem with such instruments seems to be with their very compulsion which threatens their sovereign power (Eckersley 2007). In this context, it seems appropriate to think of the related regime norms as based on a central presumption of 'hard' legal power. Thus hard normative power is implied when international regime norms take a form, for example relating to 'progress', 'development', 'security', 'peace and welfare'; 'sovereignty' or 'human rights', which is then codified in quasi-legal terms, expressed as rules or rights.

In contrast, the proposition that hungry people should be fed does not necessarily involve rules or rights in this sense; that is, the rights and obligations that the norm implies have remained implicit and relatively uncodified in the IFAR.[4] Uvin hints at the distinctive nature of this norm when he describes the international food aid regime as 'developmental' or 'humanitarian', meaning 'not-self-interested' (Uvin 1992), but this difference goes deeper than merely representing ideas such as humanitarianism. The feed-the-hungry norm appears to have a humanitarian moral ontology different to many other regime norms, meaning it has less connection to rights-based discourses, and frames the politics of the regime differently.[5]

This difference is illustrated by the WFP's voluntary funding. One important historical impact of its joint UN-FAO genesis was that from its inception the WFP was not given access to UN funding derived from assessed contributions to the UN by member-states. Consequently, unlike the UN's other operational agencies, the WFP has always relied on voluntary donations for its funding. This reliance on voluntary funding also points to the absence of quasi-legal compulsion as an implicit underpinning of the food aid regime norm.

Congruence with the US

The fact that the WFP has largely absented itself from the discourse within the UN system on the Right to Food (see Chapter Six for a more detailed discussion of this) can be interpreted not only as a reflection of US hostility to such discourses, but also as consistent with the soft normative power context in the regime. That is, the rights-based discourse on hunger can be interpreted as conflicting with the voluntarist donor ethos within the WFP. This ethos echoes the initial domestic US response to hunger in the Depression (cf Poppendieck 1986), and the early post-war policy responses by the US to international hunger (cf Bentley 1994) and is just one of many aspects of the norm which demonstrate the close normative relationship between the regime and US politics.

In other words, the characteristics of the feed-the-hungry norm that render it as a form of soft normative power are entwined with its congruence with a domestic US feed-the-hungry norm.

In fact, the international norm has a counterpart norm at the domestic US level which occupies a strong place in domestic politics, enjoying reliable bipartisan support (Zeigler 2005). The domestic political strength of this norm in the US is unusual amongst norms underpinning international regimes, avoiding as it does a reliance on international legal norms, while tapping into a strong domestic political constituency. This normative congruence is an important factor in explaining the extraordinarily strong support for the WFP within and from the US since its inception. In turn it helps explain how the WFP has achieved responsibility for control over significant material resources, even while being a typical UN organization in terms of governance structures. In combination, these factors amount to a compelling depiction of the centrality to the regime of both the feed-the-hungry norm and US hegemony.

In order to explain these propositions in more detail, I turn now to examine more closely what the 'feed-the-hungry norm' means, in both the US and in the international regime.

A normative analysis of US food aid

The standard depiction of how and why the WFP was established calls up an 'interest-based' analysis. In this analysis, the multilateral food aid program, with the US as by far the dominant donor, is portrayed as an exercise to help legitimize the much larger US bilateral food aid program, which in turn was focused on getting rid of troublesome agricultural surpluses and contributing to US export market development and strategic aims. At the domestic level within the US these aims were linked to a transfer of resources to an electorally powerful agricultural sector.[6] However, such an analysis is too narrow to adequately explain the ways in which the WFP, the IFAR and US domestic politics have entwined and influenced each other into the twenty-first century. It also begs the question of how those interests have been constructed, and why their pursuit has taken the form it has.

Though most policy can be described in terms of a mix of normative and interest-based motives, what is interesting about food aid policy is its particularly explicit rendering of this mixture. Any examination of American actions and motives in relation to food aid must take into account the interlinked normative, strategic and economic interests involved. For example, as I argue in Chapter Three, due to their entwining with agricultural protection interests since the 1930s, by the 1950s food aid norms became ranked ahead of trade liberalisation norms in the US domestic values hierarchy. This is an example not only of a norm constructing interests, but of interests contributing to the political significance of a norm.

At the normative level, the US food aid program, while in part related to and driven by economic interests, is also about a moral imperative to do good with abundance. The complex interrelationship between 'interests and morality' creates tensions between the notion that doing good should run counter to self-interest (it should be a 'burden'), and the notion that the best policy aligns the two.

George McGovern told his staff at the Office of Food for Peace (where he was responsible for US bilateral and multilateral food aid) after his appointment as Director in early 1961:

> There had been enough complaining about farm surpluses. There was no such thing as a 'burdensome farm surplus' as long as there were

> hungry children in the world. So, I said, let's praise our farmers for their skill, hard work, and productivity and tell them that they make it possible for us to have the great privilege of feeding our fellow humans (McGovern 2001, 52).

Such normative imperatives had been embedded in American public policy since at least the Depression era, as Poppendieck documents (Poppendieck 1986). Early in the Depression years, a popular, powerful and enduring depiction of the injustice of hunger and malnutrition in the context of large surpluses of food commodities was that of a 'paradox of want amidst plenty' (Bentley 1994; Counihan 2002; Levenstein 2003; Poppendieck 1986). Widespread reports in 1930–32 of simultaneous starvation in depressed areas and destruction of a range of agricultural produce rendered worthless by price fluctuations (examples cited included pigs, milk, and oranges), caused public scandal and played a role in the election of the new Roosevelt administration on the basis of a 'New Deal' (Poppendieck 1986).

Political debates have occurred in America periodically about the best means to address hunger – whether by government action or by volunteerism. These debates were framed as Hoover's voluntarism versus Roosevelt's New Deal in the 1932 Presidential election. Poppendieck cites a public statement by President Hoover in 1931 regarding the debate over Federal relief for the poor in the Depression, articulating the voluntarist view:

> 'My own conviction,' he [Hoover] asserted, 'is strongly that if we break down this sense of responsibility, of individual generosity to individual, and mutual self-help in the country in times of national difficulty and if we start appropriations of this character we have not only impaired something infinitely valuable in the life of the American people but have struck at the roots of self-government.' Local and voluntary efforts were 'the American way of relieving distress among our own people,' he contended, 'and the country is successfully meeting its problem in the American way today' (Poppendieck 1986, 51).

Bentley argues similar debates over rationing and post-war food aid policy were cut short by President Truman appointing former President Hoover to run the post-war food relief efforts in Europe:[7]

> Hoover's intense compassion for and sense of obligation toward famine victims fuelled his lifelong involvement with international famine relief. But his equally passionate belief in limited government and the ideology of voluntarism persuaded him that famine relief be

> conducted strictly outside government controls... By appointing Hoover as head of the administration's newly-formed Famine Emergency Committee, Truman was helping to reintroduce the pre-Depression ideology of voluntarism and limited government intervention – the same ideology that had been rejected as deficient and an ideological failure by the New Dealers (Bentley 1994, 6).

Poppendieck, Brown and others document the replaying of these debates in response to the US domestic hunger crisis of the early to mid 1980s, in which the Reagan administration, apart from disputing the existence of a crisis, insisted on the importance of a voluntarist response (Berry 1984; Brown and Pizer 1987; Poppendieck 1997; 1998). The feed-the-hungry norm provides the backdrop to this political debate about ways and means – reflected in the presumption embedded in these debates which places the goal of feeding the hungry beyond question.

Also, notwithstanding political debates about the place of voluntarism, Truman's appointment of Hoover amounted to a framing of food aid as bipartisan – beyond the Democrat/Republican divide. This bipartisan framing was echoed again in the 1970s when Democrat Senator George McGovern and Republican Senator Bob Dole teamed as Chair and Deputy Chair of the Senate Committee on Nutrition.[8]

The US feed-the-hungry norm acquired much of its political significance in domestic policy terms from the New Deal and can be seen as deeply embedded in the development and expansion of a domestic food stamps system during the 1950s and 1960s (e.g. Berry 1984). Such post-war developments paralleled the US policy developments concerning foreign food aid of the same period, which in their own ways had stemmed from policy responses to the Second World War.

President Roosevelt's State of the Union speech to Congress in 1941 became famous for its enumeration of the 'Four Freedoms':

> In the future days, which we seek to make secure, we look forward to a world founded upon four essential human freedoms.
>
> The first is freedom of speech and expression—everywhere in the world.
>
> The second is freedom of every person to worship God in his own way—everywhere in the world.

> The third is freedom from want—which, translated into world terms, means economic understandings which will secure to every nation a healthy peacetime life for its inhabitants—everywhere in the world.
>
> The fourth is freedom from fear—which, translated into world terms, means a world-wide reduction of armaments to such a point and in such a thorough fashion that no nation will be in a position to commit an act of physical aggression against any neighbor—anywhere in the world.
>
> That is no vision of a distant millennium. It is a definite basis for a kind of world attainable in our own time and generation. That kind of world is the very antithesis of the so-called new order of tyranny which the dictators seek to create with the crash of a bomb.
>
> To that new order we oppose the greater conception—the moral order. A good society is able to face schemes of world domination and foreign revolutions alike without fear. (Woolley and Peters nd).

This speech was made 11 months before Pearl Harbor brought America into the war, but focused on placing the nation on a war footing to fight the spread of fascism (Dallek 1979). No mention was made of hunger in it. However, the 'Third Freedom' (from Want) was to become reified by and for the feed-the-hungry norm. Norman Rockwell made a series of pictorial representations of Roosevelt's Four Freedoms for the *Saturday Evening Post* in 1943.[9] Bentley describes their significance, in particular that of the third freedom:

> The public immediately embraced the series of paintings, to such an extent that it seemed as if the paintings had inspired the themes they were intended to illustrate. These paintings, reproduced by the millions, conveyed what was at stake for American families in this global battle against fascism. *Freedom from Want*, for example, gathers up images of domesticity and material plenty. An older man, presumably the patriarch of this extended, Euro-American family, sits at the head of the table, dressed in his Sunday best, and gazes down in obvious pleasure at the oversized, succulent turkey his aproned wife has placed in front of him...Yet *Freedom from Want* was controversial as well as popular. Some, particularly U.S. allies, found the lavishly dressed turkey an inappropriate symbol during a global war which left so many hungry and undernourished. Most Americans, however, identified with the scene...[which] seemed to embody the best of what the United States stood for – stable and extended families, abundant material wealth, familiar rituals, non-denominational and patriotic celebration (Bentley 2002, 171).

In keeping with this reification, McGovern entitled his memoir, written while US Ambassador to the UN food agencies in Rome, *The Third Freedom: Ending Hunger in our Time*, placing the relevant excerpt from Roosevelt's speech before the Preface (McGovern 2001, 9), before going on to outline the significance of his experience of hunger and desperation amongst farmers as a boy during the Depression to his interest in the issue.

The power of the Depression experience is important in its demonstration of the apparent alternatives to food aid – if the surplus stocks were not being given in aid, they would be being destroyed, or stored at large cost until no longer edible. If they were to be destroyed, in the context of global hunger such actions would create a 'paradox' counter both to morality, and in a narrower sense interests: what kind of nation destroys food when there are hungry people, how can it serve US interests to be such a nation? Such a construction of (self)-interest in relation to food aid forms an important part of American identity, based on the feed-the-hungry norm.

Food aid: burden or self-interest?

It is important to clarify the different normative dimensions of US food aid policy – as burden and as virtuous self-interest.

By the 1960s, in the context of the founding of the WFP, one important element of the shift to supporting multilateral food aid came from the burden-sharing argument. This proposed that while the contribution of food aid had been pre-eminently American, given that it involved 'doing good', other countries needed to do their bit too, and a multilateral program was needed to enable such 'burden sharing'. Burden sharing was to be cited as the reason for initiating the Food Aid Convention (FAC) later in the 1960s as well (Hopkins 1987; see Chapter Three for details on the FAC). This concept of food aid and feeding the hungry as a burden had a pedigree dating from at least the end of World War II, in a context of wartime rationing having been linked to the allocation of food aid:

> President Truman took to the airwaves to alert Americans that something must be done. 'For the world as a whole, a food crisis has developed which may prove to be the worst in modern times,' Truman told the nation in a special February 1946 broadcast. 'Under these circumstances,' he continued, 'it is apparent that only through superhuman efforts can mass starvation be prevented...I am sure that the American people are in favor of *carrying their share of the burden*...Truman then outlined his plan to reduce wheat and fats

> consumption in the United States so as to donate as much as possible to needy countries (Bentley 1994, 5, emphasis added).

Bentley criticises the refusal of Truman and his post-war food aid administrator Hoover to continue with a rationing regime. Rather, in the administration of post-war food relief, food aid was completely delinked from any immediate requirement for the sort of consumer sacrifices created through wartime rationing. Food aid was designed to support agricultural interests and created consumer sacrifice only in the sense that commodity prices were being maintained at high levels through government purchase of agricultural commodities. Nevertheless, there is a strong sense of American food aid being in some sense burdensome dating from at least World War II.

If food aid were simply an exercise in economic and strategic self-interest this would imply that characterising it as a burden was no more than rhetoric or 'spin'. However, such a depiction of the burden-sharing discourse does not grasp the extent to which both domestic and foreign audiences accepted it as having some validity, despite awareness of the self-interest arguments. Rather, characterising food aid as a 'burden' demonstrates the complex interaction between norms and interests.

Food aid is a burden partly because it represents a tangible, voluntary transfer of resources – on the face of it, a transfer burdensome to the donor. The characterisation of food aid as generous gift giving and hence in some sense 'burdensome' to the giver helps undercut accusations of purely self-interested motives and reassures Americans that there really is a normative basis for their food aid programs. After all, if it were not burdensome, where would be the generosity inherent in the action?

However, the notion of the food aid program as a burden, reflecting its limits, has never been overplayed. Rather, and using a different kind of normative logic, a virtue has been made of its service of economic interests. McGovern explicitly refers to the strength of US food aid policy deriving from its unique mix of humanitarianism and service of economic interests –

> I have been in public life for most of my adulthood. During those years I have never seen a government program that was a better blend of self-interest and moral purpose than Food for Peace (McGovern 2001, 57).[10]

McGovern attributes a normative quality to this blending in itself – it is a 'better blend'. This normative quality relates to the capacity of such a blend of motivations to generate policy on a consensual basis in the complex, pluralistic political environment of the US. Thus the normative virtue of food aid policy is partly that everyone fits inside the tent. Such inclusion is a function of a norm that is widely held and deeply embedded in the national polity.

Defining the feed-the-hungry norm

> Instead of dropping bombs in Europe, we were now distributing nutritious food. In some instances American food went to hungry Germans who a few days earlier had been trying their best to shoot us out of the skies. I will wager that no European who was fed by this first American airlift after the war will ever forget it. I am even more certain that my fellow pilots and our crews will not forget the pride we felt in converting our bombers to angels of mercy at a terrible time in the life of the world.
>
> This was the spirit that later shaped the great Marshall Plan, Food for Peace, the Peace Corps, America's ongoing foreign assistance, the United Nations, and the religious and philanthropic outreach of the American people. Americans have saved the lives of countless human beings since World War II. And now we will play our part in reaching the 800 million who still hunger and thirst (McGovern 2001,68).

In an echo of this half a century later, writing four weeks after the terrorist attack of 9 September 2001, Counihan noted that 'U.S. fighter planes are dropping bombs and U.S. C-17 cargo planes are air-dropping food packets over Afghanistan' (Counihan 2002, 11).[11]

These are examples of what seems almost an American reflex to respond to crises at a public policy level with food assistance. In the course of an interview with Catherine Bertini, (WFP Executive Director 1992–2002), this was raised with her, leading her to respond that, in America, there is a strong view that 'we ought to feed everybody' (Bertini 2005b).

When Bertini was an Assistant Secretary at the US Department of Agriculture (1989–1991) she was in charge of domestic food aid expenditures of $US40 billion, compared with, at most, $US4 billion as WFP Executive Director (Bertini 2005b). Notwithstanding the still large Federal food aid expenditures (Nestle 2002; Usborne 2008), Poppendieck documents the massive food assistance voluntary sector that has grown since 1980 in the US (Poppendieck 1997; 1998), and in doing so sheds further light on the place of the feed-the-hungry norm in American society. The enormous bureaucratic and civil society apparatus in the US built around this norm is not duplicated in other Anglophone liberal democracies, such as the United Kingdom, Australia, and New Zealand, though Canada may be a partial exception to this (Davis and Tarasuk 1994; Riches 1997a).

In other words, in the US there is a domestic feed-the-hungry norm. This norm can be described largely in terms of two characteristics – its link to a distinctive set of moral claims, and its definition as politically transcendent, reflecting the interests involved in policy making in the area.

Moral claims

Poppendieck, in explaining the embrace of domestic food assistance programs by anti-poverty campaigners in America in the 1960s, describes the distinctive virtues of food as aid (in the domestic context) as follows:

> Anti-poverty activists made a strategic decision to pursue the reform and expansion of food programmes, rather than the more adequate cash assistance that might have made such programmes unnecessary...advocates for the poor identified hunger 'as the one problem to which the public might respond. They reasoned that "hunger" made a higher moral claim than any of the other problems of poverty. Federally supported housing and jobs programs could wait; but no one should go hungry in affluent America' (Poppendieck 1997, 135, citing Kotz 1984).

The 'moral claim' of the hungry suffuses most texts concerned with food aid. However, McGovern aligns it with another moral claim – that of the farmers who produce the food through honest toil (McGovern 2001, 16, 21). This claim runs deep within the American polity – as Shklar notes, 'When the founders of the American Republic equated the upright citizen with the man who works, they had a particular kind of worker in mind, the sturdy yeoman tilling his own soil or the independent craftsman' (cited in Sennett 2003, 107).

An organised and politically influential farm lobby appeared in the US during the 1920s and 1930s (Hansen 1991), and laid the foundations for protectionism in agricultural production. Food aid policy from the 1940s became closely connected to the protection of agricultural interests in American politics, and reflected the political significance of the farm sector in Congress. Yet the interactions of food aid with agricultural protection became important for normative as much as economic reasons. Food aid reminded farmers and other Americans that support for US agriculture enabled America to feed the world.

Yet, paralleling the way in which there is more to American food aid policy than narrow pursuit of national strategic or economic interest, it is not possible to reduce the moral claims of producers to being merely a function of their rationally-based economic interests. Barrett and Maxwell in their survey of the economic literature on food aid show how little evidence there is of economic benefit to producers from food aid policies – 'the benefits to American farmers come purely through image and the "warm glow" of knowing that their crops are being shipped to poor countries and peoples, even if the food aid largely displaces commercial imports of the same commodities' (Barrett and Maxwell 2005, 37).[12] Ultimately, the role played by 'economic interests' cannot be understood in isolation from the norms which help construct the perception of those interests and related policy.

The other side of the coin from the moral claim is moral hazard. Moral hazard is a term primarily used in insurance economics (Dufwenbergy and Lundholmz 1998, 2) and game theory (Dutta and Radner 1994), referring to the disincentive effects of economic support; for example, unemployment insurance removing the incentive for unemployed individuals to look for or accept work. Moral hazard is also referred to as a potential cost in connection with bail-outs of failed banks (Bovens 1998), funds or, in the case of the IMF, defaulting countries. In such contexts the benefits of systemic stability are put ahead of the moral hazard resulting from the perceived elimination of penalty or risk from failure.

While there is a considerable specialist economic literature on moral hazard, the concept derives from very old concerns with the moral implications of assistance to the poor. Since the Reformation such concerns have been prominently linked to the capitalist work ethic (Weber 1976), based on concern that excessive assistance for the poor will undermine or displace any incentives for self-sufficiency and self-responsibility, and thence undermine moral qualities essential for proper individual behaviour and effective social and political structures – concerns echoed in the citation above from Hoover. If people think they will be looked after by society, why would they, indeed anyone, choose to work? In more recent years, this reasoning has in part been applied in the neoliberal critique of 'welfare dependency' and the campaign for welfare reform (King 1999; Nestle 2002; Riches 1997a).[13]

Moral hazard arguments help explain the enthusiasm for food assistance in Depression era America. Giving individuals or groups of people money was replete with risks of moral hazard, even if they were starving. For example it could lead to indolence, or the money being wasted on vices such as drinking and gambling. Food is not fungible in the way money is - that is, it is not easily substituted for other things. The directed nature of the assistance reduced problems of moral hazard, while doing something practical to assist poor and starving people.

Conversely, applying such moral hazard reasoning to the plight of farmers required support from government linked to their production. Farmers were hard working and productive – the more so, the more they were innocent victims of 'market forces' in the context of extremely low commodity prices. To fail to support such farmers financially through the purchase of produce at guaranteed prices would be morally hazardous, as it would send a signal that hard productive work would not be rewarded. In this context, food aid was in a unique normative position – it answered moral claims (of both starving people and farmers) while avoiding moral hazard more convincingly than financial assistance could.[14]

A third moral claim, in addition to the claims of the hungry and the producers is that of a nation that both produces food efficiently enough to have surplus and distributes it to the needy. Farm surpluses, McGovern noted in 1961,

> testified to the efficiency of our farmers, who comprised only 4 per cent of the American populace and yet produced enough food to feed the other 96 per cent plus millions of people abroad. By contrast, the Soviet Union, our cold war competitor, with half of its population engaged in farming, was unable to feed the other half' (McGovern 2001, 52).

President George W Bush updated these sentiments in 2001, when he told the Future Farmers of America:

> It's important for our nation to build – to grow foodstuffs, to feed our people. Can you imagine a country that was unable to grow enough food to feed the people? It would be a nation subject to international pressure. It would be a nation at risk. And so when we're talking about American agriculture, we're really talking about a national security issue (U.S. President George W. Bush in remarks to the Future Farmers of America, July 27, 2001, Washington, DC, (cited in Suppan 2002, 1).

In light of this national moral claim, American food aid is seen as contributing to as well as reflecting a national self-image as a nation which is productive and generous. Another form of this national moral claim lies in the requirement of the US Congress that all food aid donations be clearly labelled as 'a gift of the people of the United States.' This requirement resulted in the greeting on the food aid packages airdropped into Afghanistan mentioned above.[15]

Defining the feed-the-hungry norm

While the feed-the-hungry norm is largely based on these three moral claims, its definition involves two other important elements – its construction as transcending politics, and its distinction from financial aid.

Hunger is something which is arguably universal to human experience (who has never been hungry?), and also universally regarded as a thing which can be changed with the provision of food. This is an issue on which people across a broad political spectrum can apparently agree (Poppendieck 1998, Ch9), though politics starts to intrude if, rather than just getting food to the hungry, questions are raised about why people are starving. Such questions pose problems for power structures in US domestic politics (Poppendieck 1997), and for nation-state sovereignty in the international regime, so the operation of the norm tends to avoid such issues. This means certain boundaries around the moral claims of the hungry, which tend to limit their claim to an immediate alleviation of suffering through access to food. Such limits focus organizational work and attention on practical and logistical issues – getting food to the hungry.

Another aspect of this politically transcendent definition is the use of the qualifier 'children' to define the hungry to which the norm refers. This is reflected in the emphasis given children in US domestic food aid programs, such as school feeding, and the WIC (Women and Infant Children) program. An emphasis on children has also been evident in WFP and other aid agency discourse for some time. Catherine Bertini when arguing for US support for the WFP providing famine relief to North Korea in 1997 cited Ronald Reagan to a sceptical Administration: 'a hungry child knows no politics' (Bertini 2005b; McGovern 2001, 60). Public statements from the WFP frequently make a point of mentioning hungry children in particular. For example, WFP Executive Director Josette Sheeran begins her Preface to the 2009 Annual Report with the following two sentences:

> 2008 was one of the most challenging— yet most rewarding—in WFP's history. Faced with the triple threat of the food, fuel and

> financial crises, this extraordinary organization showed once again that nothing gets between WFP and a hungry child (WFP 2009, 2; see also Morris 2006).

Uvin noted a long established 'exceptionalism' for children in the measurement of hunger, in which children's nutritional status is assessed in comparison with a baseline derived from the full growth and development of a small sample of rich country children, while the adult minimum threshold is defined at a body mass ratio 'just enough to stay alive without doing any physical activity' (Uvin 1994, 69). He suggests this '"exceptionalism" for children seems to be linked to the powerful emotional appeal of children, and the clever way in which UNICEF has been able to push through its agenda with its sister organizations.' (Uvin 1994, 69).[16]

On the other hand, the emphasis on children is not only a matter of spin or emotional manipulation. For those working in food aid, there is a constant awareness that adequate nutrition at early ages can make the difference, not only between life and death, but between normal or adequate development, and stunted growth, and a physically and mentally shortened and constrained life. For example, as one senior WFP official noted, there must be real concern as to where the next generation of leaders in North Korea will come from, given the endemic and widespread malnutrition of children in that country (Interview #11 2005).

Whether it is seen as part of a media-friendly strategy, or done for sound humanitarian reasons, the emphasis on children fits with feed-the -hungry norms that transcend politics (Interview #11 2005), both in the US and internationally. It is also consistent with the differentiation of food, as something that can directly assist children, from financial assistance, which must come to children indirectly.

Since at least the 1930s Depression, food as aid has been, for the most part, carefully distinguished from financial forms of aid, though both could take the form of grants or soft loans. To some degree the distinction can be explained in terms of pragmatics and differing backgrounds, in particular the link between food aid and surplus disposal, but this does not capture the normative dimension of the distinction. Poppendieck's suggestion of a 'double halo' effect - where food aid achieves both relief for the hungry and avoidance of waste (Poppendieck 1998, 150-2) places food aid on a different normative plane from financial aid. The distinctive nature of food as a tangible, concrete resource repeatedly comes to the fore in food aid discourse

(Byers 2005; Poppendieck 1997; 1998) in a manner that implies a subtle positive contrast to monetary assistance.[17]

Given this 'logic of appropriateness,' as food aid developed in the United States, it is not surprising that the food aid allocations in the budget before Congress in the 1950s were alone in aid allocations in never being cut back (Shaw 2001, 33). This different treatment was echoed 40 years later by the exemption of the Federal food stamps program from radical changes to 'dollar-based welfare' under the Congressional welfare reform program 'Contract with America' (King 1999). These examples do not just illustrate the political strength of the agricultural interests involved. Food aid is in a unique normative position – it answers moral claims (both of starving people, in particular children, and of farmers), and creates a kind of national moral claim on the part of a nation 'blessed with surplus', while avoiding the normatively suspect abstraction of financial assistance.

The feed-the-hungry norm in the international regime

> ...when the US Secretary of State speaks at the UN General Assembly about food aid to the Third World, he will stress the humanitarian and development objectives of the aid. The same man, or his colleague from USDA, speaking before Congress in order to get the food aid bill passed, or before the Chamber of Commerce of an agricultural region, will refer to the foreign policy and/or market creating role of food aid. This indicates that the norms applying to food aid are different on the international level than on the national US level. (Uvin 1994, 22-3).

The distinction between food aid and financial aid is also apparent in the context of the international regime, albeit with an inverse normative implication, making food aid a 'second best' to financial aid.

Before the formal establishment of the WFP important decisions had been made that established particular boundaries and hierarchies around the development issue area. In 1960, before serving on the expert panel advising the FAO Director-General on the establishment of a multilateral food aid agency, the economist Hans Singer had acted as an adviser to UN Secretary-General Dag Hammarskjöld. In that role he drafted a proposal for the World Bank to deploy food aid as an integrated component of reconstruction and development projects it supported. Hammarskjöld contacted World Bank president Eugene Black 'proposing that the Bank establish a separate management division to undertake multilateral food aid' but Black declined the proposal (Shaw 2001, 27-8). Shaw comments on these events as follows:

> The schism between multilateral soft financing and food aid, with the former going to the World Bank and the latter to WFP, was to have lasting negative repercussions. It was to result in a lower level of co-ordination of financial and food aid than might have otherwise occurred, to the mutual detriment of both types of assistance. It was also to result in different methods of appraisal, operational procedures and evaluation, even mind-sets, and odious comparisons, in which food aid came to be regarded as a 'second class' resource. This also reflected the state of affairs in bilateral aid programmes where food aid was handled differently from other forms of assistance, by separate administrative units, and with special legislative, financial and operating procedures. inhibiting the fusion of the different forms of aid. On the other hand, the birth of WFP might be seen as part of a wider compromise in which food aid and pre-investment financing were given to the United Nations as 'consolation prizes' for the loss of a soft financing facility to the World Bank (Shaw 2001, 28).

Shaw in the citation above sees the embedded distinction between food and financial aid as a mistake based largely on a preference of the World Bank President (and former Governor of the US Federal Reserve) Eugene Black, and reflecting some specific UN/World Bank trade offs. He suggests that from this decision point some sort of normative divide between the different forms of aid sprang up, but could have been avoided if a different path had been taken. This view underestimates the importance and depth of the divide between food aid and financial aid already in play in American domestic politics, reflected in the existence of a specific food aid lobby closely linked to the farm lobby in Congress since at least the early stages of the Eisenhower administration. For advocates of food aid, and for many involved with the distribution of financial forms of aid, it was important to keep them separate. In a sense, each saw the other form as a potential 'contaminant' of the different arguments for what they were doing.

This issues demonstrates the importance of differentiating between the American domestic feed-the-hungry norm and the feed-the-hungry norm in the international food aid regime. While literature such as Shaw's, written from the international regime perspective, exhibits a sense of food aid as being regarded as a 'second class' resource, such a view is difficult to discern in literature written from an American perspective. Comparing the two norms with reference to the moral claims they render highlights the complex interaction between interests and norms and between the US and the WFP.

Moral claims and local purchasing

The hungry poor are constituted quite differently in the international regime as opposed to the US context . The hungry poor in the US include both domestic and international populations. For the WFP the hungry poor are solely in developing countries. This difference reflects the fact that, unlike in the US domestic context, in the international regime the hungry poor are being viewed through the prism of the intergovernmental Executive Board of the WFP where the other two moral claims – of producers and of countries with agricultural surpluses – are operating in ways that have limited correlation with US domestic politics.

As a result, the international regime norm places the moral claims of developing country producers in a prominent position just behind the claims of the hungry poor (there is, after all, considerable overlap between the two) through the established WFP policy of preferring local purchasing of food aid, more recently given added impetus in the form of the WFP's P4P (Purchase for Progress) program (WFP 2009; Mousseau 2010). Local purchasing involves the food aid being purchased by WFP using donated cash in the recipient country where possible, or alternatively a nearby developing country. It is in a similar category to other aid purchasing modalities such as triangular transactions. In such transactions the donor countries purchase agricultural produce for donation from developing nations close to the recipient nation and send it as food aid to the recipient, thereby improving agricultural development in a third country as well as enabling the aid to arrive in a more timely fashion (Shaw and Clay 1993, 3).[18] These modalities of aid purchasing are grouped together under the heading of procurement in developing countries.

In its early phase, donor domination of the international regime was such that the claims of producers existed largely amongst competing agricultural exporters – that is, the various moral claims of US, Canadian, Australian and Argentinian farmers. This had started to change by the time of the World Food Conference of 1974:

> Food procurement from developing countries was first promoted at the World Food Conference in 1974, which called for 'improved policy for food aid' and urged donor countries to provide cash resources for commodity purchases in developing countries. In 1979, the Committee on Food Aid Policies and Programmes (CFA) adopted Guidelines and Criteria for Food Aid Programmes, which recommended triangular purchases with a view to diversifying food aid to suit beneficiary consumption habits. (WFP 2006e, 8).

The WFP's capacity to use local purchasing was initially limited by the preference of donors for giving commodities rather than cash donations. Notwithstanding this, WFP first used local and triangular purchases on a large scale 'in Asia in the seventies as a result of the influx of Cambodian refugees into Thailand', and from the early eighties introduced local and triangular purchasing practices in Africa with 'the purchase of maize surpluses from Zimbabwe' (WFP 2001a, 4).

As the international food aid regime evolved, and a consensus generating epistemic community emerged (Hopkins 1992), three overlapping characteristics of global hunger became accepted. These were, first, the prevalence of rural poverty in connection with hunger and food insecurity in developing countries (Shaw and Clay 1993; Whiteford and Ferguson 1991); second, related to this, the importance of establishing and encouraging localised agricultural production and markets in preventing hunger (Barrett and Maxwell 2005). Lastly, much economic and development research emerged on the market disruption and dependency generated by donor food aid (Bovard 1993; George 1991; Schultz 1993; Singer 1993). In this context, the pre-eminent moral claim of producers in the IFAR shifted to being that of farmers in developing countries. This normative shift was reflected in the shifts in policy in the WFP to placing an emphasis on local purchasing, and more broadly procurement in developing countries, facilitated by a shift from in-kind donations to monetary donations (WFP 2006e).

Reflecting the central role of the WFP within the IFAR, and its connection to the moral claims of developing country producers within the international feed-the-hungry norm, '[t]he likelihood that food aid is procured locally or regionally is significantly higher when food aid is channelled multilaterally rather than through NGOs or bilaterally' (INTERFAIS/WFP 2008, 10). Between 2001–04 procurement from developing countries averaged 62% of the WFP's total procurement (WFP 2006e, 10), and in 2008 the proportion reached almost 72% (2.8 million metric tons of 3.3 million metric tons distributed), up from 63.6% in 2007 (WFP 2009, 8). Table 2.1 shows that developing country procurement has long been established as the majority mode of WFP purchasing.

Table 2.1: Developing countries as source of WFP purchases (%), 1990–1997

Year	**1990**	**1991**	**1992**	**1993**
%	58	72	71	62
Year	**1994**	**1995**	**1996**	**1997**
%	60	55	62	50

Source: (WFP 2001a, 8 Chart 1).
Note – 'The [1997] substantial increase in overall purchases and the decline in the percentage of procurement from developing countries is mainly due to a fundamental change in how Canada's contribution to WFP is made. Traditionally, the Canadian Government purchased cereals from the Canadian Wheat Board for their in-kind cereal contributions to WFP. However, starting in 1997, WFP was requested to effect the purchases from the Canadian Wheat Board on behalf of the Government of Canada. Therefore, the [decline in] percentage share of purchases from developing countries in the 1997 figures is less dramatic in substance than a superficial reading of the chart would suggest.' (WFP 2001a, 4).

Chart 2.1 shows the extent to which developing country procurement has been established not only in multilateral food aid practices, but has begun to influence the other channels, both NGO and bilateral, of food aid. There has been a steady, if somewhat slow, shift from direct supply of commodities from rich agricultural exporting countries towards procurement from developing countries. This trend has increased most recently with policy shifts by major donor sources such as Europe, Australia, Japan and Canada from the mid-1990s, as well as the increasing importance of multilateral food aid.

Though donor control through tying of food aid is still a significant issue (OECD 2006), this has been a long-term normative shift in the IFAR of great significance. The differences between IFAR and domestic US food aid norms, along with the interrelated political power of vested interests, are at least partially connected to the delays in the US shifting more of its contributions from in-kind to monetary donations, though almost all other donors have done so (Barrett and Maxwell 2005). Attempts by the George W. Bush administration to shift a proportion of food aid appropriations from commodities to cash were frustrated by Congress in connection with vigorous lobbying by the US food aid lobby (Hammink 2007; Levinson 2007; Ozer 2008).

Chart 2.1: Percentage of food aid procured in developing countries, 1991-2007

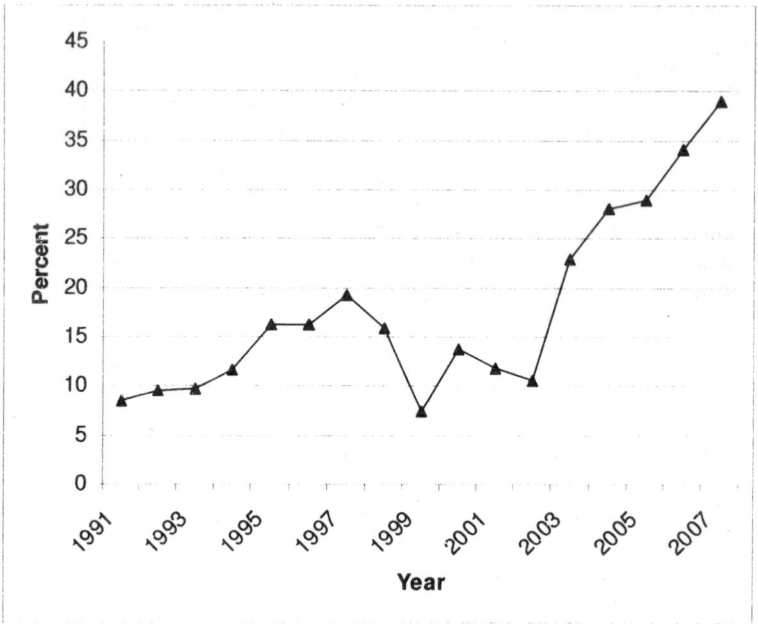

Data Sources: (INTERFAIS/WFP 2008, xi; WFP 1996, 27; WFP 2003b, Annex 1, 34).

However, the shift in the IFAR from in-kind to monetary donation has also been associated with a decline in overall resources. For example, when EU nations changed to cash from in-kind contributions there was a significant drop in the overall level of contribution (Interview #16 2005). This is a point strongly emphasised by US interests opposed to these changes. In 2005 then US Agency for International Development (USAID) Administrator Andrew Natsios gave a speech to US food aid lobbyists flagging a move to increase the proportion of cash contribution in the food aid budget – it 'went down like a lead balloon' with his audience (Zeigler 2005). Signalling the link between trade negotiations and domestic US food aid, Clapp cites a letter to then US Trade Representative Zoellick from the National Wheat Growers Association advising ".'...producers across the nation are strong supporters of humanitarian programs, but will not be willing to support cash-only programs' " (Clapp 2004, 1444).

Of course, it is not surprising that those groups in the US which actually receive, or at least perceive, a benefit from maintaining in-kind American donations would take such a position. There has been a long tradition of criticism of food aid because of its benefits to such interest groups (George 1991; Patel 2007), though such criticisms have had little obvious effect on US policies. They have had more effect at the multilateral level, contributing to the normative shift that led to the moral claims of developing nation producers receiving more attention. It is this normative shift in the IFAR, interconnected with other pressures such as WTO agricultural trade negotiations, and OECD policy contributions (OECD 2006), which seem to be contributing to signs of a shift in domestic US agricultural and food aid politics, signalled by the attempts of the George W. Bush administration to increase the proportion of food aid donated in cash.

This shift has not evaporated since Natsios' 'lead balloon' speech of 2005. Domestic US food aid policy is based on the periodic passage of the Farm Bill, most recently adopted in 2008 (Farm Bill 2008). In that context, debate emerged over the Bush Administration proposal that $350 million (approximately 25 percent) of the PL 480 Title II budget administered by USAID, which involves the bulk of US donations to the WFP, be allocated as cash rather than commodities (Murphy and Suppan 2008, 2). This could then be used in local purchasing, rather than effectively requiring that food aid take the form of US produced commodities which are required by legislation to be at least 50 percent bagged, and 75 percent processed and shipped by US companies (USAID 2006, 34).

The Director of the USAID Office of Food for Peace noted the wide array of influences on this policy, including 'academics and think tanks, ... the World Trade Organization, ... UN organizations such as FAO and WFP and ... a broad spectrum of Private Voluntary Organizations' (Hammink 2007, 1).

Such proposals continue to founder in the face of Congressional hostility, organized through food aid lobby groups such as the Alliance for Food Aid (AFA). Although the 2008 Farm Bill did not approve the President's proposal for a proportion of food aid to shift to cash from commodities (Murphy and Suppan 2008), research and pressure from critics of the tying of food aid by the US are having an influence. The Doha Round trade reform negotiations have seen American agricultural sector policies linked to food aid put on the table as potentially requiring regulation (Clapp 2004), if only as a bargaining chip for other agricultural trade reforms. Meanwhile, there is some evidence that the US food aid lobby is starting to fragment. It is difficult to maintain a status quo position of US providing in-kind donations of food aid when this is seen to, if not actively harm the poor in developing countries, fail to help them effectively – for example, as seen in the recent desertion of the lobby by the NGO CARE (Doyle 2007; Dugger 2007).

The moral claims of states

With regard to the moral claims of states, by and large the IFAR norm still implicitly accepts as of greatest import the claims of donor nations. Of course, without donations of food aid, the WFP could not function, but it reflects more than simple dependence on resources. One might posit the existence of subtle judgements amongst the donor nations that assume that a failure to feed their own people undermines any moral claim on the part of recipient nations – though not all recipient nations would be regarded as directly culpable to the extent of, for example, President Mugabe's Zimbabwe regime, or Burma in the wake of Cyclone Nargis. In those latter cases, the explicit refusal to allow the WFP (or NGOs) to mount effective relief operations in the face of famine created or exacerbated by government incompetence and brutality has rendered the authorities in Burma and Zimbabwe international pariahs.

Apart from the possibility of such judgements, recipient nations are categorised differently from donor nations in other ways. Nations might be efficient producers, and generous donors, but nations tend not to starve - people starve. This perspective is reflected by the WFP's focus on project rather than programme food aid – the beneficiaries are not countries, but starving people at the project level – though the central mechanism for projects to be funded is through Country Programmes. It is also implicit in the desire of the WFP to break down the barriers between donor and recipient countries by encouraging as many states as possible to become donors (Interview #11 2005), while at the same time acknowledging important differences between 'traditional donors'[19] and 'non-traditional donors'[20]:

> 70. WFP will accept contributions from traditional donors on the basis of full-cost recovery, which requires such donors to cover the cost of moving, managing and monitoring contributions...
>
> 71. WFP may accept contributions of commodities or services from non-traditional donors that are unable to provide cash to cover the associated costs. It will do so when such action is deemed in its interests and those of the beneficiary group(s) and does not involve a disproportionate or administrative burden on WFP. In such cases,

> WFP will seek to cover associated costs by inviting contributions from traditional donors or, for commodity contributions, monetizing part of the contribution where appropriate and cost-effective. In exceptional cases, the Executive Director may resort to the General Fund to cover associated costs. (WFP 2006c, 26).

The differentiation of recipient countries operates in a complex way. Countervailing the project focus is the fact that the WFP works with recipient country governments, coordinating projects within a country program. Also, the WFP has long emphasized targeting of the poorest countries (the UN defined Least Developed Countries, with significant net food import needs), which implicitly acknowledges structural, as opposed to solely governmental reasons for hunger. Formally, recipient countries are a majority of the WFP Executive Board as well, as Chapter Five discusses. However, there is only one group of states that exercises a moral claim sufficient to generate regular expressions of gratitude from the WFP, and it is not the recipient countries.

Conclusion

Norms do not exist in a vacuum – they both reflect and influence the perception of interests. The traditional focus in international relations on material economic and strategic interests needs to be widened to incorporate the complex interactions between norms and such material factors.

It is possible to mount a serious argument that the WFP's standing in the domestic US polity is explicable solely with reference to WFP service of US strategic or economic interests. Indeed, as Hopkins and Uvin both acknowledge (Hopkins 1992; Uvin 1992), such an argument is highly plausible when looking at the food aid regime formation, and the WFP's establishment. However, over time such an explanation would founder on two problems. Firstly, the continuing absence of benefit to US state interests from its food aid policies documented both by Uvin and more recently by Barrett and Maxwell (Barrett and Maxwell 2005; Uvin 1992). The second problem, related to the first, is the lack of an obviously negative impact from the close relationship with the US on wider WFP international legitimacy.

These problems for a more standard interest-based analysis are explicable with reference to the posited normative congruence between international and domestic US feed-the-hungry norms. This congruence is an important part of explaining the strong American support for the WFP in recent decades, though, as is argued in Chapter Four, the relationship has also been hampered by a less than monolithic approach to the WFP by the US. At the same time, the WFP's undoubted international legitimacy can be explained as due to a sufficiently complex and ambiguous relationship between the norms, and a sufficiently universal appeal from a feed-the-hungry norm. This has enabled it to avoid the more obvious legitimacy problems resulting from US dominance undermining its credibility with other state and non-state actors. It is this combination of dominance and legitimacy that suggest the US role can be seen as hegemonic in the IFAR.

Also, the normative congruence both reflects and has influenced the soft normative power exhibited by the feed-the-hungry norm in the international food aid regime, whereby the moral claims of the hungry are made without the connotations of compulsion generated with reference to justice, rights and international law.

It is important to note that the feed-the-hungry norm is not the only norm at work in the IFAR. There are other norms concerning development, equity and poverty, and trade that operate within and between the IFAR and other regimes, and have influenced the development of the IFAR and the feed-the-hungry norm itself. However, to the degree that the IFAR has some analytical clarity as a regime concept, it is useful to grasp this through the institutional prism offered by the feed-the-hungry norm. The norm is particularly useful in explaining the relationship between the international regime and the US, as well as providing analytical clarity.

The WFP operates within a distinctive normative environment constituted by the international food aid regime and its feed-the-hungry norm. This points to the importance of the impact of its institutional environment on the WFP's capacities, consistent with the argument made in Chapter One that such organizations must be understood within an institutional context.

The feed-the-hungry norm has two forms – a domestic US version and an international regime version. Both forms feature soft normative power based on moral claims – not only of the hungry, but of producers and nations - rather than the hard normative power of legal codification. The congruence between these norms is a crucial aspect of the hegemonic role of the US in the regime, but the differences between them, centered on different producer moral claims, are also significant sources of change as the regime evolves. The following two chapters now turn in more detail to tracing the historical evolution of the IFAR and the WFP.

Endnotes

[1] Arguably, over time the various sub-systemic norms will, in turn, have impacts on the systemic level norms as well.

[2] Krasner's regime elements distinguish between principles (statements of belief), and norms (statements of rights and obligations) (Krasner 1983, 1), but this is not a tenable or useful distinction at the normative level.

[3] The right to food discourse and its absence from the WFP is discussed in detail in Chapter Six.

[4] Though the right to food *has* been codified within the international human rights regime.

[5] It is not the only regime norm of this type; for example, there is arguably a different, though connected, disaster relief regime with similar characteristics. Also, while arguing the importance of the distinction, this should not be mistaken for a normative argument against legalising the expression of norms, which is important and desirable in many cases.

[6] There is considerable literature on the phenomenon of the electoral power of the agriculture sector in liberal democracies (e.g. Coleman, Grant et al. 2004). Uvin argues it has been the price of peace between urban and rural sectors (Uvin 1994); Brett and Craig & Phillips argue the importance of agrarian ideology to this phenomenon (Brett 2007; Craig and Phillips 1983; Flinn and Johnson 1974).

[7] Hoover had undertaken a similar role in the aftermath of WWI, and in the early 1920s as Commerce Secretary running the American Relief Administration, helping create a national political profile which would lead him to the White House (Zieger 1976).

[8] The close relationship is commemorated in the name of the McGovern-Dole International Food for Education Program established in 2002 (see Chapter Five). Each Senator played a national role as the losing major party candidate in the Presidential elections of, respectively, 1972 and 1996.

[9] On my first visit to the US Consulate in Melbourne I was struck by the four large prints of this Rockwell series hanging on a corridor wall on the way to a seminar room.

[10] McGovern similarly refers to the legislation underpinning American food aid (Public Law 480) as involving a 'blend of economic self-interest and humanitarian reaction' (McGovern 2001 47).

[11] Counihan cites from the *Intelligencer Journal* (Lancaster, Pa, 10 August 2001) the following description of the 37,500 food packets dropped: 'The airdrops are delivering "humanitarian daily rations," plastic pouches enriched with vitamins and minerals...The food, wrapped so that one packet has enough for one person for one day, does not contain any animal products so as not to violate any religious or cultural practices. Muslims, for example, do not eat pork...The yellow plastic packets are about the size and weight of a hardcover book. They have a picture of a smiling person eating from a pouch, a stencil of an American flag, a notation that they were made by Rightaway Foods of McAllen Texas, and this greeting in English: "This food is a gift from the United States of America." Inside are several smaller packets with food such as

peanut butter, strawberry jam, crackers, a fruit pastry, and entrees such as beans with tomato sauce and bean and potato vinaigrette. The packets provide at least 2,200 calories per day. The packets are also designed to flutter to the ground rather than drop straight down to minimize the possibility that they could hit and injure someone' (Counihan 2002, 11).

[12] Though Barrett and Maxwell make clear there are a small number of sectional interests in the American polity which do very well out of food aid policy and procedure (Barrett and Maxwell 2005, Ch5).

[13] Moral hazard is also conjured up in IR with reference to the free-rider problem posed by collective public goods (Ostrom 2003, 6) – if all benefit without reference to their contributions, at least some will choose to take the benefits without contributing; yet if all do that the goods evaporate. The risk of free-riding requires constraints (exclusions) or penalties to apply to free-riders to deter that course of action, both pragmatically to make the creation of the goods possible, and normatively, to create a system which is seen to be fair and just.

[14] This is not to suggest that moral hazard concerns have not been applied to food aid as well – they have provoked much discussion. From the mid-1970s moral hazard style welfare dependence criticism began of the American domestic food stamps program, leading to cuts to it under Reagan (Berry 1984; Brown and Pizer 1987). In recent years the relevance of this issue in the IFAR is likely to increase given the exploration of insurance-type approaches to food insecurity by WFP staff (WFP 2006f), and consequent increasing relevance of the insurance economics literature noted above.

[15] In the case of donations to North Korea in the mid-1990s the prominence of the American flag on the commodity bags initially caused some consternation on the part of the local authorities. These concerns were resolved by a decision to describe the aid donations as 'war reparations' (Anon. 2005). Noland notes the long dependence of North Korea on outside assistance, and argues that the North Koreans 'have compensated for this dependency by ferociously denouncing it, portraying aid as tribute paid to the ideologically pure North Korean state … and trying to play patrons off against each other' (Noland 2003, 4).

[16] Note de Waal points out such emphasis on children also occurs in other (non-food) aid discourses with similar logic (de Waal 1997, 74, 82-5).

[17] Wiener notes the work of Tim Breen on the importance of commodities as a tangible, unifying element of revolutionary America: 'The reason why Americans displayed such marked political solidarity beginning in 1773, writes Breen, a solidarity not evident during the Townshend protest, was that the Tea Act "affected an item of popular consumption found in almost every colonial household." an item very much like Coca-Cola which "appear[ed] on the tables of the wealthiest merchants and the poorest labourers." In creating a *material* commonalty among Americans, tea became an ideal medium through which "to transmit perceptions of liberty and rights," and a way in which *ideological* abstractions "acquired concrete meaning." Breen's analysis suggests that commodities generally can provide "a shared framework of consumer experience" that allows individuals to "reach out to distant strangers, to perceive, however dimly, the existence of an 'imagined community'" and then to take political action when the liberties and rights of that community are

infringed.' Breen, Timothy "'Baubles of Britain': The American and Consumer Revolutions of the Eighteenth Century", *Past and Present* 119 (May 1988): 73-104 cited in (Weiner 2002, 136).

[18] For detailed discussion of the operation of such modalities see (Barrett and Maxwell 2005, 159-65).

[19] Traditional donors are contributors to the WFP included in lists D or E of the United Nations/FAO Member States Listings for Elections for the WFP Executive Board (unless also recognized as a country in transition), the European Community and Saudi Arabia (WFP 2006c, 26).

[20] Non-traditional donors are those not defined by the Board as traditional donors; thus this category includes countries in transition, developing countries eligible for assistance from the International Development Association (IDA), private corporations, public or private foundations, NGOs and individuals (WFP 2006c, 26). The policy provisions above, however, are directed primarily at the first two categories of non-traditional donor states.

3
Development of a Food Aid Regime

The international food aid regime (IFAR) has evolved, largely since World War II, in conjunction with changing patterns of agricultural production and trade, as well as periodic famine crises and chronic developmental, poverty and malnutrition problems. It is the early stages of this evolution, up to the early 1980s, with which this chapter is concerned.

The first section of the chapter examines the early stages of the emergence of the IFAR from the end of World War II. Important processes contributing to this included the evolution of food aid as a tool of US policy, and the emergence of food related international organisations, in particular, the Food and Agriculture Organization of the United Nations (FAO).

While establishing multilateral food aid had been on the international agenda since at least the mid 1940s, it was not until the early 1960s that the WFP was founded. The second section turns to the specific changes and events, in particular the actions of the US and the UN and FAO Secretariats that led to the founding of the WFP in 1961.

The foundation of the WFP represented a new role for multilateralism in food aid, and was the clearest harbinger of an international food aid regime, giving it an organisational basis. The third section of the chapter considers the development of the IFAR and the WFP through to the late 1970s, in particular, the world food crisis of the early 1970s and the World Food Conference of 1974. This period was characterised by geopolitical conflicts within the UN: the Cold War; conflicts over oil, and the debates over the New International Economic Order precipitated by G77 activism. Together with these conflicts came a declining US engagement with the UN. This context tended to obstruct the coalescence of the regime, but as Chapter Four will show, further shifts in global politics in the 1980s entrenched and increasingly legitimized the WFP and the IFAR.

Emergence of an international food aid regime

Modern state deployment of aid in pursuit of a mix of foreign and domestic policy objectives – not always without charitable motivation – predates the advent of the UN system by many decades, if not centuries. Hjertholm and White, for example, speculate that gifts between kings in mediaeval times could be seen, in at least some cases, as analogous to aid. However, they adopt a definition of aid requiring a normative component of support for the populace of a different country which effectively limits the idea of aid to a modern concept (Hjertholm and White 2000, 4).

Food aid, as was discussed in the last chapter, has tended to be categorised as different from other, monetary, forms of aid. The United States has had, and retains, a dominant role globally in the provision of food aid. Even though its share of international food aid (both bilateral and multilateral) has fallen from the 1950s levels of over 90 percent, the US generally still donates more in food aid than the rest of the world put together, across all three categories of multilateral, bilateral and NGO food aid (Hanrahan and Canada 2006), as Chart 3.1 shows.

While the US dominated food aid donations over the decade to 2005 with just under 60% of the total, as Chart 3.2 shows, from year to year the proportion of food aid from the US varied from between 43.3% and 69.3%, though it was always easily the largest single donor. Nevertheless, the US dominates all governmental channels as a donor; it is the only country which gives more in bilateral food aid than multilateral food aid (Barrett and Maxwell 2005). Also,

> The United States is the principal donor that relies on NGOs to channel food aid. In 2007, 88 percent of food aid channelled through NGOs was provided by the United States, increasing from 79 percent in 2006. In terms of quantity discharged, this corresponds to 1.2 million tons of food. The other donors channelling food aid through NGOs were the European Union (European Commission and Member States: 6 percent), the Canadian Foodgrains Bank (3 percent) and the International Committee of Red Cross (ICRC) (2 percent). (INTERFAIS/WFP 2008, 12).

Chart 3.1: The major food aid donors, 1995-2005 (by volume, wheat equivalent tons)

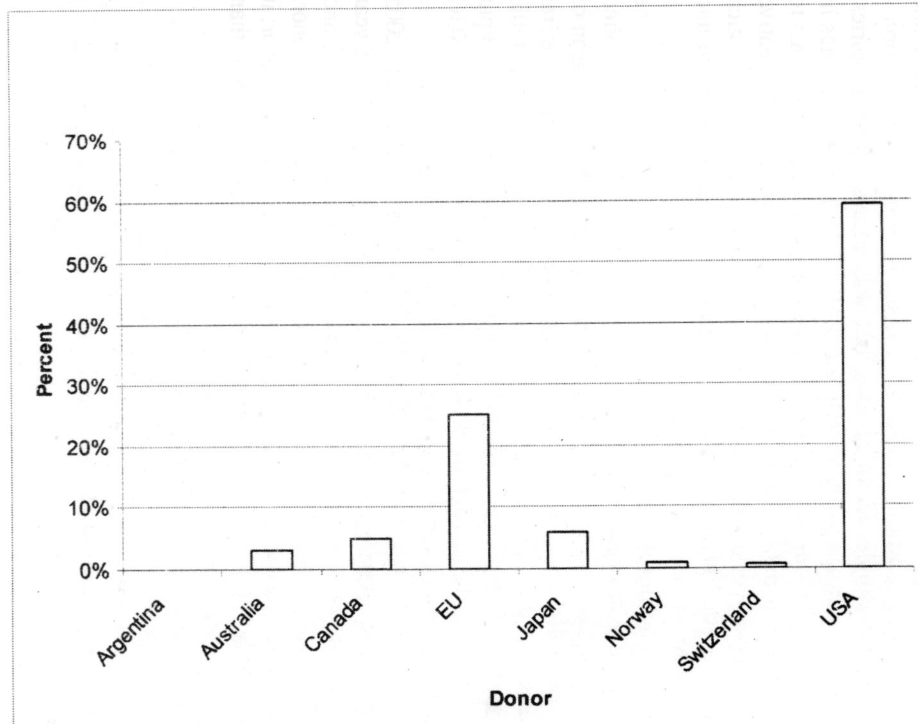

Data Source: (Hanrahan and Canada 2006, Appendix Table 1, 5).

Deployment of food as aid by the United States is generally traced back to the passage of the Act for the Relief of Citizens of Venezuela following an earthquake in 1812 (Hjertholm and White 2000, 4-7; Kanbur 2003, 3; Ruttan 1993a, 4, 229-30), though George argues that this was no simple act of charity, but was connected to a desire to support a revolt against Spain (George 1991, 192). In nineteenth century America, 'the Congress and the President generally adhered to a view that the use of public funds for charity was unconstitutional. Even the bulk of post-World War I food relief to Belgium and Russia,...came primarily from private sources' (Ruttan 1993a, 229). However, no matter how private the sourcing of the aid, administration of food aid relief both during and after World War I, and again after World War II, had a clearly strategic dimension (Bentley 1994; George 1991, 193-6).

There has long been a bifurcation of food aid between emergency aid, generally conceived of as charity (even if its distribution was affected by strategic considerations), and other forms of 'assistance' explicitly deriving from economic self-interest. Hjertholm and White note that as early as 1896 the US was consciously using food surpluses as a tool for market development in Latin America (Hjertholm and White 2000, 4), while in the 1920s the British Colonial Office had an explicit policy linking assistance to the colonies with the use of colonies as export markets to support British employment (Kanbur 2003, 3).

With substantial US agricultural surpluses in the 1930s coinciding with the Depression, the Hoover administration (1929–1933) and, more significantly, the Roosevelt administration established a food aid apparatus deploying surplus commodities for the domestic relief of hunger (Poppendieck 1986; 1998, 142-7). This apparatus eventually came to operate through the US Department of Agriculture (USDA) (Poppendieck 1998, 146) linked to a policy emphasis on providing price support to producers (Poppendieck 1997, 135), an emphasis which lasted 30 years.

Government underwriting of agricultural production was also deployed in the provision of foreign food aid in this period. During the 1930s, the Export-Import Bank was established, introducing the systematic use of state-supported concessional loans for the purchase of American agricultural products (Ruttan 1993a, 4). This remains a feature of American agricultural trade policy into the twenty-first century, as Clapp describes:

Chart 3.2: US percentage of global food aid (by volume), 1995-2005

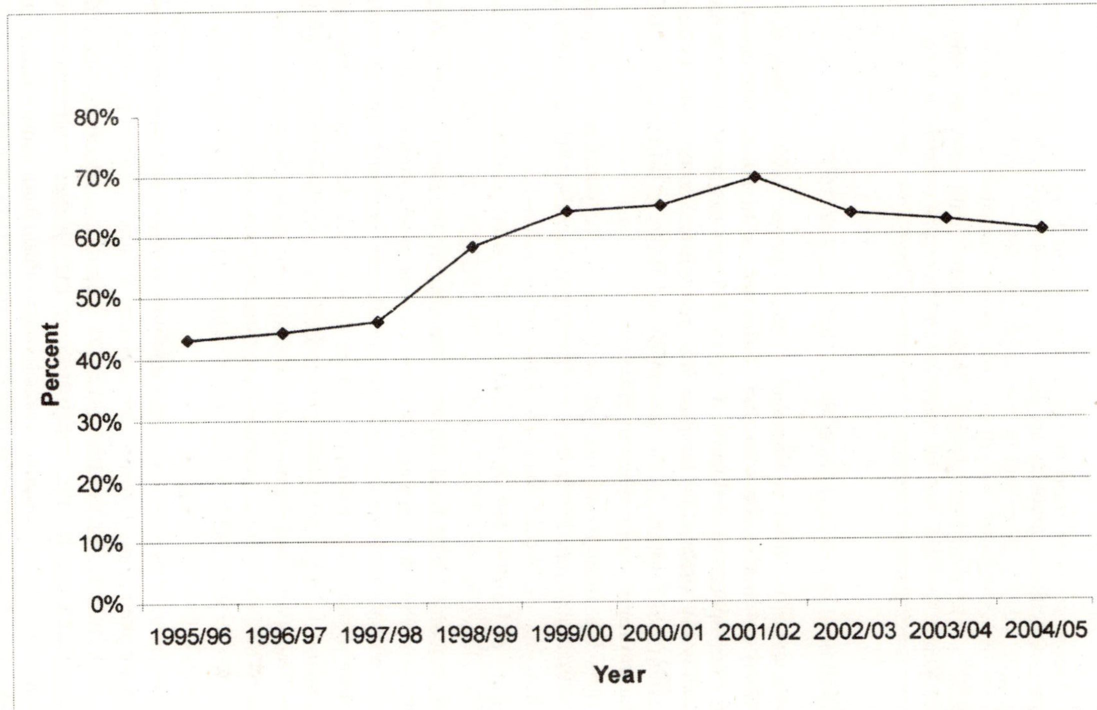

Data Source: (Hanrahan and Canada 2006, Appendix Table 1, 5).

> Some agricultural products are sold with export credits which give long periods for repayment or with credit guarantees, meaning that if the borrower defaults, the export credit agency (usually a government agency) will ensure repayment. These export credit sales are not technically 'food aid', but are perceived by the selling countries to be a form of assistance to food deficit countries. (Clapp 2004, 1440).

Establishment of the Food and Agriculture Organization

International aid – food or financial – tended prior to World War II to flow from colonial powers to their colonies, or to places deemed as within their sphere of influence. One of the key disjunctions with the pre-1945 period created by the post-war geopolitical context and system of international regimes is the advent of aid flows in wider global and multilateral frameworks (Kanbur 2003).

Thus, US foreign aid, including food aid, 'crystallized' (Kanbur 2003, 4) as an important feature of the international political economy after the end of World War II. This aid was initially linked to the rebuilding of Europe, but by the late 1940s focused increasingly on the underdeveloped world. The first step in the building of an international regime concerned with food aid was taken before the end of World War II, however. President Roosevelt convened an international conference at Hot Springs, Virginia in 1943 to commence planning for post-war food and agricultural problems.[1] The Conference set up an Interim Commission which spent two years drafting a constitution for what became the 'Food and Agriculture Organization of the United Nations' (FAO).[2] The FAO held a signatory meeting and inaugural conference in Quebec in October 1945 by the end of which 44 states had signed up as members (Talbot 1990, 17-8).

The Union of Soviet Socialist Republics (USSR) had participated at Hot Springs and in the Interim Commission. It sent delegates to Quebec, along with two of its satellite Socialist Republics, Byelo-Russia and Ukraine. However, by the conclusion of the Quebec conference the USSR had decided to remain as an observer only (Hambidge 1955, 59). Though other Eastern bloc countries joined the FAO, the USSR was to remain an observer until its collapse at the end of the Cold War (Saouma 1993), and the Russian Federation only joined the FAO in 2006. This relative lack of Soviet participation is indicative of the limited impact of Cold War politics on the FAO compared with the debates between the two blocs in the UN General Assembly and Security Council.

The FAO was initially headquartered in Washington with a British national, Sir John Boyd Orr (later Lord Boyd Orr) as its first Director-

General. It was designed as a primarily technical agency to advise and coordinate between governments on agricultural reconstruction and development post-War, both in the context of fears of a repeat of the problems of famine at the end of World War I, and a desire to harness advances in agricultural and nutrition science effectively at the global level to advance human development (Hambidge 1955, Ch4).

Specifically, the FAO's aims were, and remain, to

> Contribute towards an expanding world economy and ensure humanity's freedom from hunger by: raising the level of nutrition and standard of living of people in member countries; securing improvement in the efficiency of production and distribution of all food and agricultural products; bettering the living conditions of rural populations. (Associations 2005, 1104).

In its early days, the FAO saw debates over empowerment of intergovernmental organisations versus prohibitions on infringing nation-state sovereignty. Similar debates were to be central to the development of the international human rights regime in the UN General Assembly during the formulation and adoption of the Universal Declaration on Human Rights (Evans 1996, Ch2-3).

In 1946 Boyd Orr proposed the creation of a World Food Board (WFB) which

> was to be an international organization with power to hold, buy, and sell important agricultural commodities entering world trade, and to set maximum and minimum prices for these commodities in the international market. (Hambidge 1955, 66; see also Talbot 1990, 18).

The FAO Conference in September 1946 rejected the WFB proposal, though it set up a Preparatory Commission to examine the elements of the proposal (Hambidge 1955, 68). Reflecting the influence of producer groups and food exporting nations, the Commission recommended that 'the member-states retain their sovereign authority over agricultural and food-policy decisions' (Talbot 1990, 18), in particular via a separation of production (which the FAO was to stimulate) and trade, which was to be managed by separate commodity organisations (Hambidge 1955, 69). The Commission also recommended setting up a World Food Council – which in being accepted by the 3rd FAO Conference of September 1947 became the FAO Council.

What is interesting about the WFB proposal is not the predictably quick and effective defence by member-states of their sovereign powers against suggestions that power over agricultural trade and commerce be ceded to a multilateral organisation. Rather, it is how the political atmosphere, fluidity about the role of the FAO, and evolving norms about food governance generated a serious proposition for significant economic powers to accrue to an intergovernmental organisation.

John Boyd Orr's speech following his election as Director-General of FAO illuminates some of these issues:

> Here we have in this Organization a most valuable means of bringing about some degree of world unity...If nations will not agree on a food policy which will benefit them all, they will agree on nothing. At an early date therefore we should go before them and say, 'Here is a food policy; here is a thing you can agree upon and on which action can be taken immediately.' And we can prophesy that if action is taken immediately it will begin to solve some of the apparently unsolvable economic problems of the world of the present day...Then I think you will begin to develop...a technique of co-operation in getting this policy applied on a world scale. It should be easier then to develop international cooperation in other fields. (Hambidge 1955, 59-60).

These statements demonstrate a perception of the FAO as an actor independent of its member states – the 'we' which plans to 'go before' the nations. They also demonstrate the concept of international food policy, related to the alleviation of hunger, as a norm capable of generating genuine international cooperation, which in turn will serve as a model for effective international institutions in other areas. The FAO secretariat from the start established itself as an actor independent of the states, prepared to portray food and agricultural problems as not only related to improving production and distribution in a technical sense, but also to market failure requiring multilateral governance intervention.

It is important to contextualize these propositions. The exigencies of wartime had placed such a premium on the management of food resources that the Allies had instituted supranational cooperation via the Combined Food Board (CFB) – the US, the UK and Canada were its members. The CFB was seen as a useful and effective mechanism for ensuring the feeding of populations that were at risk of starvation due to wartime pressures on supply and markets. Hambidge notes that the overall nutritional status of the UK population actually improved during the war, due to the systematic improvement of the nutrition of poor people under the rationing system (Hambidge 1955, 48).

After World War II ended, the US was the only country with higher agricultural production than pre-war levels, and there were significant food shortages in Europe and Asia (Bentley 1994). The CFB was replaced, post-war, with the International Emergency Food Council (IEFC, later IEF Committee), run by the FAO. The IEFC was much larger than the CFB, with 34 member states.[3] It made recommendations about how to distribute scarce commodities which were almost all accepted by member countries during the period of operation – for example, out of 475 recommendations on allocations between September 1947 and August 1948, only 13 were not concurred with by member states (Hambidge 1955, 62-4). This suggests the extent to which norms of international cooperation were emerging around the food distribution issue area.

Hambidge was heavily involved as a staff member of the Interim Commission that planned the FAO, then as a senior staff member of the FAO – one of the first three staff appointed to the FAO following the Quebec conference. His account of the establishment of the FAO conveys the sense of opportunity, prevailing in the mid to late 1940s. This was created by the unusual fluidity of relationship and cooperation between the Allies in the face of wartime mobilisation; as well as the widely held belief that the world needed to be ordered differently in face of the conflagration and the Depression and world war which preceded it. However, he notes a debate about 'the fundamental nature of the proposed agency':

> One group favored establishing a strong food and agriculture organization which could take positive steps to foster economic expansion and help prevent disastrous crises, the recent depression still being much in men's minds. The other group wanted a rather narrowly limited fact-gathering and advisory agency which would be carefully insulated from positive action. (Hambidge 1955, 53).

Hambidge characterizes the eventual FAO outcome as a compromise, albeit leaning towards the latter group perspective. This was reflected in the annual budget allocation of $5 million - between the activist $10m and the advisory $1m propositions - though it was left open for the organisation to expand its operations more into the activist direction in the future (Hambidge 1955, 53). Notwithstanding Boyd Orr's activist inclinations, the view of the most powerful member-states was decidedly at the non-activist end of the spectrum.

At the end of the early contretemps over the WFB proposal, the FAO Secretariat was merely empowered to circulate recommendations (Talbot 1990, 19) and Boyd Orr decided not to seek re-election as Director-General (Hambidge 1955, 70). In 1949 under new Director-General Norris E. Dodd (former US Under Secretary of Agriculture),

FAO tried again to give itself a concrete management role over agricultural production and trade with a proposal for an International Commodity Clearing House (ICCH). Again the FAO member-states at its governing conference declined such a proposition, establishing instead a Committee of member-states on Commodity Problems (CCP) (Hambidge 1955, 71-2; Talbot 1990, 19). A pattern was emerging of FAO Secretariat attempts to expand an activist view of the organisation's role in relation to agricultural trade as well as production, while member-states insisted on constraining such ambitions.

Also in 1949, a vote was held on the permanent location of FAO headquarters, which saw a narrow ratification of its establishment in Rome ahead of Washington (30 votes to 28) (Hambidge 1955, 79-80; Talbot 1990, 20). This decision in turn led to the establishment of all the newer major UN food agencies in Rome,[4] a location that has had some relevance to WFP governance and reform as will be discussed in Chapter Six.

Food surpluses and food aid debates in the 1950s

In the early 1950s, as Europe's recovery from the war proceeded and the Marshall Plan wound down, the fact that American agricultural production kept going at a massive pace was becoming a significant economic and political problem for the US Government. At the same time, conflicts, slow reconstruction and underdevelopment contributed to starvation in many countries.

Following the end of the Korean War, in the latter part of 1953, there was a collapse in agricultural commodity prices (Ruttan 1993a, 3). This compounded a growing problem with surplus agricultural produce in the US. McGovern gives the following description:

> Seeking to prevent surplus grain production from destroying market prices for farmers, the government agreed to help individual farmers by granting them loans against their stored surplus grain until it could be sold at a fair price, at which time the loans would be repaid. But as the surpluses grew, they depressed farm prices even as they lay in storage. Beyond this, the cost to the government of holding the grain off the market soon reached $1 billion annually. Also, some of the grain began to deteriorate, having been held too long. (McGovern 2001, 47).

Thus in 1953, the newly elected Eisenhower administration confronted an increasingly significant political problem managing conflicts between farmer constituent expectations of government support for agricultural prices through government purchase of surplus stocks, a massive and growing surplus stockpile with increasing storage costs, and a foreign policy based on liberalisation of trade (Ruttan 1993a, 7). In accordance with the prevailing paradigm of agricultural trade policy (Coleman, Grant et al. 2004, 20), conflict between policy makers concerned with trade liberalisation and agricultural producers concerned to maintain price supports and protection was resolved in favour of the agricultural interests. By 1954 these interests had evolved into 'a political constituency for food aid – consisting of farm commodity groups, shippers and handlers, and private relief agencies' (Ruttan 1993a, 5). Demonstrating its institutional strength, fifty years later this constituency continues to operate, being referred to as an 'Iron Triangle' (Barrett and Maxwell 2005, 87).

A number of Government agencies and departments were involved in devising and implementing the relevant policy instruments for food aid. Considerable bureaucratic conflict continued in this area between the Department of Agriculture (USDA), representing the farming interests, the State Department, representing the foreign policy view, and the Bureau of the Budget, representing the Treasury (Ruttan 1993a, 6-9). There is a long history of tension between the USDA and the State Department, with both departments running foreign services.

The link between US agriculture and diplomacy has a provenance going back to the birth of the American state, with the first agricultural representative role in US foreign missions being held by Thomas Jefferson in France during the Revolutionary period (Mustard 2003). The USDA, established in 1862 by President Lincoln, began sending its own staff overseas from 1905, with its Foreign Agricultural Service (FAS) being established in 1930. While Roosevelt shrank and downgraded the FAS during the Depression, it was re-established in March 1953 by the new Eisenhower administration (Mustard 2003), reflecting the need for measures to improve its capacity to deal with the agricultural surplus issue.

Demonstrating the political confusion of the new Eisenhower administration around this complex issue,

> [a]t the urging of the Bureau of the Budget, the White House brought Charles Francis, chairman of General Foods, into the White House to serve as surplus disposal coordinator. The incredibly naive Francis assured the President that if he was given a free hand to "get rid of surpluses" the burdensome stocks could be reduced in about ninety days. Francis attempted to move aggressively to dump surpluses onto the world market with little of [Senator Hubert] Humphrey's sensibilities about trading with the Soviet bloc or [Secretary of State]

> Dulles's concerns about relations with our trading partners. (Ruttan 1993a, 7).

In this context it became increasingly a point of political consensus that the management of agricultural surpluses would need to be done at least partially through a structured foreign food assistance program. Hubert Humphrey, Democrat Senator from Minnesota and future US Vice President and Presidential candidate, was prominent in proposing a surplus disposal package in the Senate, keeping pressure on the Republican administration to develop a legislative package of its own (Ruttan 1993a, 7, 230).

Also prominent in proposing a link between surplus disposal and foreign assistance was a Marshall Plan veteran, Gwynn Garnett (Mustard 2003; Swanson 2003):

> While working to implement Marshall's vision, Garnett, then a young army officer, suggested an idea that would change U.S. farming forever. Garnett's plan had an appealing simplicity: use the U.S. agricultural surplus to feed a hungry Europe. In fiscal terms, Garnett proposed that the United States accept local currencies, many of which were virtually worth-less outside their own borders after the war, in exchange for agricultural products. These local funds could then in turn be used to rebuild foreign markets. Garnett presented his plan to officials of the Eisenhower Administration and to members of Congress when he returned from Germany to serve as a Farm Bureau official. The plan rapidly found support because it allowed Congress to help U.S. farmers, feed hungry nations and foster future markets. (Swanson 2003, 5).[5]

By mid-1954 the Eisenhower administration had negotiated legislation through Congress establishing authority for a range of food aid activities. On 10 July 1954 the President signed into law the *Agricultural Trade Development and Assistance Act of 1954* (Public Law 480) (Ruttan 1993a, 7; Shaw 2001, 31-2). The Act, best known as PL 480, though amended and revised several times, continues to form the legislative basis for US food aid policy more than fifty years later (Barrett and Maxwell 2005).

International agricultural trade and food aid

US trading partner concern with the surplus disposal issue combined with the long-standing interest at the FAO in international food assistance led the FAO Committee on Commodity Problems to propose in the early 1950s the establishment of an Emergency Food Reserve to deploy surpluses for the relief of famine through an international mechanism. However, this proposal was rejected by the FAO Conference in 1953. (Hambidge 1955, 72; Talbot 1990, 19). This rejection reflected the fact that the US and other major industrialised countries 'were adamantly opposed to any centralized and multilateral world food management arrangement' (Shaw 2001, 20).

This opposition was not surprising given the highly politicised interrelationship between surplus disposal and agricultural trade and foreign policy. While a potential relationship between surplus disposal and famine relief was well recognised, in the values hierarchy of developed countries generalised famine relief seemed to rate well below trade and foreign policy objectives. In spite, or perhaps because of, this the issue of surplus disposal was a source of conflict between the US and its Cold War allies, especially Australia and Canada who were the other major agricultural exporters during the 1950s. The need to manage this conflict led to the use of the FAO as a forum for negotiating differences through establishing a Subcommittee on Surplus Disposal (CSD) in 1954. The CSD was (and remains) based in Washington, reporting to the FAO Committee on Commodity Problems. The CSD established Principles of Surplus Disposal, mainly to constrain dumping of agricultural surpluses onto world markets. The FAO describes the principles as:

> A code of international conduct adopted by the FAO Council in 1954 which encourages the constructive use of surplus agricultural commodities and at the same time safeguards the interest of commercial exporters and local producers. (FAO, 2001, iii).

Thus, through the CSD a multilateral mechanism was being used to manage conflicts over global agricultural markets, though it is important to note that this mechanism was set up through the FAO, and not the General Agreement on Tariffs and Trade (GATT) that had emerged out of the Havana Charter of 1948. As discussed in Chapter One, agriculture was to effectively be quarantined from the international trade regime until the Uruguay Round of the GATT resulted in the Agreement on Agriculture in 1994 (FAO 2006a).[6] The Agreement itself explicitly mandates the application of the principles of surplus disposal to food aid (FAO 2006a, 1; Clapp 2004, 1441).

Three basic principles of surplus disposal were agreed: It should increase consumption rather than reduce production ('additionality'); it should be orderly to avoid sharp price falls; and it should occur while maintaining normal patterns of trade (Shaw 2001, 21; FAO, 2001, 33–41). The Principles (see Appendix 2) have since provided the basis for 'an effective international code for monitoring food and agricultural commodity assistance programmes' (FAO, 2001, 2).

The Principles remain central to the relationship between food aid and trade in formal terms, with explicit reference to them in the Agreement on Agriculture established by the Uruguay Round of the GATT, and as a consequence the CSD (now known as the CSSD[7]) continues to meet and report on food aid transactions. However, its significance has been in long-term decline. Even before 1994, Hopkins was noting that as food aid became increasingly concerned with emergency relief from the early 1970s, the CSD was becoming less relevant to food aid and trade –

> In this period, when Bangladesh was desperately short of cash and famine threatened the lives of an estimated one million people there, adherence to the additionality principle seemed onerous, irrelevant, and even perverse. Consequently, since the mid-1970s, the number of food aid proposals questioned by the CSD has dropped... Although the CSD continues to meet every two weeks in Washington, it deals with few issues of any substance. (Hopkins 1992, 253).

As was discussed in Chapter One, the advent of the Agreement on Agriculture resulted in the shift of the international agricultural trade regime into a closer connection with the international trade regime (Coleman, Grant et al. 2004). This led in 1997 to revision of the post-Uruguay Round CSSD arrangements (FAO Committee on Commodity Problems 2005), with a significant drop in notifications of food aid transactions and a move to quarterly meetings (FAO Consultative Subcommittee on Surplus Disposal 2005). Then in 2000, the proportion of global food aid transactions notified to the CSSD dropped from 50 percent to 5 percent (FAO Consultative Subcommittee on Surplus Disposal 2003, Table 2), a drop noted in CSSD reports to the FAO Committee on Commodity Problems ever since as an issue of concern. The following excerpt from the CSSD report to the April 2007 Committee meeting illustrates the extent to which the CSSD has been sidelined from both international agricultural trade and food aid regimes:

> Following previous discussions where members raised the drop in food aid notifications since 2000 as a matter of considerable concern, the CSSD sent letters in 2005 inviting members to join the CSSD. Countries invited to join the CSSD included major donors (China and South Korea), various major recipients, key players in agricultural

> trade, and potential observers. Unfortunately, none of the countries approached accepted the invitation. (FAO Committee on Commodity Problems 2007, 4).

The decline of the CSSD implies that the food aid and agricultural trade nexus is no longer as strong as it used to be. This is due to further increases in the use of food aid in emergency relief since Hopkins noted the trend, and changes in the agricultural trade regime in the context of the Agreement on Agriculture and Doha Round negotiations. Nevertheless, there are still significant tensions between agricultural exporting nations over trade, and concern that US food aid practices still amount to forms of protection (Clapp 2004; FAO Committee on Commodity Problems 2007; FAO Consultative Subcommittee on Surplus Disposal 2005) – tensions evident at the WFP Executive Board, as will be discussed in more detail in Chapter Five.

Looking back to its original establishment, however, the CSD/CSSD was the first discrete element of an intergovernmental body focused on food aid related matters. At that point, the international food aid regime is probably best thought of as existing at the cusp of the dual international regimes of agricultural trade and agricultural development, rather than having its own discrete existence. It is only with the benefit of hindsight that the beginnings of an international food aid regime can be read back into the setting up of the CSD. At this point, the modern multilateral system was barely ten years old, and in the midst of what Hopkins argues was a first wave of post-World War II regime building – 'the liberal wave of 1944–1960 that aimed at harmonisation of commercial interests and the coordination of information standards and research' (Hopkins 1990, 178).

The CSD highlights the heterogeneous nature of intergovernmental organisations with multiple roles such as FAO, and the complexity of interaction between organisations, regimes and issue areas. Coleman et al. argue that reasonably clear cut delineations between issue areas and related international regimes have become complicated since the 1980s with processes of fragmentation and integration arising from globalisation (Coleman, Grant et al. 2004).[8] While this is true to some extent, international regimes have always had fuzzy boundaries and, in some areas, complex interrelationships between actors and other regimes. The case of CSD and FAO shows how such complexity existed within the first post-war period of multilateral institutions, before the acceleration of globalisation.

Although theoretically the surplus disposal principles are concerned as much with the effects of surplus disposal on developing country markets as with their effects on competing exporter countries, in effect the latter concern has always been the primary focus of the CSD. Along with the practicalities and symbolism of CSD being based in Washington DC, while the FAO Council, Conference and Committee on Commodity Problems (CCP) to which it reports are in Rome, its membership reflects the dominance of developed countries in establishing and operating multilateral agricultural trade institutions.[9]

For example, of the membership of CSSD at November 2000, the only African nations listed were Ghana and Malawi; with no other African countries listed even as observers (FAO Consultative Subcommittee on Surplus Disposal 2003). The only objections and concerns about notified food aid transactions (almost all of which involve the US as donor) come from export competitors such as Canada, Australia, New Zealand or the European Commission. They do not come from recipient states, who presumably would either not accept food aid donations if they agreed that they disrupted domestic agricultural markets,[10] or would not want to draw attention to the fact that they did. Thus the CSSD has an entrenched focus on competing exporters as interested parties, ahead of the poorest countries in which surplus disposal actually takes place, despite the risks to markets in recipient countries from inappropriate food aid.

Given 90–95 per cent of global food aid was from America in the 1950s, CSD information sharing was primarily concerned with the operation of PL 480 (Talbot 1990, 19). Hence the agreement of the US to establishing the CSD in 1954 was crucial, yet it involved a policy shift from previous opposition to any multilateral constraints on its actions in relation to food and agriculture. This shift can be explained as reflecting a combination of two different agendas. Firstly, it reflected the fact that all significant agricultural exporters were aligned with the West in the Cold War context, and that potential agricultural trade conflicts needed to be managed in order to protect the security relationships. Secondly, the CSD provided a mechanism that could help manage the domestic policy tensions between trade liberalisation on the one hand, and surplus disposal on the other. The US lacked a domestic capacity to resolve this tension, while also acknowledging concerns on the part of a number of 'friendly' countries with its surplus disposal activities. The FAO created another policy option for the US to manage these problems.

The agricultural trade hegemon

PL 480 was important in its setting apart of food aid from other forms of aid and its institutional linking of food aid to farm legislation and the USDA (Barrett and Maxwell 2005; Shaw 2001). Shaw describes the distinctiveness of food aid in American policy as follows:

> Strikingly, while the US Congress never refused a food aid budget below the president's requests, other economic assistance budgets always received a mauling. Since the time PL 480 was enacted in 1954, food aid has traditionally been treated separately from other forms of US aid, and as an inextricable part of an omnibus farm bill which has been passed at periodic intervals of four to five years, financed out of US Department of Agriculture appropriations. This, in turn, has led to marked differences in responsibility for policy, programming and operations between food aid and other forms of US assistance, and a lack of coordination among the different types of aid in country assistance programmes. (Shaw 2001, 33).

PL 480 created three categories or titles for provision of food aid. Title I authorized concessional bulk sales of surplus commodities for foreign currency to 'friendly' governments; Title II authorised government to government grant aid for famine and other urgent relief assistance, both for friendly nations and 'friendly but needy populations without regard to the friendliness of their government' (Ruttan 1993a, 7). Title III authorised donations to private voluntary organisations (PVOs) for distribution in domestic US food relief programs as well as projects in foreign countries; it also provided for barter of the food aid commodities 'for strategic materials and goods not produced in the United States' (Shaw, 2001, 32).

Ruttan details how bureaucratic conflicts over food aid continued to dog the operation of PL 480. Ultimately the 'concern by [US Department of] Agriculture that food aid not displace commercial sales and by [Department of] State that it not obstruct State's efforts to negotiate a more liberal international economic order gave way to pressure from Congress and its agricultural constituencies' (Ruttan 1993a, 8). Even non-food surplus commodities were brought into the ambit of a program focused almost entirely on surplus disposal:

> Some of the recipient countries began to see it as simply an American dumping operation to get rid of costly storages. This attitude was encouraged when the administrators forced Greece to accept unwanted tobacco while India was required to accept cotton, in each case as a condition for obtaining American food. The Greeks had their own

> sources of tobacco and the Indians had local supplies of cotton. (McGovern 2001, 48; see also Ruttan 1993a, 8).

The significance of PL 480 can be seen in the fact that by the late 1950s it accounted for approximately one third of US grain exports, and more than one fifth of US foreign aid expenditures (Ruttan 1993a, 9), but the problems created by its sheer size extended past commodities to currency issues arising from Title I sales.

Ruttan gives a detailed description of how such sales worked:

> The first step was for the U.S. government and the foreign government to reach an agreement that enabled the latter to pay for some farm product imports with its own currency rather than with dollars. The agreement specified the quantity of the product involved, the price, and, usually, the uses that could be made of the foreign currency acquired by the United States. The farm products were usually sold to the foreign government by a private exporter who was paid in dollars by the U.S. government. The foreign government in turn usually sold the imported commodities in its domestic market to recoup the funds paid to the United States for the imported commodities. Under PL 480, the United States was authorized to lend the funds back to the country for use in its development program. In effect this meant that the foreign government found itself borrowing its own currency, and paying interest on it, when it could just as easily have printed additional money. The primary reason the U.S. government engaged in such fictional transactions is that they appeared more acceptable to Congress and the American people than outright grants of food or of dollar aid. The primary reason the importing countries were willing to engage in the fictional transactions is that they realized it was unlikely they would be forced to repay the loans or the United States would ever find a way to use for its own purposes a significant share of the countries' currency that it controlled. (Ruttan 1993a, 231, fn18).

Title I sales proceeds could be used for a range of purposes, including development of markets for US agricultural commodities; purchase of strategic materials or military equipment; financing goods and services from 'friendly' countries; and promotion of economic development and trade (Shaw 2001, 32). However, use of proceeds was not always easy to agree on with the recipient countries, and these 'soft' currencies 'continued to accumulate to the point where concern was expressed that the United States had control over too much of the money supply in recipient countries' (Ruttan 1993a, 9). Barrett and Maxwell note that Title I programs 'are explicitly targeted at promoting American agricultural export markets and at advancing US strategic interests. In the fifty years of... [PL 480's] history, there has rarely been any serious pretence of Title I serving development objectives' (Barrett and Maxwell 2005, 21).

Despite the importance of PL480 in aligning US strategic and domestic farm policy and getting rid of agricultural surplus commodities, still the surpluses continued to mount, with four year's annual production of cereals in storage by 1960 (Cathie 1982, 8). Also, European agricultural production was starting to recover from the depredations of the war, and the development needs of the poorer nations were coming to the fore. In the late 1950s, policy debates about food were acquiring more intensity within the US and the UN.

The founding of the World Food Programme

By 1958, prominent Democrat critics of PL 480 operation including Senator Hubert Humphrey and Congressman George McGovern, were criticising its excessively narrow focus on surplus disposal. The solution they advocated was to boost the humanitarian focus of the program, renaming it the 'Food for Peace' (FFP) program, and linking it more strongly to the US strategic interest in development of poor countries. The solution to ongoing bureaucratic struggles for control (and implicitly the narrow focus of USDA, which ran most of the PL 480 program) was to locate a Director for the FFP in the White House (Ruttan 1993a).

This was in the context of increasing Australian and Canadian objections to American use of commodity bartering as part of its surplus disposal program, in particular with Europe (Cathie 1982, 6).

Also in the late 1950s, it was becoming clear to US policy makers that agricultural surpluses were not merely a short-term problem but were assuming a structural character that would require an approach based on a longer-term strategic frame (Ruttan 1993a, 12). US development aid at this time was closely related to its Cold War security agenda,[11] but the opportunities for deploying food aid as part of a non-securitised strategic framework were beginning to develop a higher profile.[12]

In 1959, legislation influenced by Hubert Humphrey extended PL 480 for two years and established the Food for Peace Administrator position (Ruttan 1993a, 10-2); and during the 1960 election campaign both presidential candidates – Republican Vice President Richard Nixon and Democrat Senator John F. Kennedy – proposed the establishment of a multilateral organisation for food aid (Shaw 2001, 13). Two months before the election, in September 1960, President Eisenhower addressed the UN General Assembly and called for the establishment of a committee by the FAO to examine proposals for co-ordinating food aid multilaterally:

> The United States is already carrying out substantial programs to make its surpluses available to countries in greatest need. My country is also ready to join with other Members of the United Nations in devising a workable scheme to provide to Member States through the United Nations system relying on the advice and assistance of the Food and Agriculture Organization. I hope the Assembly, at this session, will seriously consider a specific program for carrying forward the promising food for peace program. (President Eisenhower address to UN General Assembly. Fifteenth Session, 868th Plenary Meeting, 22 September 1960, cited in Shaw 2001, 13–14).

This speech articulated a crucial policy shift in US politics that had emerged from the critiques of surplus disposal policy in the late 1950s. From the start of the surplus disposal problem in the early part of the 1950s, implicit in resistance to multilateral food aid mechanisms was an opposition between bilateral and multilateral programs. The understanding was that one or the other had to be chosen, and that the bilateral option was more clearly and reliably attuned to advancing the national interest than the alternative. With both presidential candidates advocating the use of a multilateral organisation for food aid, a new bipartisan consensus based on an assumed *complementary* relationship between multilateral and bilateral food aid had emerged. In a report to President Kennedy in March 1961, following a review of the Food for Peace program, McGovern stated

> we should support an expanded role for the FAO – a role where it will have responsibility for developing and executing a multi-lateral food distribution program. There should not be fear that a multi-lateral approach will conflict with the US Food For Peace Program. On the contrary, world food needs are so great that there is need for both approaches. (cited in Shaw 2001, 6–7).

Shaw notes Nixon was the first to present such a proposal publicly, and suggests part of the motivation was to 'out-innovate' his opponent (Shaw 2001, 13). This is consistent with a largely ascendant Eisenhower administration in the 1950s finding itself constantly on the back foot in Congress against Humphrey, and later McGovern too, on surplus disposal and food aid issues, as attested by their effective agenda setting of legislative approaches on the issue. In turn this can be linked to some extent with the agricultural interests bloc in Congress and its role in US electoral politics (Hansen 1991). However, apart from this domestic political dynamic, Shaw also suggests another relevant motivation for Nixon's policy: 'It would not be subjected to criticism directed against US unilateral aid as it would be administered through the UN. It would project a positive international image for the United States.' (Shaw 2001, 13).

This suggests the toll taken on US foreign policy interests by criticisms of its relatively naked self-interested disposal of surplus commodities during the 1950s, but such an instrumental analysis does not entirely capture the nuances of domestic US political debate over the appropriate balance between self-interest and humanitarian motivations for food aid policy – McGovern's 'better mix' cited in Chapter Two. This balance issue in food aid policy points to the distinctive relationship that the evolving IFAR had with American interests at both political and normative levels. From its earliest beginnings, the regime has been characterised by a significant level of US control, not only as the most significant donor, but as the leading norm-maker. In other words, a crucial aspect of the US role in the regime involved its capacity to mesh the international regime with its own bilateral aid programs via the imperatives of both its domestic and an emergent international feed-the-hungry norm.

UN role in the foundation of WFP

In 1956, B. R. Sen of India was elected the first person from the developing world to head the FAO as its Director-General. In fact the American nominee had sufficient support to be elected ahead of him in a later ballot, but withdrew due to a policy desiring solid majority support for the position (Talbot 1990, 20). Sen's election reflected the steadily increasing prominence of developing countries in the UN, in the context of a growing interest in the potential role the UN could play in assisting their development. Along with this came an increasing emphasis on analysis and policy concerning development within UN agencies, with the economist Hans Singer playing a leading role in this.

A former student of John Maynard Keynes, Dr (later Professor Sir) Hans Singer, had begun working for the UN in 1947. Working independently from each other, in 1950 he and Argentine economist Raul Prebisch developed what became known as the Singer-Prebisch hypothesis. This hypothesis predicted an ongoing decline in the terms of trade between the developing and developed world due to the dependence of the former on raw commodity exports and the latter's dominance of processed exports (Murphy 2001; Telegraph 2006). This structural problem with the world's economy necessitated, in Singer's view, a compensatory shift of resources to the developing world in the form of aid from developed countries, something which also accorded with the Keynesian belief in stimulating demand as a tool of macroeconomic management (Shaw 2001, 27-9).

These views had impacts on the development of various UN programs, such as the Expanded Program of Technical Assistance (EPTA),[13] and the proposal for a multilateral development financing facility, the Special UN Fund for Economic Development (SUNFED).[14] SUNFED was opposed by the US and not approved as a UN Agency, though the idea of a soft-loan multilateral finance facility was later adopted by the World Bank, in the form of its soft lending window, the International Development Association (Kanbur 2003, 6; Shaw 2001, 27). Shaw suggests US concurrence with this latter move reflected their greater voting power in the World Bank compared to the UN (Shaw 2001, 27).

Singer himself attested to the links between this work and food aid as follows:

> It was also in casting around for possible financing for SUNFED that I became very interested in 1954 in the establishment, under Public Law 480, of the US food aid program and in the possibility of an international food aid program which had begun to emerge in Rome...This interest led me to my involvement in laying the ground for the UN/FAO World Food Programme. (Cited in Shaw 2001, 27).

The FAO's attempts to develop a multilateral approach to food distribution began to be influenced by this wider context of deployment of aid for economic development. The FAO sponsored a number of studies from the mid-1950s designed to make the case for deploying agricultural surpluses, both as emergency relief and as a form of income transfer for development (Shaw 2001, 21-2). One was based on a pilot investigation in India and 'showed in detail how the large amounts of capital represented by food surpluses could be used to finance a general expansion of investment programmes in developing countries' (FAO 1955). Others were focused on the case for international food reserves in the absence of national food reserves in many developing countries (FAO 1956). These studies derived from the FAO tradition of proposing practical interventions to relieve hunger and deploy agricultural surpluses via multilateral mechanisms, though to this point such proposals had come to very little due to obstruction from developed nations. Yet the ongoing surplus production in developed countries along with significant development needs in other nations was increasingly making such opposition difficult to maintain.

On 27 October 1960 the UN General Assembly accepted the propositions from President Eisenhower and resolved to invite the FAO to undertake a study into multilateral procedures for deploying surplus food to alleviate hunger.[15] This decision reflected both the long-term efforts by the FAO to put multilateral food aid on the agenda, crystallised in its Freedom from Hunger Campaign (FFHC, adopted in October 1960), and the shift in the US position articulated by President Eisenhower's speech, cited above.

The FAO set up an Intergovernmental Advisory Committee to do this task, along with an expert panel which assisted the Director-General to prepare a study to inform the Committee's work (FAO 1961). The five panel members included Professor Singer, along with another two former students of Keynes, and two other Keynesian style economists (Shaw 2001, 22). Consistent with the principles of surplus disposal and reflecting the Keynesian consensus of the time, the study placed emphasis on stimulating demand rather than restricting production to deal with surpluses. Demand stimulation was to be accomplished by income transfers from the developed world, with food surpluses forming an important part of the resource transfers. The panel

> estimated that about $12,500 million of agricultural commodities would become available as 'surpluses' over a five-year period for use outside normal commercial market channels, either bilaterally or through the United Nations system. It recommended that about two-thirds of these resources should be used in economic development programmes and one-third for social development (Shaw 2001, 23).

Economic development programs would use food aid as a capital resource to deploy, for example in feeding workers involved in building infrastructure and/or to free up scarce financial resources. In turn this development would assist in overcoming poverty which was the only means to achieve freedom from hunger. Social development programs would deploy food aid to offset temporary effects on food production from land reform programs, or via school feeding or other relief and welfare programs. In addition, the panel recommended the deployment of a small proportion of food aid (6 percent) into the establishment of an international emergency food reserve, and a further 8 percent to assist the establishment of national food reserves (Shaw 2001, 23–5).

George McGovern, who had lost a bid for the Senate in the 1960 US elections, was appointed Director of the Office of Food for Peace by

President Kennedy in one of his first executive actions on taking office in January 1961. In April 1961 McGovern went to Rome to attend a meeting of the FAO Intergovernmental Advisory Committee. After realising the main stumbling block to establishing something concrete was the lack of member-state willingness to commit resources, McGovern took advantage of his political seniority and the newness of the Kennedy administration, which meant a relatively fluid process for obtaining finance outside of the budget process. After some intensive lobbying via phone from Rome over a weekend, McGovern secured Presidential authorisation to make a concrete proposal for establishing a World Food Program with a commitment of US$40 million, so long as it was matched by other countries up to a starting stake of US$100 million.

This proposal was put to the committee meeting on Monday 10 April, 1961. After a brief adjournment to allow FAO officials and member-state representatives to recover from their 'visible shock' at the sudden concrete proposal, the proposal was adopted, and went forward for approval by the FAO Conference and UN General Assembly in parallel resolutions on 24 November and 19 December 1961 respectively. (McGovern 2001, 57-9; Shaw 2001, 6-9). Those parallel resolutions established the World Food Programme. (See Appendix 3 for McGovern's proposal; Appendix 1 for the UN resolution, including at Annex 1 the relevant FAO resolution text).

Historiography of the founding of WFP

The title of the relevant chapter in Shaw's book is "The Birth of WFP: One Man's Inspiration", though this is really a reference to McGovern's decisive role in making something happen in April 1961 rather than crediting him with having the idea of such an agency. Indeed, Shaw cites B. R. Sen stating in his autobiography that "This bold initiative by Senator McGovern…finally got *my proposal* off the ground…" (Shaw 2001, 9; emphasis added). Leaving aside the compelling individual stories, however, the story of the founding of the WFP needs to be understood from (at least)[16] two broader perspectives.

From the first perspective, the WFP originates in the cosmopolitan ideals of activists and believers in international institutions. Since at least the founding of the FAO there had been many attempts to manage the distribution of food and reduction of global hunger multilaterally, but they had always been frustrated by the narrower national interests given priority by food exporting nation-states. The work of the FAO Directors-General and staff, and others in the UN system was crucial in developing, advancing and persisting with the arguments for multilateral food assistance that were eventually successful in 1961.

This version of the genesis of the WFP suffers from lack of reference to the crucial role of the US – in first blocking such an organisation, then catalysing it. Thus, from the second perspective, the United States is the driving force behind the WFP; the source of inspiration and resources for it, motivated largely by self-interest.

Within this perspective there are some differences about the extent to which that self-interest could be said to be 'enlightened' by normative considerations, or complicated by bureaucratic turf wars, or the significance of the election of Kennedy. McGovern and Shaw in particular emphasise the importance of Kennedy's presidency as opposed to the Republican administration he replaced, with Shaw even mentioning the counterfactual of a Nixon administration (Shaw 2001, 16). McGovern's approach is not surprising given he was a member of the Kennedy administration and a Democrat legislator and, later, a presidential candidate himself (unsuccessfully opposing President Nixon in 1972).

However, McGovern also emphasizes the bipartisan nature of American political support for food aid (McGovern 2001, e.g. Ch3), and it is important not to overstate the relative importance of changes in US Administration. That issue is relatively peripheral to the analyses of Cathie, Ruttan and Talbot (Cathie 1982; Ruttan 1993a; Talbot 1990), who (along with Shaw and McGovern) all emphasize the political economy of surplus disposal during the 1950s, the role of agricultural constituencies and Congress, and the adoption of PL 480 as important to the founding of the WFP. From this perspective, the WFP could be said to have effectively extended American food aid policy into an international regime in order to give it both additional legitimacy, and an additional operational arm for delivery. Consistent with this argument, Hopkins adds a desire for burden sharing by other developed nations (Hopkins 1990, 180), in the context of emerging European agricultural surpluses and a desire to divert the Europeans from establishing their own bilateral programs (Shaw 2001, 64).

Most of those adopting the US perspective draw on Wallerstein, who gives the definitive history of US food aid up to the late 1970s (Wallerstein 1980). However, it is important not to miss the UN perspective on the WFP's foundation. In fact, the different perspectives on the establishment of the WFP point to the complexity of how such organisations get established – not just in the range of actors, interests and institutional contexts, but in the layers of politics interacting between national and international arenas.

An innovatively cautious intergovernmental organisation?

Three months before formally passing the resolution to establish the WFP, the UN General Assembly adopted a proposal from President Kennedy to officially designate 'the decade of the 1960s as the United Nations Decade of Development' (Kennedy cited in Shaw 2001, 28). What Hopkins refers to as the second wave of post-war regime building – 'the development wave of 1960-1973 that sought to accelerate the expansion of economic modernization, especially in non-industrial, poorer states' (Hopkins 1990, 181) – was underway with the WFP in the vanguard. Meanwhile, McGovern suggests that the WFP 'is not only the UN's major food arm, but also the single largest humanitarian project of the U.S. government.' (McGovern 2001, 62). It is the intertwining of internationalist and hegemonic norms and interests which characterized these decisions and continues to characterize the WFP.

Reflecting the slow transition within the US towards accepting a multilateral approach to food aid, and then only as a supplement to its bilateral programs, the propositions from McGovern took a cautious and limited form, proposing the WFP as a trial program.[17] This gave his own government and others the option of backing out if the new organisation proved to be too expensive or in other ways problematic for their national interests. Also reflecting this caution was the WFP's complex parentage – it was to be a creature equally of the FAO and the UN, with each organisation nominating half the member-states on its governing body, called the World Food Programme Intergovernmental Committee (IGC). In line with this parentage, the appointment of the WFP Executive Director (ED) was to be decided jointly by the FAO Director-General and the UN Secretary-General. The ED was to be responsible for reporting, not only to the IGC, but to the FAO Conference and the UN's ECOSOC. Also, the FAO was to house and provide administrative systems and support to the WFP. Such arrangements had the virtue of drawing from existing UN systems and organisations, and implicitly encouraging if not requiring cooperation amongst them whilst simultaneously creating a distinctive check and balance element to WFP governance.

One other innovatively cautious (or cautiously innovative) characteristic should be noted at this point – the adoption of what is today still referred to as the dual mandate. This refers to the WFP's mission to use food aid both for development work and emergency relief. As will be discussed in more detail in later chapters, the tension between those roles remains prominent in the WFP today, although the balance between them has changed significantly over time. Establishing a dual mandate from the outset reflected the ambiguity in the international norm towards the uses for food aid (an ambiguity which continues to the present day as will be discussed further in Chapter Six). However, the initial emphasis was on food aid's potential capacity to substitute for financial aid.

IFAR as inchoate regime, 1961–1981

The establishment of an intergovernmental organisation dedicated to multilateral food aid was a significant step in the development of the nascent international food aid regime. However, the nature of the WFP, at least initially, placed some important constraints on the development of the regime. The characteristics of the WFP as temporary, experimental, and marginal come to the fore as relevant to these constraints. After its initial trial period, while the WFP became more securely established, the global food crisis of the early 1970s attested to the fragility of global food security. The subsequent World Food Conference led to more changes which, in limited ways, assisted the development of an international food aid regime, though the IFAR was not to solidify as an institution until at least the 1980s.

Early WFP and IFAR developments

The WFP's initial establishment was to be on a trial basis for three years (1963–65), subject to assessment of operations and some UN mandated studies on aspects of the Programme at the end of 1965 (Shaw 2001, 37). This reflected a general view of the Programme as experimental, partly given its focus on development *projects* based on food aid, in contrast to the standard form of bilateral food aid as *program*, or government to government in form. The FAO research into food aid in the 1950s referred to above was aimed at assessing whether multilateral, project food aid could credibly contribute to rural development in poor nations, but the WFP was the first serious test of the prospects for project food aid as the basis for serious multilateral development work.

Standard technical categorisations of food aid are based on a tripartite categorisation – *program*, *project*, and *emergency* (Shaw and Clay 1993, 1). The apparently neat functional distinction between bilateral, program food aid and multilateral, project aid (reflecting the different Titles within PL 480), left some uncertainty about where the operation of multilateral emergency relief fitted. While the WFP's first operations commenced with responses to emergencies in September 1962 (Shaw 2001, 38), it soon became apparent that the WFP lacked the ready access to both food and cash resources which would enable it to respond rapidly to emergencies. All food aid resources were pledged by donor countries and only actually supplied in response to WFP decisions to allocate them; the WFP had no stockpiled reserves of its own and was also perennially short of the cash reserves necessary to fund the transport and distribution of emergency food supplies (Shaw 2001, 148ff). As a result, in his evaluation of the WFP's emergency operations at the conclusion of the trial period, the Executive Director commented as follows:

> The conclusion is reluctantly reached that it is important to make clear to countries suffering disasters the inevitable limitations to which the supply of World Food Program emergency food aid is subjected, in order to avoid the raising of hopes which cannot be fulfilled. (Cited in Shaw 2001, 148).

These problems led to the IGC placing constraints on the proportion of WFP resources allocated to emergency relief,[18] albeit with ongoing debate as to ways to either improve the WFP's capacity to respond to emergency needs, or to shift responsibility more effectively to bilateral aid and NGOs (Shaw 2001, 149). Despite these problems, and the WFP's focus on development as its primary role, Shaw interestingly notes that a role in emergency aid was never eliminated from the WFP mandate in an implicit reference to the feed-the-hungry norm – WFP 'could not stand aside and not move to help countries and people stricken by disasters. The humanitarian impulse of food aid was too strong' (Shaw 2001, 149).

Another issue constraining the formation of the international food aid regime distinct from the WFP's experimental nature was what was seen to be its *temporary* nature (Charlton 1992, 635). This reflected a view, deriving from the successful processes of post-war reconstruction and the generation of large agricultural surpluses, that the issue of countries with lagging economic development was a temporary problem amenable to technical solutions. This view was present in the 1960–61 study led by Singer, linked to the notion that a Marshall Plan-type approach to development assistance could accomplish development objectives over approximately 15 years (an initial five years of transfers, and a decade of reduced transfers) (FAO 1961; Shaw 2001, 22). In this context, one of the WFP's key characteristics, according to Charlton, was its 'lean structure which could be easily dismantled once the need for multilateral food aid disappeared' (Charlton 1992, 635). This leanness links to the WFP's status as the only UN organisation with no mandated or specific allocation from the UN budget, relying totally on voluntary contributions.

The advent of the world food crisis of the early 1970s saw the end of such optimistic thinking, to the extent that the conception of hunger as a temporary problem at the global level is now barely discernible. These ideological shifts concerning the nature of the problem of global hunger are discussed in more detail below and in Chapters Six and Seven.

Consistent with its temporary and experimental nature, the WFP had only marginal significance in terms of the wider global movement of food aid in its early years. Charlton describes the WFP in its first decade as remaining 'a largely marginal actor in the global food aid system', handling only 'about 4 per cent of the food aid provided world wide' by 1971 (Charlton 1992, 8). Instead, the vast bulk of food aid was bilateral, program food aid based on government to government bulk grants or concessional sales of food commodities.

If the initial trial set-up of WFP was based on a view of multilateral food aid as experimental, temporary and marginal, this view was to evolve, along with a range of developments in the latter part of the 1960s and early 1970s. In the first instance the WFP was accorded an indefinitely extended existence following the end of its initial trial period in 1965. This was followed by the signing of the first Food Aid Convention in 1967; the global food crisis (1972–74), and the World Food Conference in 1974, resulting in changes to WFP governance and the establishment of the International Emergency Food Reserve (IEFR). These developments, detailed below, all contributed to the consolidation of the IFAR, though the regime was not to fully develop until the WFP achieved substantial organisational autonomy from the FAO – a process which took most of the 1980s – and the US re-assumed a clear leadership role in the WFP in the early 1990s.

The Food Aid Convention

It was not under the auspices of the WFP, but within the context of the Kennedy Round of the GATT that the US (and to a lesser extent Canada) successfully moved to link food aid with the International Wheat Agreement in 1967 (Shaw 2001, 72–4; Talbot 1990, 51). They did this by establishing the Food Aid Convention (FAC), reflecting the centrality of bilateralism and trade to food aid. The motivation for initiating the FAC is generally described as a desire for 'burden sharing' amongst other wealthy nations, given the US and Canada dominated food aid donations; the GATT context enabled trade concession carrots and sticks to be used to cajole the other states into signing the Convention (Shaw 2001, 73; also Uvin 1992, 303).

The FAC, periodically reviewed and still in operation, commits the signatories[19] to 'provide guaranteed aid in the form of cereals or cash to purchase grains for shipment as aid. Each member agreed to provide a minimum quantity of food aid in physical terms irrespective of fluctuations in production, stocks and prices'. The first aggregate minimum was set at 4.5 million tons (Shaw 2001, 73); the current aggregate is 4.9 million metric tons (Hanrahan and Canada 2006; International Grains Council 2007). Despite some encouragement in the FAC to use multilateral channels (i.e. donating through the WFP), 'only 5 to 6 per cent of the aggregate shipments of FAC grains were channelled annually through WFP during the three years of the 1967 FAC, which mirrored the proportion of food aid handled globally by WFP' (Shaw 2001, 73-4). FAC requirements have been well below the actual levels of food aid being donated, and are generally regarded as providing a very low floor for food aid donations, rather than pushing higher levels of donation. The real purpose of the FAC was to make as many agricultural exporting nations as possible part of a global food aid system, but, as Ruttan notes, the 'U.S. interest in burden sharing stopped short of letting multilateral programs become large enough to interfere with the political leverage of the bilateral program'. (Ruttan 1993a, 17).

The 1974 World Food Conference

The early 1970s saw a transformation in the post-war system of large developed country surpluses contributing to a mix of bilateral and multilateral food aid. A sudden, if temporary, disappearance of agricultural surpluses and consequent price increases led to a 'food crisis', a UN sponsored World Food Conference in 1974, and changes to the UN system in relation to food.

Global food shortages emerged as a problem, commonly referred to as a 'world food crisis' in the period 1972–74 (Talbot 1990, 11) due to a complex array of factors both reducing supply and affecting demand. US food surpluses had fallen from a peak of 1 billion bushels in 1962 to less than 20 million bushels at the end of 1973 (Ruttan 1993a, 22). This drop was partly due to the adoption of policies in the latter part of the 1960s to discourage production through incentives to reduce the amount of land under cultivation (George 1991, 29; Shaw 2001, 80). However, the importance of this factor should not be overemphasised given, as Friedman notes, the structural biases towards overproduction continued and US agricultural surpluses returned fairly rapidly as a concerned

USDA introduced new production incentives in the context of the shortages (Friedman 2002, 333). Other factors affecting global production included production cost increases – in particular fertiliser costs and the oil price increases implemented by the Organisation of Petroleum Exporting Countries (OPEC) from the end of 1973 (Horton 2009, 33), though George points out the importance of separating those two issues:

> during 1970–74, the cost of *energy* necessary to produce one hundred pounds of anhydrous ammonia went from 47c to 70c. The price for the same quantity of *fertilizer* during the same period rose from $3.79 to $9.15...Prices for all types of fertilizers had *already* increased 100 per cent between June 1972 and September 1973, or well before the December 1973 oil increase. (George 1991, 143; emphasis in original).

In fact, given the emphasis on use of fertilisers in the changes to production from the 'Green Revolution', it is likely that the increase in demand for fertilizers (and for its hydrocarbon origins) would have contributed to both oil and fertilizer price increases.

Also important were harvest failures due to climactic events. In the context of the détente period thaw in US relations with the USSR, harvest failures in 1972 in the Soviet Union led to the US supplying grain (at concessional prices) to the USSR for the first time. The Soviet Union received 'more than' 17 million metric tons[20] of (largely US) grain in 1972–73 (Shaw 2001, 80).

> This led to a record level of world trade in cereals, which could only be achieved by drawing on food stocks, which were reduced to their lowest level in over two decades. Prices, triggered off by Soviet Union purchases, rose abruptly to four times their previous level. (Shaw 2001, 80).

In the early 1970s, there were devastating famines in Bangladesh (de Waal 1997, 17-8; Sen 1981, Ch9) and the Sahel region of Africa, which suffered drought from 1968–1973 (Meredith 2005, 290; Sen 1981, Ch8). At the same time, a sudden drop in supply led to rapid food price increases, and a greater demand for food aid together with a simultaneous and related loss of surpluses available for food aid (Cathie 1982, Ch1).

The crisis eloquently demonstrated the problem of food aid's pro-cyclical nature. At the same time that production failures created the need for access to surplus stocks, those failures meant that surpluses were not available as food aid. Also, when the price of commodities increased significantly, this meant much less food aid could be purchased for a given budget allocation (Rothschild 1993, 91), even as price increases also triggered starvation and an increased need for food aid as the poor were priced out of access to food.

Food aid flows dropped from a peak of 16.8 million tons of cereals in 1964–65 to less than seven million tons in 1973–74, shrinking 'at a time when they were most needed.' (Shaw 2001, 80). Steady falls in PL 480 food aid from a high of 18 million tons in 1966 to 11 million tons in 1970 (Rothschild 1993, 90) suddenly accelerated and between 1972 and 1974 US food aid fell from 12 million to 3 million metric tons (Hopkins 1992, 241). In the face of direct competition between food aid and commercial transactions the US froze its food aid in the Northern spring-summer of 1974 (Ruttan 1993a, 22).

Apart from the grim realities of food market failures at the global level, three other developments in the period are relevant to the context of the international response to the food crisis.

Firstly, the late 1960s and early 1970s had seen a growth in NGO interest in and campaigning on humanitarian relief following the Biafra airlift of 1968 (de Waal 1997, 72ff). Consequently, in rich countries public awareness of 'Third World famines' grew.

Secondly, along with this heightened world public interest came certain systemic kinds of analysis of hunger which saw it as a global issue requiring a global level response. For example, the well known Club of Rome Report *The Limits to Growth* (Meadows, Meadows et al. 1972) argued, on the basis of computer modelling, that without change to human behaviour growth in the Earth's human population would outstrip food production capacities limited by pollution and industrialisation (see also Uvin 1994, Ch6). Also Hardin (1974) suggested a metaphor of the earth being a lifeboat into which the starving masses of the Third World not only would not fit, but in their desperate efforts to climb aboard placed everyone else in jeopardy of drowning. This led to debates within moral philosophy about the nature of global hunger and the response it required from wealthy countries (see Singer 1993).

Thirdly, the devaluation of the US dollar led to a breakdown in the Bretton Woods post-war international financial arrangements in the early 1970s (Gilpin 1987). This exacerbated the price increases in agricultural produce, but also stimulated a slow-burning debate about the nature of the international economic system. The developing, 'Third World' nations overcame internal differences and solidified an alliance begun a decade earlier in the UN as the Group of 77 (G77), based on articulating the New International Economic Order (NIEO) in opposition to developed country economic interests (Murphy 2001, 270; Traub 2006, 19–21). The NIEO analysis drew on Marxism and the work of economist Raul Prebisch arguing that the world economy was divided into rich, 'core' states, and poorer, peripheral ones (Hobden and Wyn Jones 2001, 205–6), in which the latter were structurally disadvantaged. Prominent in the NIEO argument was a claim for aid as reparation for historical colonial exploitation, linked to continuing unfair advantages for the center compared to the periphery in the global economy (Murphy 2001, 269). Hopkins characterises the period 1973–1981 for the UN as 'the structural conflict wave ... in which coalitions of southern or G77 states sought to control issues, agendas, and budgets in [intergovernmental organisations]... in order to exercise power and extract resources from industrialized states.' (Hopkins 1990, 178). In the context of this North-South divide within the UN, the FAO was seen as under the control of the G77, and became increasingly distrusted by the developed nations (Hopkins 1990, 182).

These three developments along with the food crisis led many member-states to question 'the utility and relevance of the FAO itself' (Thompson 1981, 195) while considering how to improve international institutions concerned with food. In particular, a perception on the part of the developed world that the FAO had failed to achieve its mandate in realising and warning of the impending crisis placed the FAO 'under shadow of opprobrium' (Talbot 1990, 10). Given the FAO's lack of control over world food markets and their role in the crisis such views do not seem to have had an entirely reasonable basis. As with most 'blame the UN' rhetorical moves, whatever elements of truth in the accusation that FAO had been negligent, it was also a convenient distraction from any suggestions that member-state government policies had played a role in generating the crisis.

A World Food Conference was convened by the UN Secretary-General in November 1974 following a proposal by the US Secretary of State Kissinger in his first address to the UN General Assembly in September 1973 (UN General Assembly 1973). That it was convened by the UN Secretariat rather than the FAO highlighted the extent to which the FAO was being held culpable for the food crisis, though the Conference was held in Rome.

Ruttan notes evidence that Senator Humphrey required Kissinger to commit to supporting a World Food Conference as the price of his confirmation as Secretary of State getting through the Senate (Ruttan 1993a, 235, fn60). Humphrey himself put it this way:

> Recognizing the necessity of international coöperation in approaching the issue of world food security, Dr. Henry Kissinger, in his first address to the General Assembly of the UN as U.S. Secretary of State, proposed a UN conference on food to be held in November, 1974 following a suggestion that I posed at the Secretary' confirmation hearings before the Senate Foreign Relations Committee. (Humphrey 1970).

Within the US, the Soviet grain deals of 1972 had been driven by the State Department under the rubric of State's détente policy. The mid-1970s saw a renewed period of competition between the Departments of State (under Secretary Kissinger) and Agriculture (under Secretary Butz) over control of international food policy (Friedman 2002, 333). The Department of State saw food aid as a key bargaining chip in Middle East strategy, while the USDA opposed food aid in a climate of strong commercial sales and high prices. Meanwhile church activists were pushing for more to be done to relieve hunger (Ruttan 1993a, 22ff).

These internal US conflicts, along with the impact of the resignation of President Nixon over the Watergate scandal, led to a 'disorganized' (Ruttan 1993a, 25) US delegation at the World Food Conference.

Butz chaired the delegation but Kissinger gave the keynote address.

> At the Conference itself delegates from developing countries took turns blistering the U.S. government and the Soviet Union for 'rationing' the world's food supply. The U.S. delegation, including members of the World Hunger Action Coalition and the Inter-religious Task Force on U.S. Food Policy, and Senators Richard Clark (D-Iowa) and Humphrey, pressured Secretary Butz to cable the President to approve a minimum volume increase in food aid of one million tons for 1975. Bolstered by his budget and treasury officials, Ford...refused. (Ruttan 1993a, 24-5).

Apart from its pro-cyclical nature, another problematic feature of food aid is its volatility (OECD 2006). This was classically demonstrated by the decline in food prices during the Northern hemisphere 1974–75 winter. Within three months of the Conference at which any increase in US food aid had been rejected, in February 1975, USDA Secretary Butz was announcing the biggest food aid budget since the late 1960s of $1.6 billion (Ruttan 1993a, 25).

There were four principal outcomes of the World Food Conference, all endorsed by the UN Economic and Social Council and General Assembly (UN General Assembly 1974). Firstly, it adopted a Universal

Declaration on the Eradication of Hunger and Malnutrition. In this it declared, *inter alia*, that

> every man, woman and child has the inalienable right to be free from hunger and malnutrition...It is a fundamental responsibility of Governments to work together for higher food production and a more equitable and efficient distribution of food between countries and within countries...
>
> ...within a decade no child will go to bed hungry, no family will fear for its next day's bread, and no human being's future and capacities will be stunted by malnutrition. (cited in Uvin 1994, p60).

Secondly, it resolved to restructure the WFP ruling body, the IGC, renaming it the Committee for Food Aid Policies and Programs (CFA) and expanding its remit to deal with all food aid policy issues, not just those associated with the work of the WFP. The WFP secretariat did not have the resources to engage in much effective policy work on food aid, and member states had no interest in multilateral interference in their bilateral food aid programs. However, the concept of a broader mandate in the policy realm helped inspire efforts to broaden the WFP's work (Ingram 2006), which can still be seen in some of its contemporary advocacy work. This broadening also provided an important conceptual mandate for the IFAR, with the WFP governing body at its heart.

Thirdly, the World Food Conference resolved, despite Kissinger's view prior to the Conference that no new bodies would be agreed to (Talbot 1990, 103), to create two new bodies. One was the ministerial level World Food Council to maintain high level commitment to dealing with hunger issues (Talbot 1990, Ch4) while avoiding FAO control by working through ECOSOC (Hopkins 1990, 182). This Council struggled with articulating a relevant role on top of the other food agencies and lack of member-state support (Ingram 2006, 56-7).[21] The second new body was the International Fund for Agricultural Development (IFAD), set up principally as a mechanism for bringing in OPEC nations as a source of development funds in a multilateral setting (Talbot 1990, Ch5). IFAD continues to operate, based in Rome; in 2006 it distributed US$556.8m in grants and loans (International Fund for Agricultural Development 2008).

Lastly, the Conference resolved to recommend 'measures for meeting international food emergency requirements particularly in order to enhance WFP's capacity to render speedy assistance in emergencies' (FAO Committee on Commodity Problems 2005, 4). This led to the UN General Assembly establishing an International Emergency Food

Reserve (IEFR) in September 1975. The IEFR had 'a minimum target of 500, 000 tonnes of cereals, placed at the disposal of WFP, in addition to regular WFP pledges, and subject to the existing WFP procedures for approval of emergency requests. The CFA approved modalities for the operation of the IEFR at its First Session in 1976' (FAO Committee on Commodity Problems 2005, 4). However, there were a number of obstacles to its operation reflected in the fact that the necessary pledges for the IEFR did not get made until 1979 (Ingram 2006; Shaw 2001).

The FAO was largely absent from these principal outcomes of the Conference, though it did also establish an FAO Committee on World Food Security (FAO Committee on Commodity Problems 2005, 4). Its absence from a role in these new developments was a glaring indication of the perception that it had become a partisan player in the NIEO debate and failed to prevent the world food crisis. However, given the dominance of developed countries in food production, and the role of market inequities in the food crisis, the NIEO analysis strongly suggested that the blame did not lie with the FAO. Thus the FAO was to become more and more identified with the G77. The new FAO Director-General, Lebanese national Edouard Saouma, fostered this relationship skilfully following his election in 1975.

Another important absence from these developments was clear leadership from the US, reflecting domestic policy uncertainty and disarray in the context of Nixon's resignation as President earlier in 1974, and conflicts between the hunger lobby, Congressional Democrats and the Departments of State, Agriculture and Treasury. The World Food Conference marked the beginning of a period of relative policy neglect of multilateral institutions by the US (Hopkins 1990, 178-81, 197-9), which increasingly were seen as tools of the G-77 and other critics of US power. This period, during which the US withdrew from various UN organisations such as the International Labor Organisation (ILO) and UNESCO was to last until the end of the Cold War in the late 1980s.

The developments arising from the World Food Conference provided significant impetus to the formation of the IFAR, not least demonstrated by the assumption lying behind the Conference itself that the nature of the food crisis required a global, multilateral response. In hindsight, the events of the 1970s had contributed to a divergence of the IFAR feed-the-hungry norm from its domestic American counterpart norm. However, by the early 1980s, with little consistent leadership by the US, and the WFP still very much a subordinate division of the FAO, the IFAR had only developed some limited institutional solidity, mainly in the evolved technical understandings of more effective deployment of food aid.

Endnotes

[1] Hambidge documents the antecedents of this Conference in the development of nutrition and food work in the League of Nations led by former Australian Prime Minister Stanley Bruce, and his economic adviser, F. L. McDougall. McDougall was in Washington in the early 1940s and influenced President Roosevelt's decision to call the Hot Springs conference. McDougall was also to chair the important Reviewing Panel of the Interim Commission. (Hambidge 1955, 44ff, 54).

[2] Note that the FAO was established before the UN itself – see Hambidge for explanation of how this precise name was adopted. (Hambidge 1955, 53-4).

[3] Member states at July 1947 were: Australia, Austria, Belgium, Brazil, Canada, Chile, China, Cuba, Czechoslovakia, Denmark, Ecuador, Egypt, Finland, France, Greece, Hungary, India, Ireland, Italy, Mexico, Netherlands, New Zealand, Norway, Peru, Poland, Portugal, Philippine Republic, Sweden, Switzerland, Thailand (Siam), Turkey, Union of South Africa, UK, USA (Hambidge 1955, 250).

[4] Rome derived an argument to be the hosting city from the location there of the International Institute of Agriculture (IIA), an intergovernmental organisation established in 1905 after the King of Italy hosted an international conference on agricultural issues. IIA was concerned primarily with data collection and sharing of agricultural production information, and was subsumed into the FAO when it was established (Hobson 1931; 1932; Hodgson 1932).

[5] After working for the key farm lobby group and writing a draft of legislation for disposal of surplus commodities as food aid as early as 1950 (Mustard 2003, 40), Garnett was appointed USDA FAS Administrator 1955–58 (Agexporter 2003, 12).

[6] Though there were various commodity agreements (Coleman, Grant et al. 2004, 113ff) – e.g. wheat and sugar – arguably these agreements formed part of an international agricultural trade regime separate from the international trade regime.

[7] In 1995 the subcommittee changed its acronym to CSSD – Consultative Subcommittee on Surplus Disposal – to 'avoid conflict with a sister organization in the UN family' (FAO 2001, 2).

[8] In response, Coleman et al. have developed the concept of the transnational policy space to grasp the complexity and interdependence of supranational governance processes (Coleman, Grant et al. 2004, 164).

[9] Coleman et. al. note it was the developed OECD and GATT member nation-states which shaped the 'transnational agricultural policy space' during the 1970s and 1980s (Coleman, Grant et al. 2004, 165).

[10] Refusal of food aid is a rare occurrence, though there are isolated examples such as Zambia's refusal to accept Genetically Modified maize from the US in 2002 (Clapp 2005, 467).

[11] 'Between 1952 and 1956 military assistance, primarily to Greece, Turkey, and [Republic of] China accounted for over 50 per cent of all U.S. aid. Much of the economic assistance budget was justified as defense support' (Ruttan 1993a, 232, fn20).

[12] For example, Ruttan notes the issue of food aid to (communist) Poland in 1956–57 (Ruttan 1993a, 231-2, fn19).

[13] EPTA was to merge with the UN Special Fund to become the UN Development Program (UNDP) in 1966 (Murphy 2006).

[14] It was Singer's suggestion to add 'Special' to a name which otherwise would have resulted in the acronym 'UNFED' (Telegraph 2006).

[15] "Provision of food surpluses to food-deficient peoples through the United Nations system", UN General Assembly resolution 1496(XV) adopted at the 908th Plenary Meeting, 27 October 1960 (Shaw 2001, 6).

[16] Additional research would be needed to comment meaningfully on the perspectives of other nation-states on the founding of the WFP. The perspectives given here are, in my view, the most significant for understanding the international food aid regime. (See Charlton 1993 for the Canadian perspective).

[17] Though this was not the first time a trial period was used in setting up a UN operational agency; The UN High Commission for Refugees (UNHCR) was also set up on a trial basis (Barnett and Finnemore 2004, 73).

[18] For example, in its first year of operations 'up to 25 per cent of the commodities pledged to the Programme were earmarked for use in emergencies, including the establishment of national food reserves' (Shaw 2001, 147).

[19] The original signatories of the 1967 FAC were 'Argentina, Australia, Canada, Denmark, the Commission of the European Communities (for EEC community aid), Finland, Japan, Norway, Sweden, Switzerland, the United Kingdom and the United States' (Shaw 2001, 259, fn2).

[20] Friedman puts the figure at 30 million metric tons of grain, 'which amounted to three-quarters of all commercially traded grain in the world' (Friedman 2002, 333). Luttrell states it as 440 million bushels of wheat, 'more than the total U.S. commercial wheat exports for the year beginning in July 1971' (Luttrell 1973, 2). (For details of US/USSR grain trade in this period see Balaam and Carey 1981, Ch4). The sales to the USSR were made secretly in circumstances which allowed private interests involved to make large sums of money on the inevitable price increases which followed when their scale became public. The subsequent scandal in the US, referred to as the 'great Soviet grain robbery', led to grain embargoes on the USSR from July 1973 through 1975 (Friedman 2002, 333).

[21] The eventual winding up of the World Food Council in 1996 could be portrayed as the final nail in the coffin of a putative world food regime.

4

The Evolution of the World Food Programme

In the short history of the international food aid regime there have been substantial changes in the use and direction of multilateral food aid. This chapter analyses these changes by considering the evolution of the WFP and IFAR since the 1980s, concluding the historical analysis of the IFAR begun in the last chapter.

The first section examines the period when James Ingram was WFP Executive Director (1982-1992). During this period the WFP's relationship with the FAO became a focus of controversy, while, as was noted at the end of the previous chapter, the US, though remaining the largest donor, stepped back from a significant leadership role. The reasons for this stepping back are complex, but are at least partly linked to changes in the political economy of US food aid.

When the WFP was founded, food aid was a relatively large proportion of overall aid, predominantly in the form of bilateral program (government to government) aid, and largely driven by the surplus disposal needs of agricultural producers. By the late 1990s, food aid had become a much smaller part of overall aid, but now a much larger share was multilateral in modes at least partially separated from donor country surplus disposal. However, multilateral food aid itself had changed from predominantly developmental to an emergency relief focus. These shifts both reflected and contributed to the evolution of the IFAR feed-the-hungry norm, and its changing relationships with perceived state economic and strategic interests, and the domestic US feed-the-hungry norm. The second section of the chapter details the early stages of this process of shifting away from development and into humanitarian assistance, in the context of other important changes in the international regime.

The final section of the chapter considers WFP development under Executive Director Catherine Bertini (1992-2002). Like Ingram, Bertini served two five year terms in the role, during which period there were important managerial reforms to, and growth in, the organization as it emerged as the largest and one of the best regarded of the UN operational agencies. Of particular interest are the continued depoliticization of WFP operations, the continued intensification of the emergency relief focus, the shifting and complex relationship between WFP and US food aid policy, and attempts to reconcile the dual development/emergency relief mandate. Understanding the historical development of these changes is an important part of explaining the legitimacy of the WFP and the IFAR, as Chapter Six will demonstrate in more detail.

The WFP under James Ingram

James Ingram was appointed to a five-year term as WFP Executive Director (ED) in 1982, after a career in Australia's foreign service. His was the first ED appointment in some years that was not on a short-term or acting basis. The main factor in that instability was the increasingly problematic relationship the WFP had with the FAO. The eventual establishment of the WFP as an autonomous UN agency occurred only at the end of Ingram's second five-year term as ED, and the struggle between the FAO and the WFP over control or autonomy was one of two major issues defining his tenure. That it took ten years to resolve reflected an uncertain and partial engagement of the US with the WFP for much of the 1980s, though the appointment of American Catherine Bertini as Ingram's successor presaged an important transition in the US relationship. The second issue of Ingram's tenure was the defined shift into emergency aid, which will be discussed in more detail later in this Chapter.

Ingram was undoubtedly successful as ED, as reflected by his successful campaign for reappointment in 1986–87 despite attempts by the FAO Director-General (D-G) Saouma to end his tenure. This success resulted from a combination of management and political skills. While the former was important to ensuring the WFP was able to deliver food aid in an efficient manner, the latter refers to his ability to manage the politics of donor and recipient nations on the CFA, based on a hard-headed assessment of the nature of CFA politics:

> Despite their rhetoric, developing countries were realistic enough to recognize that the donors wrote the basic music to which all must dance if contributions to the Programme were not to decline precipitately. Because WFP's funding was provided by the donors on a voluntary basis, the Executive Director could not afford to alienate

> them. For their part the donors, including the United States, at bottom recognized that the Executive Director must strike a balance between their interests and those of developing countries. With a reasonable amount of political skill it was not that difficult to find an acceptable balance. (Ingram 2006, 96).

Ingram would not have survived his battle with Saouma without some fundamental credibility of his own with both donor and recipient countries. To this end, Ingram worked hard to cultivate his own image as a UN honest broker between the two groups:

> The best way to make this clear to all was to continue as I had begun, by bringing forward projects for any deserving country even if they were out of political favour with the United States. This I did. The result was that I always had the positive support of some developing countries and never lost the confidence of the G77 as a whole. (Ingram 2006, 95).

Thus under Ingram CFA decision making managed to maintain and enhance its consensual tradition which helped reinforce the politically transcendent aspects of the feed-the-hungry norm. In the face of a serious political struggle with the FAO this was no small feat.

The WFP – FAO relationship

As outlined in Chapter Three, the FAO was the principal UN organization responsible for the establishment of the WFP. Formally, the FAO is one of the WFP's parent organizations, and it housed and administratively supported the fledgling program from its establishment. The first WFP Executive Director, Dutch national A.H. Boerma (ED 1962–67), came from the FAO to the WFP, and returned to the FAO as Director-General in 1968 (Shaw 2001, 291). Boerma's successor as WFP ED, El Salvadorean Francisco Aquino (ED 1968–1976) attempted to take the same path to the FAO D-G position, but lost an election for that position to Edouard Saouma in 1975 (Shaw 2001, 291). Saouma's election came at a critical time for the FAO and for food aid, in the context of the 1974 World Food Conference, and the emerging North-South conflict within the UN.

Saouma was to win three six-year terms as FAO D-G (1976–1994), a feat requiring strong ambition and political skills. Saouma's power base lay in the G77 (Ingram 2006, 95), which, as discussed in Chapter Three, had become the most electorally powerful group within the UN during the 1970s (Murphy 2001). The G77 defined itself increasingly in opposition to the developed nations who were members of the Organisation for Economic Cooperation and Development (OECD) (Ingram 2006, 95). During the 1970s and early 1980s, as 'Third World states sought to capture control of international organizations and to channel a greater share of these organizations' budgets to developing countries' needs', conflict between G77 and developed countries 'was manifested in every food organization, particularly in efforts to control organizational resources, policies and personnel.' (Hopkins 1990, 181).

Saouma's behaviour towards the WFP suggests that he saw it as a potential source of rivals for his position and threats to his authority, as well as a useful source of development largesse which could help maintain his electoral support in the FAO Conference. A less pejorative analysis might argue he saw it as important to keep control of the WFP in order to integrate the UN's food and agriculture related development resources in the service of the world's poorest countries. Whatever the motivations, Saouma kept in place a series of acting and short-term ED appointments: four in less than six years from May 1976 until Ingram's appointment in March 1982. One such appointee 'left the WFP in frustration, having served his entire term on a series of three-month contracts approved by Saouma.' (Charlton 1992, 639). While formally the WFP ED was appointed jointly by the UN Secretary-General and the FAO D-G, Saouma had ensured that in practice he controlled the position by dint of his organization's considerable financial and administrative dominance of WFP, and his support from the G77.

In the early 1980s, under the General Regulations and evolved organizational practice, the WFP's status was equivalent to an FAO Department, with the Executive Director equal in rank to an FAO Assistant Director-General, and the WFP was still housed within the FAO building in Rome. As Charlton noted,

> All general financial and administrative services were to be provided by the FAO on a reimbursable basis. This meant that, although the executive director was responsible to the CFA for administration of the WFP, the director-general of the FAO would be responsible for the maintenance of accounts and records, the preparation of financial reports, and the custodianship of the WFP's Trust Fund. (Charlton 1992, 635).

When put together with reliance on the FAO for technical advice, the WFP had a relationship with the FAO which Charlton characterised as 'dependent'. In 1987, 'approximately one-third of the WFP's annual administrative budget' was transferred to the FAO for these services

(Charlton 1992, 636). The WFP was also, in staffing terms, a much smaller organization. In 1986, the FAO had 6,594 professional and general staff in Rome and the field, compared with 650 HQ and 207 field staff for WFP (Charlton 1992, 636).

The WFP General Regulations had been designed for a temporary, experimental program, mostly without its own organizational infrastructure (Charlton 1992). However, by the early 1980s the gradual expansion in WFP resources, and its now clearly ongoing nature had rendered some of these aspects of WFP formal governance out of date. Despite its much smaller staff, by 1987 program operations for WFP were budgeted at US$900m, while the FAO program budget for 1986/7 was less than half that figure at US$437m (Charlton 1992, 636). The disparity between budget and staff sizes points, not only to how 'lean' WFP was, but to the difference between its mandate to disburse food resources compared to the FAO's as a service organization collecting information and disbursing policy and technical advice.

Saouma's determination to interpret the General Regulations as giving him effective control over the WFP had, for Ingram, brought into question whether he had any meaningful independent authority as WFP ED. This was important to Ingram as he was determined to use his position at WFP as a career capstone, and to lead the organization in a manner which would result in real achievements (Ingram 2005b) –

> An important reason why I had sought the post at WFP was my view that, legally speaking, the head of WFP was more 'independent' than the heads of other UN programmes. (Ingram 2006, 88).

One of Ingram's first actions as ED was to request a legal opinion from the UN on his powers (Ingram 2006, 86ff). The opinion confirmed his perception of the WFP as being more autonomous from the UN than other programs such as UNDP or UNICEF, as the Executive Director was not a part of the UN Secretariat, thanks to its mixed FAO/UN parentage (Ingram 2006, 88). Despite this opinion, Ingram found he had no control over any senior[1] appointments in the WFP all of which had to be approved by the FAO D-G (Charlton 1992, 641). This limited his capacity even to develop a minimal policy function in the WFP (Ingram 2005b). His first public battle with Saouma was over his capacity to submit policy papers to his own governing body (the CFA) without first getting them approved by Saouma (Charlton 1992, 642; also Ingram 2006).

The story of the battle led by Ingram for WFP autonomy from FAO is covered in great detail by Ingram (Ingram 2006; see also Charlton

1992; Shaw 2001, Ch8). It ended with the adoption of new General Regulations by the CFA, and the UN and FAO parent bodies in 1991 as Ingram's second term as Executive Director drew to a close. This clarified the WFP's autonomy, and established a new, enlarged CFA. Given Saouma's efforts to cast the WFP autonomy struggle in terms of the North- South conflict, its eventual resolution in revised General Regulations for WFP involved an expansion in developing country representation on the CFA. Out of an overall increase of 12 positions (from 30 to 42), most were allocated to developing countries, which had a total of 27 positions in the new structure (Ingram 2006, 290). As noted in Chapter One, the CFA was subsequently transformed into a smaller, 36 member Executive Board by UN General Assembly resolution in 1993 which harmonised the governance arrangements for WFP, UNICEF, UNFPA and UNDP.

Ingram's appointment was only made possible by Saouma's backing (Ingram 2006, 40–50); given subsequent events it seems relevant to ask why Saouma supported his candidacy. The two had met when Ingram was contemplating becoming a candidate and got on well (Ingram 2006, 40) – indeed even now Ingram retains some respect for Saouma as epitomising the sort of strong leader the UN needs if it is to overcome member-state timidity and lack of interest (Ingram 2005b). Undoubtedly, Saouma was concerned that the appointee not come from a country, such as the United States, which had sufficient power to potentially challenge him, and an Australian appeared a relatively safe choice. Other candidates, especially Brazilian Bernardo Brito, who was Acting WFP ED at the time, were seen as operating from a G77 power base and likely future challengers for Saouma's job if they were made ED. Ingram speculates that important factors were that he would clearly owe his position to Saouma and, as an Australian, lacked an obvious power base of his own (Ingram 2006, 50). Whatever logic had led Saouma to support Ingram's appointment, from Saouma's perspective it proved flawed as Ingram set out to articulate a role for the WFP that did not subordinate it to the FAO.

This portrayal of the WFP/FAO dispute may appear overly one-sided and imply an over-reliance on Ingram's account. In fact there is little or no literature that credibly refutes or rebuts Ingram and Charlton. Saouma's own book (Saouma 1993) barely mentions the WFP, and its overall argument is entirely consistent with Ingram's portrayal of Saouma's perspectives. In contrast, Talbot referred to the dispute as a case of WFP attempting to obtain autonomy, with an implication of empire building behaviour. He also argued that Saouma had been unfairly vilified as corrupt by a regressive American campaign in the media due to ideological opposition (Talbot 1990). However Talbot's account is not detailed and does not contend with the operational issues at stake between the WFP and the FAO in the 1980s.

Throughout the battle, Saouma attempted to portray the WFP and Ingram as American pawns attacking and undermining the FAO's attempts to maximise resources for developing nations (Ingram 2006; see also Saouma 1993). In contrast with this, Ingram suggests that the most problematic member-state relationship he had as ED was with the United States (Ingram 2006, 164ff).

Role of the United States

The United States was an ambivalent and unclearly positioned player in the food agencies during the period of conflict between the WFP and the FAO, reflecting both a broader US disengagement from multilateralism over the decade before the end of the Cold War (Karns and Mingst 1990a), and policy confusion in the food issue area (Hopkins 1990). During the 1970s, US perceptions grew that the UN had gone from being a venue for US global leadership to a venue for condemnation of the US by the developing world, egged on by the Soviet bloc. In comparison with its earlier role in the UN, the US 'found itself increasingly on the defensive,' with its influence over agendas and secretariats slipping, and its support for the UN tested 'by programs and activities regarded as detrimental to American interests' (Karns and Mingst 1990a, 6)

The late 1970s saw US withdrawal from significant UN agencies such as UNESCO and the International Labor Organization (ILO). The Reagan Administration elected in late 1980 had relatively little interest in multilateralism which reinforced this trend in disengagement (Traub 2006, 21). Since 1961 Congress had mandated the US proportion of 'assessed' UN budgets (that is, budgets which required member-state contributions at an assessed amount) not exceed 25 percent. Concerns that some of the budgets during the 1970s appeared 'both retributive and redistributive' resulted in 1985 in the passage of the Kassebaum Amendment (Talbot 1990, 36) This amendment required the reduction of assessed contributions for the US to 20 percent unless the UN introduced voting weighted to give more say to the large contributors (Talbot 1990, 28-9)

Meanwhile, in the food issue area concerning both the FAO and the WFP, policy conflicts within the US continued to cause some policy confusion. Hopkins notes a number of differences between USDA and State Department interests at this time (Hopkins 1990); Ingram's account of his re-appointment campaign in 1986 also highlights the complexity of different personal and institutional positions within the US establishment (Ingram 2006, Ch8).

Saouma's campaign in 1986–87 for a third term as FAO D-G involved a serious challenge from OECD member states, led by the Canadians, disgusted with what they saw as his divisive and self-serving administration that bordered on corrupt. The reformists were backing an alternative candidate from Benin (a G77 country), Moise Mensah. However, the US only belatedly and uncertainly decided to support Mensah's candidature (Hopkins 1990), due at least in part to suggestions from Saouma that in return for US support he would back an American candidate to replace Ingram at the end of his first term as ED in 1987 (Ingram 2006, 172, 178). Ultimately the manoeuvring over Ingram's re-appointment campaign resulted in an understanding that the US would nominate Ingram's successor, presaging a greater and clearer commitment to differentiating WFP governance from the FAO on the part of America.

Meanwhile, during this period as in others, US food aid flows and donations closely tracked the varying levels of surplus stocks without reference to any of these political debates over governance reform or nomination of the ED (Barrett and Maxwell 2005, 28). The apparent imperviousness of American multilateral food aid flows to the contingencies of policy conflict over WFP reforms is usually taken to point to the power of the material agricultural and business interests involved. However, as will be outlined in more detail below, the configuration of these interests in American politics was changing during the 1980s, both with reference to domestic policy and foreign food aid. These changes must be comprehended in normative terms as well as with reference to the material interests that, quite literally, the feed-the-hungry norm made a virtue of.

US domestic federal food aid in the 1980s

Soon after taking office in January 1981, the Reagan Administration was faced with a surplus problem involving large stocks of dairy produce held by the Federal government, especially cheese, which was unable to be stored for long without deteriorating.[2] In late 1981 the Reagan administration initiated the Special Dairy Distribution Program (SDDP) which was mainly concerned with giving away cheese to Americans (Poppendieck 1998, 88–91).

Following anecdotal evidence of increasing malnutrition in the Boston region and requests from groups working with the poor,

Professor Larry Brown of Harvard University public health school put together teams of physicians who, over two years (1983–85), travelled extensively in four regions of the US – New England, the South, the South West, and the Mid-West (Brown and Pizer 1987). Their research found there were significant and increasing numbers of hungry people in America, concluding that at least once each month some 20 million Americans went hungry (Brown and Pizer 1987, 161). This signaled the public re-emergence of domestic malnutrition as a social problem, though concerted government action from the late 1960s, in particular through expansion of the Food Stamps Program, had been seen as largely effective in eliminating it (Berry 1984; Brown and Pizer 1987; Nestle 2002).

Hunger advocates explained this re-emergence as due to the combined effects of the early 1980s recession and significant cuts to the Federal Food Stamp program by Congress over the period 1982–85, just as the need for access to it increased (Berry 1984). The cuts to Food Stamps came within a wider context of neoliberal hostility to government from the Reagan administration (Krugman 2007; Stiglitz 2003). Apart from the context of a Republican Congress and Presidency committed to 'small government' at least in relation to non-defense related areas, there had been some years of sustained attack on the Food Stamps Program as an example of excessively generous welfare allowing widespread cheating and fraud. Attacks on food stamps began in the period 1974–76 (Berry 1984, 77), at just the same time as surplus stocks had disappeared and the price of food (and hence the costs of the program) had shot up, and the need for surplus disposal it represented had shrunk (Bowers, Rasmussen et al. 1985). These attacks functioned to partially separate the Food Stamps Program from the feed-the-hungry norm and redefine it as part of a more suspect 'welfare state norm'.

The Federal government engaged in considerable criticism of the methodology and accuracy of measuring the number of hungry people. Edwin Meese was appointed by President Reagan to examine hunger in the US and sparked outrage when he claimed there was 'no real evidence' that it existed (Poppendieck 1998, 103). Another infamous example of the incumbent administration refusing to accept hunger as a public policy problem was President Reagan telling a schoolboy that hungry people were just too ignorant to know where the food was (Brown and Pizer 1987, 179). Underlying these rhetorical gambits was a normative shift of domestic food aid programs from being an important instrument of the welfare state back to having a *voluntarist* response to food related emergency relief, echoing a return to the debates of the early 1930s between Hoover Republicans and the Roosevelt New Deal.

In 1983 the SDDP was broadened to include other commodities and was replaced by the Temporary Emergency Food Assistance Program (TEFAP) with an expanded role for the burgeoning number of private voluntary relief organizations (PVOs, otherwise known as NGOs) (Berry 1984; Poppendieck 1998). The late 1980s saw an increasing institutionalisation of non-government food relief organizations (Poppendieck 1998).

Domestic hunger in the US had become a sort of permanently institutionalized emergency by the end of the 1980s (Poppendieck 1998). In 2005, according to the USDA, 35 million Americans were exposed to food insecurity, down from 38 million in 2004, but the first such decline for six years (Associated Press 2006b). Since the early 1980s crisis, the proportion of the American population actually hungry, or at such risk of hunger they can be defined as food insecure had remained consistently at or over 10% - around 30 million people (Hotakainen 2007; Usborne 2008), until the significant recession and food price increases in 2007-2008 caused a big jump in these figures. Large increases in the numbers accessing charitable food providers and Food Stamps reported in 2008 (The Food Research and Action Center 2008; Turse 2009) was followed with the release of findings from a December 2008 USDA survey showing that 49 million Americans suffered from food insecurity (DeParle 2009; Goldstein 2009). The 36 million Americans accessing food stamp assistance in 2009 is a 40 percent increase on 2007 (DeParle 2009). One domestic food aid activist made a telling comment in response to these reports: "This is unthinkable. It's like we are living in a Third World country," (Goldstein 2009).

The domestic Food Stamp program (now called the Supplemental Nutrition Access Program: SNAP) remains the main government funded response to this, and the largest of the food and nutrition programs, with expenditure in 2004 of $28.6 billion, despite significant cuts in the 1996 welfare reform bill (Nestle 2002). However, recent studies estimate it reaches only half of those eligible to access the assistance (Hotakainen 2007), with the voluntary sector still playing a major role in assisting the food insecure in America. Other liberal democracies have problems with poverty (and implicitly, hunger). None has a comparable discourse and policy apparatus focused on hunger.

Such food aid controversies at the domestic level seem to have little direct impact on US food aid policy at the international level. Yet it is difficult not to see a certain dovetailing of the emphasis on emergency relief that was coming to the fore in both arenas in the 1980s, and an increasingly important role for NGOs – points that are explored further below.

US industry structure and lobbying

Barrett and Maxwell show in some detail just how small the number of domestic beneficiaries of US foreign food aid policy have been in recent decades (Barrett and Maxwell 2005). This stems from changes linked to and reinforcing the continuing decline in the proportion of small family farms (Ritchie and Ristau 1987; Wise 2005), and increasing vertical integration of the food production industries (Coleman, Grant et al. 2004; George 1979; Patel 2007; Wagenhofer 2005; Ziegler 2005).

Thus structural change in the political economy of US agriculture was considerably more complicated than simply the size and frequency of surpluses. By the early 1980s, there had been a shift in lobbying access to Congress, with a decline in the importance of the traditional generic farmer organizations such as the American Farm Bureau Federation, and the growth in importance of the processor dominated specialist commodity organizations (Hansen 1991). That there was deep-seated hostility towards processor groups from farm organizations originating in the Depression era (Hansen 1991) adds some piquancy to this shift.

In the early 1980s as noted above, there was a significant political shift towards market-based and small government policy on the part of the Reagan Administration and the Republican dominated Congress. Following the 1980 elections not only was Ronald Reagan elected president, but Republicans took control of the Senate Agriculture Committee for the first time since 1955 (Bowers, Rasmussen et al. 1985, 37). In the arena of agricultural policy, this resulted in the 1981 Farm Bill being subordinated to budget policy - the first time this had happened (Bowers, Rasmussen et al. 1985, 36). This is generally taken as reflecting a loss of influence on the part of the farm lobby, linked to the long term decline in the proportion of the population engaged in farming, which by 1980 had fallen below 4 percent (Hansen 1991, 167). As a result, agricultural subsidies and the food stamps program were cut, and the importance of exports was emphasised, with the establishment of a revolving export credit fund and standby export subsidies. This added importance to PL 480, which 'had the ceiling on its donations abroad raised from $750 million to $1 billion (Bowers, Rasmussen et al. 1985, 40)

Consistent with free market ideology, there was a shift from surplus disposal (in which USDA purchased, stored and made available surplus stocks for food aid), to open market purchasing of food aid. This was partly linked with a trend started in 1973 to move agricultural policy away from a mixture of price support through government purchase of surplus stocks, and incentives to reduce production, to more direct income support for farmers via 'deficiency payments' (Ritchie and Ristau 1987, 6; Bowers, Rasmussen et al. 1985, 29). These trends were also connected to structural economic changes in agriculture that saw increasing dominance of large farms, and vertical integration of production and processing. By the 1980s, while the influence of the farm lobby in Washington was well past its peak (Hansen 1991), agribusiness – business which involved and often integrated inputs, production and processing of agricultural commodities – was increasingly influential.

In relation to food aid, this caused some conflict between large-scale processors pushing 'for increased levels of procurement of bagged, processed, or fortified commodities,' and the bulk commodity purchases favored by agricultural producer groups (Barrett and Maxwell 2005, 89). Reflecting the success of agribusiness lobbying, the 1985 Farm Bill required at least 75 percent of non-emergency minimum tonnage be 'fortified, bagged or processed' (Barrett and Maxwell 2005, 89).

Another example of the interaction between agribusiness and food aid policy dating from this period is the establishment of the Bill Emerson Humanitarian Trust. The Trust acts primarily as a grain reserve for increasing food aid available for Congress to deploy when demand is high (Landis 2005; Zeigler 2005). In 1980, the placing of a trade embargo on the USSR because of its invasion of Afghanistan led to the US government purchasing the wheat from the contracts that the embargo had abrogated. Private agribusiness was paid to store the resulting reserves, which were then sold back to industry at a 'sharp discount'. Industry, impressed with the profitability of this process, then lobbied to create an ongoing wheat reserve, operating on the basis that the more in storage, the greater the profits – 'the agribusinesses that benefit from the Emerson Trust have historically been very successful in minimizing releases from this facility.' (Barrett and Maxwell 2005, 92).

A change allowing processed products to be held by the Trust rather than only bulk grain, shifted benefits to processors in the late 1990s. Now,

> [s]ub-coalitions of agribusinesses jockey for the greatest spoils from this system, lobbying for relatively minor rule changes that effectively redistribute the profits within a relatively small group of corporations that make handsome profits out of what is intended to be a humanitarian mechanism. (Barrett and Maxwell 2005, 92).

The advent of the agribusiness lobby both reflected and intensified the practical displacement of the traditional service of farmer interests in US food aid policy. However, shipping interests were not displaced; indeed they managed to expand their entitlements in the same period. The Cargo Preference Act was enacted alongside PL 480 in the 1950s. This Act required that a minimum 50 percent of gross food aid tonnage 'be shipped on privately owned, registered US-flag commercial vessels.' (Barrett and Maxwell 2005, 93). The 1985 Farm Bill increased this minimum to 75 percent over opposition from USDA, USAID and farm groups. Also, the maritime industry is a strong supporter of bagged/processed food use as there are bigger profits from ships transporting such product than from bulk containers.

The US Government Accountability Office (GAO) estimated in 1994 that the average annual cost of preference in food aid shipping (i.e. the *addition* to what it would have cost without the preference requirement) was US$200 million. From 2000 to 2002, 'nearly 40 per cent of total costs of US food aid programs were paid to US shipping companies.' (Barrett and Maxwell 2005, 95). Moreover, limits on the availability of US-flagged ships constrain the location of commodity purchases, again often increasing the price paid. Barrett and Maxwell argue that these subsidies have not stopped the decline of the US maritime industry, just padded the bottom lines of a few shipping lines (Barrett and Maxwell 2005, 97).

The way the American feed-the-hungry norm incorporated a link between morality and self-interest – making a virtue out of food aid's service to both the hungry and producers has contributed to an expectation in US Congress that such profiteering is merely consistent with moral policy settings, smoothing the path for the effective lobbying by food aid interests. Barrett and Maxwell's critique comes from the standpoint of the international regime norm which focuses more strongly on the hungry poor and turns a critical eye to the self-serving policy settings of wealthy interests in rich countries. I will discuss the monetization policy debate further below as another illustration of the role of domestic US interests in food aid policy.

Evolution of the IFAR

From development to emergency assistance

The process of WFP/FAO disentanglement reflected a wider shift within the frontline UN agencies from a focus on development in the 1960s to the 1990s focus on humanitarian assistance in the context of 'complex emergencies' (Natsios 2001). If the FAO-dominated WFP cast itself as a development agency, it is no coincidence that the expansion of the WFP's emergency assistance role occurred at the same time as its struggle for autonomy from the FAO.

Ingram notes the FAO's lack of interest in the problems with food aid, compared with WFP concern to improve technical design of projects. Poorly designed food aid assistance could do more harm than good (Barrett and Maxwell 2005; Ingram 2006; Maren 1993; Shaw 2001; Shaw and Clay 1993; Singer 2001), and the WFP acknowledged this required engagement with critics of food aid and endeavours to improve its operation. Meanwhile the FAO conflated the championing of the interests of the poor with demanding more food aid and applying it (largely uncritically) mainly to agricultural development projects, even when it demonstrably did more good in social development projects such as maternal and infant nutrition and school feeding (Ingram 2006, 283–4). Saouma demonstrates the relatively narrow FAO perspective emphasising quantity, donor obligations and logistical arrangements around a hard normative frame as means to enhance food aid effectiveness in his memoir:

> I had on several occasions, without great success, proposed to the WFP and FAO Governing Bodies that measures should be taken to make multilateral food aid more effective, for example by making IEFR legally binding for the countries that participated in it, doubling the level of that reserve (unchanged since its establishment in 1975), prepositioning reserve security food stocks at certain strategic points (such as Dakar for the Sahel countries) in order to be able to deliver food aid rapidly in the event of emergencies. (Saouma 1993, 82).

Saouma's record of his time at the FAO indicates the extent to which FAO thinking was defined by the NIEO and pursuit of resources for development, even in the face of developed nation indifference and hostility (Saouma 1993). These differences, as well as the political conflicts between Saouma and Ingram were displayed when, in 1984, the WFP and FAO submitted conflicting policy papers to the CFA on reforming emergency food aid processes. The FAO expressed a view that, simply, more aid was needed. The WFP argued for clear criteria to target such aid to the most needy, given the need to ration insufficient resources (Ingram 2006, 129–31).

Emergency relief in the WFP

As noted in Chapter Three, typically food aid is categorised in three ways – as *program aid*, as *project aid*, and as *emergency aid* (Shaw and Clay 1993, 1). The WFP defines these categories as follows:

> *Emergency* food aid is destined to victims of natural or man-made disasters. It is freely distributed to targeted beneficiary groups, and is usually provided on a grant basis. It is channelled multilaterally, through NGOs, or, sometimes, bilaterally.
>
> *Project* food aid aims at supporting specific poverty-reduction and disaster-prevention activities. It is usually freely distributed to targeted beneficiary groups, but may also be sold on the open market and is then referred to as 'monetized' food aid. Project food aid is provided on a grant basis and is channelled multilaterally, through NGOs, or bilaterally.
>
> *Programme* food aid is usually supplied as a resource transfer for balance of payments or budgetary support activities. Unlike most of the food aid provided for project or emergency purposes, it is not targeted at specific beneficiary groups. It is sold on the open market, and provided either as a grant, or as a loan.
>
> (INTERFAIS/WFP 2005, vi).

While a role in emergency assistance had always been seen as an important part of the WFP mandate, and indeed McGovern's original proposals had emphasised this, in the context of the Development Decade and UN priorities in the 1960s the WFP had developed as first and foremost a development agency (Charlton 1992, 636). In other words, the WFP deployed food aid as a resource to assist development through projects. This meant using food aid in two broad categories: agricultural and rural development (for example, as part or full payment for work, usually involving infrastructure building such as roads and bridges – 'food-for-work'), or for human resource development (for example, to improve nutrition for mothers and infants through feeding projects) (see Shaw 2001, 89ff).

Effective delivery of emergency aid requires quick access to nearby food resources and cash to pay for transport and distribution. Especially in its early years, along with a desire to focus on development, WFP had no capacity to access food rapidly enough to be effective in much emergency relief, and little or no cash to fund hard transport and distribution costs (Shaw 2001, 148). In its first year of operations, no more than 25 percent of WFP resources were used for emergency relief. Between 1963 and 1975, the total value of WFP development aid commitments was US$1,822m (Shaw 2001, 84), while in the same period emergency aid commitments totalled only US$209.1m (Shaw 2001, 155) – that is just over 10 percent of the total.

Despite the fundamental barriers to WFP acting on emergency aid, however, 'it was recognized that a multilateral organization administering food aid could not stand aside and not move to help countries and people stricken by disasters' (Shaw 2001, 149). Shaw makes his comment on the overwhelming strength of the 'humanitarian impulse of food aid' (cited in Chapter Three) as an explanation of this. In fact, rather than imbuing food aid with such powers it seems more appropriate to explain WFP emergency relief as a demonstration of the power of the moral claim of the hungry in the feed-the-hungry norm.

The main barrier to WFP engagement in emergency relief was seen as lack of prompt access to food stocks, and various attempts were made in the 1960s to establish a world food bank or reserve (Shaw 2001, Ch3). The decision of the World Food Conference in 1974 to establish an International Emergency Food Reserve (IEFR), managed by WFP, finally broke the impasse.[3] WFP emergency aid increased at more than triple the rate of increases to its development assistance in the 1970s (Shaw 2001, 154). This increase, however, came from a low base, and up to the late 1980s relief assistance accounted for no more than one-third of WFP operational expenditures. The truly significant proportional increases occurred between 1982 and 1994, when emergency relief and development aid swapped positions as the dominant mode of WFP food aid, as Chart 4.1 shows.

In the early 1990s emergency relief accounted for two-thirds of WFP resources (Shaw 2001, 154). By 2004, the WFP estimated it spent 91 per cent of its operational budget on relief aid (including recovery) and only 9 per cent on development aid (WFP 2006d). In 2008 the proportion of resources deployed on development operations 'fell to the lowest level ever' (WFP 2009, 37): just over 8 percent, albeit in the context of a global food crisis leading to big increases in contributions to assist with emergency relief.

There were many factors implicated in this shift (Clay 2003), but three stand out as important.

Firstly, the creation of the IEFR established an accessible and larger resource base for emergency relief, albeit at some cost to development assistance donations (Talbot 1990, 70).

Chart 4.1: WFP contributions for development and relief, 1990-1999

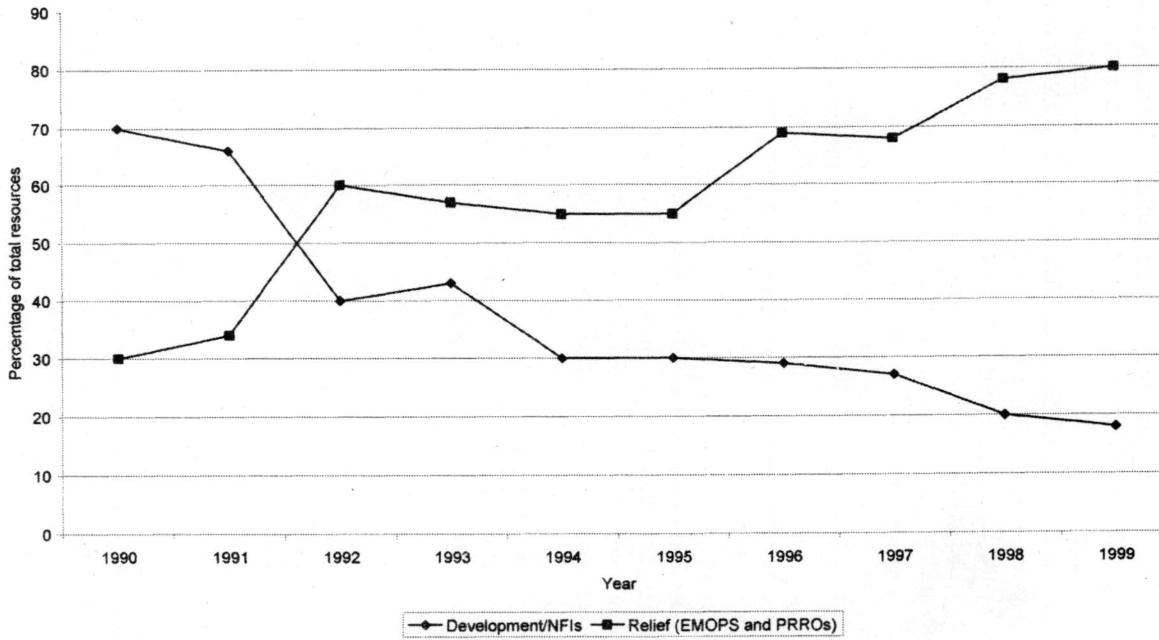

Source: (WFP 2000, Annex VI).
Notes: NFIs - Non-Food Items; EMOPs - Emergency Operations; PRROs - Protracted Relief and Rehabilitation Operations.

Secondly, the heightened NGO activism around and media awareness of famine crises which had helped play a role in the World Food Conference continued.

This was boosted enormously by the publicity over the Ethiopian famine of 1984 (de Waal 1997, 121–4). These things both led to increased recognition of needs for emergency assistance, and public pressure in the donor countries to act, leading to strong donor interest in emergency relief work. This was one factor in the evolution of policy settings by the US in the 1990s, which happily accommodated the WFP within its larger food aid policy arrangements as primarily an emergency relief agency (Barrett and Maxwell 2005; Landis 2005), complementing a policy emphasis on NGOs as the channel for US development food aid. However, as noted earlier, an American assumption of a strong role in emergency relief for the WFP had been evident since McGovern's original proposal. Also, as noted above, the domestic US hunger situation became institutionalised as an emergency, which dovetailed with the increasing emphasis on multilateral (voluntary) food aid as most appropriately donated in response to emergency needs.

Thirdly, critiques of the use of food aid for development (see Chapter Six) had had an impact on the WFP. This was, perhaps, assisted by Ingram's newness to food aid (Ingram 2005b), which meant he was not locked into long established positions defending food aid as a development tool from its critics. Ingram observes that by 1984 he held the view 'that food aid found its clearest justification in emergency feeding' (Ingram 2006, 129). Emergency relief work played to the WFP's undoubted strengths in logistics, and in a virtuous cycle, helped strengthen its logistical expertise more and more. Emergency relief operations also had the virtue of creating a role for the organization more clearly distinct from the FAO than agricultural and rural development assistance, which tended to be more closely connected to the work of the FAO. In the context of attempts to free the WFP from the FAO's close oversight, Ingram was also able to use the emergency food aid issue 'to argue for more rapid and flexible decision making' (Charlton 1992, 643).

These factors came together during the 1980s to create an organizational logic or a 'path of increasing returns' (Pierson 2000) for the WFP to change from a development organization to a relief organization. From the late 1980s, there has been a significant expansion in refugee numbers and camps (Barnett and Finnemore 2004, 74; Shaw 2001, 225; Terry 2000). Together with the advent of 'complex emergencies' this phenomenon has tended to involve an increasing array of emergency responses from UN agencies, and attempts to develop much more effective coordination of responses (Natsios 2001). WFP logistics and infrastructure have become important parts of such a response. Moreover, emergency food aid donations have both increased and largely displaced development food aid donations. This has made it difficult for the WFP to maintain capacity in development aid.

Changes in IFAR norms and principles

Hopkins suggested that the international food aid regime had originally been based on a 'package' of four original principles, which had then evolved, under the influence of an epistemic community of food aid experts, into a new set of regime principles.

Hopkins' proposed four original regime principles were that food aid should:

1. be provided from donor surplus stocks;
2. supplement the usual commercial imports in the recipient country;
3. be given under short-term commitments sensitive to political and economic goals of donors; and,
4. directly feed hungry people.

(See Hopkins 1992, 229).

Similarly, Uvin proposed that the IFAR was originally based on two basic norms. First, that food aid 'was to reflect only the changing political and economic goals of the donor'; second, that the additionality principle applied to food aid in order that it did not displace US farmers' exports (Uvin 1992, 302).

Chapter Two noted the centrality of surplus disposal, especially for the US, to the early IFAR. Uvin's and Hopkins' posited norms and principles also emphasise the centrality of donor interests to the early regime; only the fourth of Hopkins' principles refers specifically to the moral claim of the hungry. The early form of the feed-the-hungry norm provided an underpinning normative logic to these principles, linking the moral claims of donor producers, donor nations and the hungry together.

The early regime version of the feed-the-hungry norm was very close to the domestic US version, reflecting the dominant role of the US in the regime. However, the changes of the 1970s and 1980s discussed above diminished that dominance, making the regime 'more multilateral' (Hopkins 1992, 230; also Uvin 1994, 142). Reflecting this, and the growing importance of an epistemic community of food aid experts, Hopkins argued in 1992 that the original regime principles had changed, and proposed the following as now applying:

Food aid should

1. be supplied in the most efficient manner possible;
2. substitute for usual commercial food imports;
3. be given under long-term commitments; and,
4. 'serve as the basis for the recipient's economic development aimed at addressing long-term food security problems, rather than merely serving as a vehicle to alleviate immediate food shortages.'

(Hopkins 1992, 246).

These renovated principles were more oriented to the interests of recipients and creating stability and efficiency for multilateral food aid (i.e., in effect, the WFP). This reflected reforms to food aid both in technical literature, and in the IFAR/WFP, which by the late 1980s had 'become the major arena in which new norms for all food aid were being articulated' (Hopkins 1992, 230). Yet thirteen years after Hopkins proposed these renovated regime principles, Barrett and Maxwell were talking merely of food aid (and implicitly the international food aid regime) 'edging slowly toward a more recipient-oriented system' (Barrett and Maxwell 2005, 107). This reflects the fact that there have always been significant gaps between the expert consensus on optimal food aid practices and policies, and the behaviour of states, in particular the US, within the IFAR (Barrett and Maxwell 2005; OECD 2006).

At least with hindsight, the third and fourth of Hopkins' 'new' principles seem to have misread the trend to an emphasis on short-term emergency relief ahead of development assistance on the part of donors to the WFP.[4] However, the principles do correctly identify the shift of the IFAR feed-the-hungry norm away from the domestic US version of the norm, and towards a more recipient-oriented version. Barrett and Maxwell acknowledge the extent to which the WFP in its strategic planning articulates an approach to food aid consistent with their recommendations, while focusing their attention on the US policy settings which they see as lagging behind best practice in which the WFP and most other donors are already engaged (Barrett and Maxwell 2005, Ch6).

Uvin, while agreeing that the regime changed substantially in the 1970s and 1980s, was sceptical about Hopkins' claim for the role of 'consensual knowledge' in the food aid regime, arguing it was more appropriate to think in terms of 'dominant knowledge', as there was still too much debate to be able to claim any consensus. (Uvin 1994, 174). Rather, Uvin argued, change to the regime had been triggered by the world food crisis and the watershed of the 1974 World Food Conference (Uvin 1992, 302). These events, along with domestic US political shifts meant that 'food aid donation is increasingly governed by multilateral institutions, norms and procedures. The objectives the regime now promotes changed from economic and foreign policy interests to developmental/humanitarian preferences' (Uvin 1992, 303).

Uvin pointed to the influence of thinking on food aid policy within the international regime on domestic US policy making. For example, it has long been clear that many of the negative effects of food aid, such as its depressing of local commodity prices, come from its supply to people who do not really need it (Barrett and Maxwell 2005; OECD 2006; Schultz 1993). Such arguments had particular relevance in the context of concern that the Nixon and Ford administrations were using food aid to get around Congressional constraints on funding the war in Vietnam (Ruttan 1993a; Uvin 1992). They were deployed in Congress in 1975, resulting in legislation to require that food aid be closely targeted to the poorest countries, and to cut off counterpart funds (i.e., funds generated from the sale of donated food, generally granted or concessionally lent to the recipient government) from military uses (Uvin 1992, 302).

Another American legislative change reflecting the influence of international policy thinking on food aid was the 1979 Bellmon Amendment to PL 480. The Bellmon Amendment requires an assessment be made to ensure there will be no negative impacts from American food aid on the food markets of the recipient country (OECD 2006; Ruttan 1993a; Uvin 1992; Zeigler 2005). The operation of the Bellmon amendment has little contemporary credibility – Barrett and Maxwell cite a private remark of a 'senior US government official' that "Bellmon Analyses are sheer fraud… no one believes them" (Barrett and Maxwell 2005, 190). However, in formal terms at least, the Amendment suggests constraints on the operation of US interests in food aid, acknowledging potential adverse impacts on recipients. For Uvin, these changes in the seventies signaled more of a humanitarian focus to US food aid policy (Uvin 1992, 302).

Such changes to US policy on food aid during the 1970s and 1980s undoubtedly point, amongst other factors, to the influence of the international regime. At the same time, given the WFP's history, its reliance on donors for resources, and the pre-eminence of the US amongst the donors, the WFP and the regime itself remained largely dependent on US policy.

The significance of the US to the regime was only to increase with the appointment of, effectively, the first[5] American Executive Director of WFP, Catherine Bertini.

The WFP under Catherine Bertini

As noted above, in the context of reappointment manoeuvring by Ingram and Saouma, an understanding had been reached that the US would nominate the next ED on conclusion of Ingram's second term. The American nominee was Catherine Bertini.

Bertini's career began as a New York state Republican activist in the mid-1970s, who went on to a business career in the Mid-West state of Illinois, before going into government service. She was a nominee of the Reagan administration as Director of the Office of Family Assistance, then in the George H.W. Bush administration she held a senior appointment as an assistant secretary in the Department of Health and Human Services. This was followed by two years as assistant secretary for Food and Consumer Services of the USDA (Bertini 2005b; Shaw 2001, 293). In the latter role she was responsible for administering the American federal (domestic) food aid program.

Bertini was the first woman to head the WFP, and at 41, by far the youngest appointee. She was also the first ED to be born after World War II. Her appointment began at the same time as the commencement of WFP's newly established autonomy, meaning that WFP was to some extent about to be remade as an entity within the UN system, creating a unique situation for organizational change and reform. This context saw a new emphasis on managerialism as both a driver of reform and a generator of political consensus, while continuing to base credibility with both donors and recipients on continued operational effectiveness and efficiency. This reform agenda was closely tied together with skilful management of the politics of the US relationship to the food aid regime.

Bertini placed WFP at the forefront of UN management reform, for example making it the first agency to adopt a four year strategic and financial planning cycle (WFP 1996, 25). However, managerial reform was linked to two rather more significant changes - the intensification of American dominance in the management and donor processes; and an acceleration of the shift in operations to almost a complete focus on emergency relief. This latter change can be linked to a struggle which continues within the WFP to articulate a credible place for development work in its role (Clay 2003).

These two changes can be portrayed as merely exhibiting continuities with long-standing trends in WFP: the shift to emergency relief as described above had begun as long ago as the 1970s, and gathered pace under Ingram. Also, while US dominance had waxed and waned to some degree over the years, it had been embedded in WFP since its foundation, as discussed previously. Nevertheless, the changes to these things during the 1990s were of great importance to the evolution of global governance in the IFAR and WFP.

Before looking in more detail at the accelerated shift from development to emergency aid and the intensified role of the US in the WFP, it is important to set the context for them with a brief examination of Bertini's focus on management systems and governance reforms, and the implications for the feed-the-hungry norm in the IFAR.

Bertini's reform agenda

In 2002 the WFP secretariat produced a paper for the Executive Board documenting 10 years of reform under Bertini. This document told a story of reform focused on how the WFP 'built its *capacity* to deliver programmes for the hungry poor, *not* its achievements in serving them.' (WFP 2002, 4, emphasis in original). As this implies, the focus of much reform was in the development of effective management systems and a strategic approach to running WFP. Management consultants were deployed to assist in these processes (Bertini 2005b), as the prominence of generic management language and concepts suggests.

For example, in the period 1992–95, this involved 'early change initiatives' in seven areas, only the first of which could be said to be specific to WFP's mandate:

> targeting the hungry poor;
> delivering integrated and more effective programmes;
> mobilizing resources;
> building a more robust management culture;
> matching the organization to its operations;
> establishing financial controls; and
> strengthening accountability and oversight.
> (WFP 2002, 5).

In 1994 the WFP undertook a review of its 'Policies, Objectives and Strategies' (WFP 1994). This in part reflected the impacts of a comprehensive assessment of the WFP by Norway, Canada and the Netherlands, known as the Tripartite Evaluation (Chr. Michelsen

Institute 1994) which had run over the previous two years (WFP 1994, para2). These reviews contributed further to the reduced emphasis on development projects and an increased emphasis on emergency relief, albeit with an agenda to integrate the various stages of relief, rehabilitation and development into a more integrated approach (Shaw 2001). The outcomes of these reviews, combined with an ED review of progress in reform, resulted in an announcement in July 1996 by Bertini of

> A new vision for the organization. WFP was to become a much more strategic organization, capable of responding flexibly and rapidly to the situations of greatest need and integrating emergency, recovery and development programmes. (WFP 2002, 5).

This new vision focused on a number of 'organizational themes' consistent with a managerial agenda. As with the early change initiatives, the themes listed were all, bar one, generic concepts deriving from mid-1990s managerial thinking: 'strategic thinking'; 'letting managers manage'; 'teamwork'; 'leadership'; 'communication'; 'flexibility and adaptability' (WFP 2002, 5). The one exception to these generic managerial themes was 'keeping the field at the center'(WFP 2002, 5). This latter theme illustrated three important characteristics of the Bertini reform agenda.

First, keeping the field at the center grasped an important element of WFP's effectiveness during previous periods – its logistical competence and field expertise – and the need to organizationally support this strength, rather than succumb to the bureaucratic tendency to centralise. A key mechanism for this was a strictly enforced staff mobility policy requiring all staff to rotate into the field if they had been based in Rome for more than a couple of years as a condition of advancement (WFP 2002, 34).[6]

Second, making the field central to WFP functioning was one of a series of decentralisation reforms, begun under Ingram (Ingram 2005b; 2006), which had a political as well as managerial aspect. This political aspect involved the building of political capital for the WFP (and its ED) with both recipient and donor countries by ensuring competent operation and responsiveness to real beneficiary needs. The WFP made an apposite comment about a later step in this process (decentralising regional bureaux):

> One of the key objectives of the change process was to bring senior managers, programme and administrative staff closer to the

> beneficiaries so that decisions would be better informed and programmes more effective. (WFP 2002, 45).

Third, the nature of 'the field' appears objective and timeless in this managerial discourse. In turn this relates back to the way the reform focus on 'capacity' begs the rather more political question of what the capacity is *for*. It is here that the managerial reform agenda can be seen as functioning politically to 'depoliticise' – i.e. remove political contention from - WFP operations as much as possible.

Such depoliticization was not new. For example, Ingram details various efforts to avoid the derailment of worthy projects by political objections in the context of his work to build a consensus culture noted above. Bertini certainly shared Ingram's political skills when it came to building on the consensus culture on the governing body. Nevertheless, the techniques of making project proposals as politically uncontentious as possible through embedding the decisions within strategic and policy frameworks already agreed on by the CFA (from 1996, the Executive Board) were a new development.

The latter stages of Bertini's second term saw a shift from management to governance as a focus for reform – meaning, in particular, the functioning of the EB and its interactions with the secretariat. In 1999 the EB adopted Bertini's proposal to set up a Governance Steering Committee (WFP Governance Group 2005), chaired by then EB President, Anthony Beattie of the United Kingdom.

> The origin of the project lay in informal discussions between the then Executive Director, Ms Catherine Bertini, and members of the Board as to the best way of governing a changing organization. The challenge was to develop ideas to make the Board more strategic, more effective and more efficient. It was suggested that a successful project might offer lessons for other parts of the United Nations. (WFP Governance Group 2005, 5).

The Governance Group made a report to the Board in 2000 with 23 recommendations for improving or streamlining the functioning of the Board. These were focused on enabling the EB to have a clearer strategic, policy, oversight and accountability focus, reducing its meeting times and volume of paper flow, planning leadership succession, induction, and increasing both delegations to the ED and the use of informal consultations to prepare the ground for formal meetings. The only one of the recommendations not adopted was to redraft the WFP Mission statement, as, tellingly, 'some members felt that this might expose unproductive differences of view about WFP's role...' (WFP Governance Group 2005, 7).

Such a sentiment of concern about exposure of differences points again to the centrepiece of the WFP's particular depoliticised style of governance – what the Governance Group describes as the 'tradition of consensus decision making' by the Board. The nature and political implications of this style of governance will be discussed in more detail in Chapter Six.

Tensions in the dual mandate

The benefits from and limits to these managerial techniques come to the fore in the case of the tensions between development and emergency relief aspects of WFP's dual mandate. The 2002 Secretariat paper on ten years of reform hinted at some of the issues at stake when it posed the question '*What would have happened if WFP had not engaged in its process of change?*':

> The answers are fairly clear. First, the pressure of the massive emergencies during the decade has been enormous. A less resilient, less effective organization would have buckled under the strain. Its attractiveness to donors for emergency programmes would have been diminished and its emergency funding would have decreased significantly. Since WFP is a voluntarily funded organization, the implications would have been serious. Second, it would probably have lost even more of its development programmes, which might have threatened its dual mandate of development and emergencies. (WFP 2002, 44).

The advent of 'complex humanitarian emergencies', and significant growth in refugee numbers since the 1980s meant that emergency relief needs were perceived to have increased at a rate outpacing the resources available for assistance. These needs, which by their urgent and imminent nature tend to take organizational and logistical precedence, also generated public concern and interest in donor countries. This concern was propitious for increasing donations ('mobilizing resources' in the language of the time) to fund WFP operations. Also, as the WFP endeavoured to develop its corporate identity (and concomitant public image), such work had particularly important resonances.

The issue of what the WFP should be doing lay at the heart of considerable debate focused on the tensions between emergency and development aid – indeed Bertini describes the WFP as having to be dragged 'kicking and screaming' into emergency aid (Bertini 2005b).

This statement suggests that the increasing role for the WFP in emergency relief was not merely the continuation of a trend already established in the 1980s, as noted above. Under Ingram this process had involved an extension of its emergency work mainly through access to the IEFR, albeit with the funding arrangements indirectly displacing funding for development work. Under Bertini this process accelerated to involve a more active redistribution of resources away from development assistance (see Chart 4.1, also Clay 2003, 701, Table 1). In a very real sense, WFP was publicly reinvented during the 1990s as a relief agency (Clay 2003).

Apart from the US, most other donors shifted away from in-kind donations to cash donations during the 1990s – but this shift also brought reductions in the aggregate amount of resources going to WFP, and increasing pressure to allocate larger proportions of this resource to emergency priorities. It also increased the relative proportion of resources coming from the US. At the same time, US food aid policy changes also contributed to these changes in the WFP. These changes require some explication before going on to consider the normative implications of the dual mandate tensions within WFP.

US food aid policy from 1990

The 1990 Farm Bill formally shifted the focus of PL 480 food aid away from export development to 'enhancing food security in the developing world' (USAID Office of Food for Peace 2005, 7; see also Barrett and Maxwell 2005; Hopkins 1992). This was consistent with and reinforced a long term decline in Title I food aid – government to government concessionary sales, managed by the USDA - which had been historically the largest component of US food aid from the 1950s (see Table 4.1; also Barrett and Maxwell 2005, 23).

Apart from PL 480, other sources of authorized food aid in the US system include:

- The Agriculture Act 1949, s416(b) authorising donation of surplus commodities held by the Commodity Credit Corporation (CCC administered by USDA);
- Food for Progress, created in 1985 under the Food for Progress Act to authorize food aid donations from Title I or CCC resources under s416(b) to countries engaged in economic liberalisation reform in their agricultural sector (administered by USDA);

Table 4.1: Average annual expenditures in US food aid under PL 480 Authorization, per decade, 1960-2006 (nominal US$ million)

PL 480 Program	Years				
	1960-1969	**1970-1979**	**1980-1989**	**1990-1999**	**2000-2006**
Title I	$849.75	$748.85	$800.29	$525.84	$185.87
Title II	$437.97	$442.97	$711.83	$975.54	$1,449.41
Title III	$0.00	$0.00	$0.00	$114.35	$0.00

Sources: Based on data from the US Agency for International Development Greenbook (http://qesdb.usaid.gov/gbk/index.html); US Department of Agriculture. Note – The PL 480 Title III program represents government to government donations of commodities, with their sale by recipient governments generating funds for development programs. Title III has had no allocations since 1999, being effectively privatised into the Title II development food aid program, with US NGOs acting as the recipients who monetize and deploy the consequent resources for development projects.

- The McGovern-Dole International Food for Education and Child Nutrition program, a school feeding program initially piloted 2000-2002 as the Global Food for Education Initiative (administered by USDA); and,
- The Bill Emerson Humanitarian Trust, known from its establishment in 1980 to 1998 as the Food Security Wheat Reserve, designed to supplement PL 480.

Despite these various other categories, by the early twenty-first century, grants and donations of food aid for emergency relief and development projects, administered by USAID under Title II, represented the bulk of US international food assistance. For example, in Fiscal Year (FY) 2006, expenditures in these various programs were dwarfed by the PL 480 Title II allocations, primarily in emergency food aid – over 80 percent in Fiscal Year (FY) 2006 (see Table 4.2).

From the mid-1990s, the USAID Office of Food for Peace has organized food aid resources around the emergency/development distinction (USAID Office of Food for Peace 2005). Emergency food aid is now the primary source of US resources allocated to the WFP while development food aid is now allocated primarily to the NGOs (or in USAID terminology, Private Voluntary Organizations: PVOs). Of the Title II allocations to emergency projects in FY 2006, 79 percent went to the WFP as a Coordinating Sponsor (see Table 4.3), involving funding totalling $US1.16 billion (calculated from data in USAID 2006, Appendix 5, 26-8).

WFP received no USAID Title II Non-emergency activity funding (totalling $US341,128.1), which all went to various NGOs as cooperating sponsors (USAID 2006, Appendix 6, 29–31).

This separation of emergency/non-emergency function reflected a mix of pressures from US NGOs concerned that the WFP was competing with them in development work (Barrett and Maxwell 2005, 63), but also reflected a direction of change within WFP itself – it was congruent with the operation of both international and domestic US food aid regimes.

NGOs had long had involvement with US food aid distribution, but the advent of monetization policy changes had structural effects, linking them with the domestic US groups with an economic interest in maximizing in-kind American food aid (agribusiness food processors and shipping).

Together with USAID focusing on NGOs as service organizations for its development food aid resources (while the WFP was given the bulk of emergency relief food aid), US NGOs were increasingly allowed to monetize the food aid received from USAID – that is, sell it on the market in recipient countries, and deploy the resultant funds in their development projects. Monetization had been introduced initially into the Title II program in the 1985 Farm Bill 'as a means of making additional cash available for transporting and handling commodities.' Subsequent Farm Bills in 1990 and 1996 introduced further increases in the monetization minimum to 10 percent, then 15 percent of the total value of non-emergency commodities and 'expanded the uses of these

Table 4.2: Total US international food assistance, Fiscal Year 2006

Program^	$US Million	Percentage
PL 480 Title II (emergency)	$1,197	54.5
PL 480 Title II (non-emergency)	$342	15.6
PL 480 Title II Misc*	$300	13.7
Subtotal PL 480 Title II	$1,839	83.8
Food for Progress (Title I funded)	$73	3.3
Food for Progress (CCC funded)	$147	6.7
Subtotal Food for Progress	$220	10
Food for Education	$86	4
PL480 Title I	$50	2.2
s416b	No allocation	0
BEH Trust	No allocation	0
PL 480 Title III	No allocation	0
TOTAL	$2,195	100

Source: (USAID 2006, Appendix 10, 35).
^ Does not include the Farmer to Farmer program which rates as international food assistance, but in the form of technical assistance rather than food aid (expenditure in FY2006 of $10m).
** This refers to non-food support in the form of cash disbursements in association with food aid including $41.6m in cash for WFP, and $157.7m unallocated appropriations when demand for food aid exceeds them (administered by USDA).*

Table 4.3: Proportion of USAID/USDA food aid projects with WFP as cooperating sponsor (CS), Fiscal Year 2006

Program	No. of Projects	No. with WFP as CS	% of funding to WFP
Title II Emergency Aid	67	44*	79%
Title II Non-Emerg. Aid	75	0	0
Food for Progress (CCC purchased)	22	2	<2%
McGovern-Dole IFECNP	16	4	39%

Source: (USAID 2006, Appendices 5–8, 26–33).
**36 of the 44 were designated as Protracted Refugee Relief Operations (PRRO), and only 8 as International Emergency Food Reserve (IEFR) – hence Emergency Operations.*

proceeds to include income generation, health, nutrition and agricultural activities.' (USAID Office of Food for Peace 2005, 15). The actual rates of monetization remained low until 1996 when they went to 20 percent, and by 2001 the rate had reached a peak of 70% (Barrett and Maxwell 2005, 101, Fig.5.4). In 2006, of $US342 million in Title II non-emergency food aid, approximately $180 million (53 percent) was monetized (Alliance for Food Aid 2007b).

The practice of monetization has created considerable controversy (USAID Office of Food for Peace 2005, 14). Barrett and Maxwell provide an important critique of the potentially destructive nature of monetization practices on recipient country producers, through displacement and depression of prices (Barrett and Maxwell 2005, 133-8); they are particularly concerned with the way in which US NGOs have apparently become dependent on the revenue it generates (Barrett and Maxwell 2005, 98-105). In turn this dependency has helped lock the NGOs into a lobbying alliance with producer and shipping interests in the US, bolstering the commercial self interest of the latter two groups with their capacity to, in the words of former President Jimmy Carter, 'speak from the standpoint of angels' (cited in Dugger 2007). As discussed in Chapter Two, these interactions are central to the functioning of the American food aid 'iron triangle', which has been the key lobby group alliance maintaining US food aid as primarily in-kind, despite trends away from that mode in the international regime. The integration of these NGOs in the food aid lobby would not have been possible without the underpinning normative logic provided by the feed-the-hungry norm. It is through drawing on the notion that food aid serves both the moral claims of the hungry and the moral claims of the producer (generally perceived, however inaccurately, as the small scale family farmer), while creating a strategically important national moral claim that such sectional interests have been able to profit to the extent they have.

In August 2007 one of the major NGOs involved in the system, CARE, announced its phased withdrawal from the use of US government commodities by 2009 (Doyle 2007; Dugger 2007). This decision was influenced by Barrett and Maxwell (Dugger 2007), and came after a Government Accountability Office (GAO) Review criticising the operation of food aid monetization by NGOs in April 2007. However, other NGOs in the system insist that in-kind food aid and monetization remain appropriate through their lobby Alliance for Food Aid (Alliance for Food Aid 2007a; 2007b; Doyle 2007; Dugger 2007; Shaw and McKay 2006; USDA Foreign Agricultural Service 2001).

In the WFP there had been debate over monetization policy since the mid-1980s. However, the issue was put to rest when, in 1997, the WFP resolved not to engage in monetization outside of exceptional circumstances (Barrett and Maxwell 2005, 263, fn41; Russo, Luzot et al. 2005, 6; WFP 2006c, 23–4). This resolution reflected the divergence of the IFAR feed-the-hungry norm from the US domestic norm; it also points to the significance of the WFP as a policy space that has helped enable concerns with monetization within the US to be legitimized and advanced. In turn this suggests the importance of developments in the US/WFP relationship during Bertini's tenure.

US/WFP relationship in the 1990s

The primary and most obvious impact on the WFP from Bertini's US background came with the use of her political skills and connections to build more effective links with the US political system – as she puts it, 'I knew how to work the system' (Bertini 2005b). This began when then Assistant Secretary of State for International Organizations John Bolton organized cash contributions from the US to the WFP on her commencement to 'help out' (Bertini 2005b). Until then, the US had provided almost no cash to the WFP (Bertini 2005b), despite the WFP's General Rule XIII.4 requiring donors to 'provide sufficient cash, acceptable services, or acceptable non-food items to cover the full operational and support costs related to their commodity contribution' (WFP 2004a). WFP had been subjected to periodic cash crises due to the absence of sufficient cash to go along with large commodity donations to pay for its logistical and administrative infrastructure needs (WFP 2000, 12–13).

In the 1996 Farm Bill, USAID was authorised to make additional cash donations to the WFP to assist with administrative and support costs for the first time, with the 2002 Farm Bill increasing the amounts available for this considerably (USAID Office of Food for Peace 2005, 15). Bertini's working of the US system involved knowledge of when surplus resources, cash as well as commodities, were around and available to be accessed; as well as how to get such resources sent the way of the WFP through relationships with the food aid lobby, Congress, the USDA and other parts of the executive branch. She also recruited staff to the WFP who had Washington backgrounds and could help build important relationships (Bertini 2005b).

In the mid 1990s Bertini set up a new organization – *Friends of WFP* (FoWFP) – based in Washington DC (WFP 2000, 13). This was done primarily to provide a mechanism enabling private and corporate donations to the WFP that would attract domestic tax concessions. In 1997 a lawyer, lobbyist and consultant, Rick Leach, was employed as the first Executive Director of FoWFP. His remit was not only to funnel donations to WFP, but also to do some lobbying work that the WFP, as a non-domestic entity, could not do, and to pull together a leadership group of US supporters as the FoWFP Board. Leach's position was funded by grants from WFP (Leach 2005).[7]

In recent years, FoWFP has expanded in size and significance. Revenue (in US$) grew from $674,871 in 1999 to around $1.5 million in 2000 and 2001, just under $5 million in 2004, and $8,958,894 in 2005 (Friends of WFP Inc. 2006). Of the 2005 revenue, $7,041,685 was donated to the WFP (Friends of WFP Inc. 2006, 17). From having just two employees in 2004, FoWFP has expanded to a staff of eleven (Friends of WFP 2007).

The Board of FoFWP demonstrates blue chip, bipartisan credentials, including two former Agriculture Secretaries (one each from Republican and Democrat administrations), former Senators and Congressional representatives from both major parties, a former Clinton speech writer, and a former Republican Governor of Illinois (Friends of WFP 2007).

As Murphy shows in relation to UNDP, the fact that a UN agency is being led by an American neither predicts the direction in which the organization will go, nor its relationship with the United States (Murphy 2006). These are ultimately contingent on factors such as the US domestic political situation, the historical relationship with the agency, and the aptitude and political skills of the leader. Like Ingram before her, Bertini's largest problem with re-appointment to a second term as ED came from the US, where elements within the Democrat Clinton Administration saw her links with the previous Republican Bush Administration as requiring her replacement with one of their own (Bertini 2005b). As with Ingram, Bertini's credibility as a capable and progressive administrator, and respect from both an array of member-states and a broad spectrum of US domestic players made the difference. The seriousness of this political struggle is reflected in the fact that her re-appointment was not formally confirmed until a very late stage – February 1997 – only weeks before the expiry of her first term, although she had clear G77 support from early 1996 (Bertini 2005b).

The interaction of the depoliticised operation of the WFP, and Bertini's management of the US relationship came to the fore when she successfully lobbied the US in early 1997 to contribute to an humanitarian aid package for North Korea.[8] American support was vital in the capacity of the WFP to become the first and most significant intergovernmental organization to mount a humanitarian operation in that notoriously isolated and paranoid country. As noted in Chapter Two, getting US participation derived first and foremost from the politically transcendent appeals on behalf of starving children.

WFP's involvement in North Korea can be taken as a good example of the WFP's strengths as simultaneously influential with the US and credible in the wider international community in a way which is capable of overcoming deep-seated political hostility, though this example also involves some typical provisos on such a positive reading: There have been considerable problems with WFP operating in North Korea posed by the regime there (see Bourn 2007). Medicins Sans Frontière (MSF) became the first of several NGOs to withdraw from North Korea in 1998, condemning the regime's control over food aid resources and criticising WFP for continuing to work there (see Chapter Six for further discussion; Noland 2003, 11).

Norms and the operation of the dual mandate

Clay suggests that as a result of the shift to emergency relief a problematic gap has emerged between a reality of negligible development operations, and rhetoric referring to a development mandate (Clay 2003, 702). Similarly, Hopkins noted a debate

> between those who assign top priority to emergency food aid, which has less clear long-term development value, and the members of the [IFAR] epistemic community, who favor an early transition from emergency feeding to development activities among refugee and famine victims. (Hopkins 1992, 260).

As discussed above, Hopkins argued that under the influence of an epistemic community of food aid experts, the principles governing the international food aid regime had evolved. New principles were now 'embedded in the institutional practices of multilateral agencies, particularly the WFP, and of bilateral agencies as well' (Hopkins 1992, 246). According to these principles food aid should, *inter alia*

> serve as the basis for the recipient's economic development aimed at addressing long-term food security problems, rather than merely serving as a vehicle to alleviate immediate food shortages. (Hopkins 1992, 246).

Both Hopkins' depiction of the epistemic community's emphasis on development, and Clay's argument point to the way in which development norms have strongly influenced WFP. These norms valorize as more legitimate and desirable aid (through structured projects) which empowers the recipients and enables them to reduce and eliminate their need for it.[9] The norm assumes a hierarchy of types of assistance, with 'assistance' that fails to address structural forces causing poverty and hunger of questionable worth. When considered through the lens of development norms, emergency relief tends to be problematic as it is reactive and has little capacity to change the conditions which generate its necessity in the first place, though it is generally acknowledged as necessary in some circumstances (Isenman and Singer 1993, 244, fn1).

On the other hand, emergencies are generally simpler and easier to manage in terms of measurable outcomes; unlike development aid they are almost universally perceived as legitimate and important. Most literature on food aid suggests they are less problematic than development projects as a means of using food as aid (Barrett and Maxwell 2005; OECD 2006). Importantly, they are much more effective as a motivator for public support and donations. Intuitively, they fit the bill for a feed-the-hungry norm, while requiring a more immediate response than other forms of aid.

Bertini cites WFP's norms as twofold:

> 'nobody should be hungry'; and 'nobody should be dependent - except children' (Bertini 2005b).

The relationship of these two norm-statements is complex. While the first seems like a straightforward paraphrase of the feed-the-hungry norm, the second has at least two meanings which can be read as either adding to or qualifying the first.

'Nobody should be dependent…' can be interpreted first as a call to deploy assistance in aid for longer-term development - the notion of assistance that empowers and therefore eliminates dependency. On this reading, the twofold norms seem to equate respectively to the two elements of the emergency-development dual mandate. A second reading, however sees 'nobody should be dependent…' as qualifying the operation of the array of emergency and development uses to which the first statement might lead.

It is this second reading that is reflected in the record of WFP policy since the 1990s, and demonstrates how the emergency/development issue was normatively delimited and removed from being a significant political problem for WFP. First and foremost, the feed-the-hungry norm did not mean a constant competition between short-term emergency demands and longer-term more strategically desirable development work. It meant doing both, subject to the test of not creating dependency. Signifying the centrality of this approach, one senior WFP officer I interviewed argued that the distinction between emergency and development work is deeply problematic, and only formally exists as part of the construction of differentiated operational categories designed to help maximise contributions from donors (Interview #11 2005). (USAID has also identified this problem with its use of the emergency/non-emergency distinction for funding purposes - see USAID Office of Food for Peace 2005, 13–4).

In applying these norms, WFP took two approaches. First, there was an attempt to shift from an 'either/or' depiction of emergency relief and development. Echoing critiques of such distinctions in development literature, and in the context of refugee camps operating for extended periods, WFP sought to develop 'an integrated approach to prevention, preparedness, relief, recovery and development'. This was done through the policy document *From Crisis to Recovery* (WFP 1998) and the associated development of the aid category of protracted relief and recovery operations (PRRO) (Shaw 2001, 175-6; WFP 2002, 30).[10]

This approach was, however, largely confined to medium-term refugee situations and did not deal with other non-emergency operations. Here the problem was defined as a lack of resources for development programs. Initial attempts to narrow allocation of development resources to the poorest countries were not sufficient to alleviate concern for the future of the WFP development mandate:

> During the 1990s, resources for development programmes continued to decline, and there were major concerns that WFP's dual mandate – emergencies and development – could be threatened. This was despite the fact that the CFA set targets for the development resources that at least 50 percent should be spent in LDCs [least developed countries], at least 90 percent in LIFDCs [low-income food-deficit countries] and no more than 10 percent in countries outside these categories. (WFP 2002, 29).

This led to the second approach, which was based on further focusing and narrowing the circumstances in which development work could take place. In 1999 the Executive Board adopted an 'Enabling Development' policy 'designed to revitalize WFP's development programme' (WFP 2002, 29). The policy (at paragraphs 31-33) explained the role of WFP food aid in relation to development as follows:

> 31. Families facing chronic food insecurity are caught in a hunger trap. The very inadequacy and uncertainty of their food supply make it difficult for them to improve their situation. Development opportunities may exist, but poor families often cannot take advantage of them. For them, there is no long-term solution without a short-term solution.
>
> 32. This is where food aid can help. Assisting a poor household with food consumption in the short term can enable it to invest time or resources in a better future. Food aided projects should give poor people scope for their ingenuity and efforts, leveraging their access to the benefits of development. This should be the special niche of WFP food aid.
>
> 33. By some definitions, this is not "development". Certainly, it differs from the kind of contribution that capital projects, technical assistance or structural adjustment lending can make to mainstream development. WFP food aid should play a different role, which is not to promote development in the same ways as other organizations but to enable marginalized people to be a part of it, and share in its benefits. Food aid is an enabler, a pre-investment which can free people to take up

> development opportunities which increase human capital or acquire assets. Whether this is called "development", "pre-development", "pre-investment" or something else, it fulfils a vital role in enabling millions of families to escape their hunger trap.
> (WFP 1999, 7).

In order to better define the 'niche' of WFP food aid, the policy proposed to 'limit' WFP development activities to five objectives:

> Enable young children and expectant and nursing mothers to meet their special nutritional and nutrition-related health needs;
> Enable poor households to invest in human capital through education and training;
> Make it possible for poor families to gain and preserve assets;
> Mitigate the effects of natural disasters, in areas vulnerable to recurring crises of this kind;
> Enable households which depend on degraded natural resources for their food security to make a shift to more sustainable livelihoods.
> (WFP 1999, 16).

The evidence was clear that the WFP needs to focus on the neediest – the hungry poor – both in response to emergencies and to avoid considerable problems with displacement and economic disruption caused by poorly targeted development food aid. Two things followed from this. One was that its systems, for identifying who and where the neediest are, needed to be state-of-the-art. This led to considerable investment in a system known as Vulnerability Analysis and Mapping (VAM), linked with the Financial Management Improvement Programme and WFP Information Network Global System (FMIP/WINGS) – investment only partially covered by specific donor contributions (WFP 2002, 44). The other implication was that the WFP would not only need to develop new projects each time a new emergency occurred, it would have to stop some existing projects, even in the face of beneficiary and recipient state protests.

This occurred most significantly in relation to Latin American and Caribbean nations. Clay notes that the number of WFP country programs in the Americas shrank in the ten years to 2001 from 24 to 11, with regional expenditure down by 39 percent (Clay 2003, 702). That this shift occurred relatively smoothly - though not without some controversy (Bertini 2005b) - suggests amongst other things the effectiveness of the managerial strategies in depoliticising reforms, and the political culture of consensus underpinned by the feed-the-hungry norm.

Conclusion

At the end of Bertini's tenure, Clay argues that despite the WFP's undoubted organizational success two important tensions had emerged. The almost complete displacement of development work with relief work led to disjunction with the WFP's mandate which still assumed a considerable role in development work; and an increase in American donations and a decline in EU contributions were contributing to an erosion of the WFP's 'multilateral character' (Clay 2003). These points are of central importance in Chapter Six which considers effectiveness as an aspect of the legitimacy of the WFP and IFAR. Before turning to effectiveness, however, we need first to consider the aspects of legitimacy concerning state and non-state actor interaction – inclusion and accountability.

Endnotes

[1] D1 (Principal Officer) and above.

[2] And thus was not a viable commodity for use in bilateral or multilateral food aid. Federal cheese inventories were to peak in 1983 at 933 million pounds, though USDA policies to reduce production brought this down to 83 million pounds by 1988 (Poppendieck 1998, 149).

[3] Though the operation of the IEFR was complicated by a requirement for FAO D-G approval of emergency relief operations – a requirement which WFP fought against unsuccessfully in 1976 (Charlton 1992, 637–8). Charlton notes an alleged example of the politicization of such powers, where 'the director-general of the FAO was accused of delaying approval of emergency food aid requests from Ethiopia as a lever to force the dismissal of Ethiopia's representative to the FAO.' (Charlton 1992, 643).

[4] Though the relationship between emergency and development food aid is more complex than a simple either/or, as will be discussed further in Chapter Six.

[5] US citizen Thomas C. M. Robinson became Acting ED May 1976–July 1977, and was appointed ED briefly from July 1977–September 1977. However his limited and stop-gap tenure and Saouma's then dominance over the WFP make it impossible to meaningfully describe him as 'running' the WFP in the same sense that Bertini did as ED. (See Shaw 2001, 212).

[6] Though the genesis of this policy, like many in the 1990s, can be traced back to the Ingram period (Ingram 2006, 67–9).

[7] Other UN Agencies made similar arrangements, e.g. UNHCR (WFP 2000, 33).

[8] North Korean food production failures result from a number of factors, in particular heavy reliance on industrial inputs which were severely disrupted by the cessation of support from the Soviet Union in the early 1990s. By the mid-1990s North Korea was suffering from chronic famine affecting a significant proportion of the population (Noland 2003). WFP assistance to North Korea continues to be significant (Interview #11 2005; Anon 2005; Associated Press 2006a; Bertini, 1998; Bertini 2005b; Bourn 2007; Toy, 2006 #606; WFP 2006g).

[9] Other more critical analysis suggests that aid itself, even while claiming to empower and undermine poverty inducing circumstances, often is fundamentally connected to the exercise of donor power in ways which make it part of the problem (Maren 1993; 1997).

[10] The bulk of USAID Title II emergency funding for WFP went to PRRO designated operations in 2006 (see Table 4.3).

5
Inclusion and Accountability

In the framework for analysing legitimacy proposed in Chapter One, three features were proposed – inclusion, accountability and effectiveness. Having established the historical and organizational underpinnings of the international food aid regime, I turn now to examining the first two of these features within the governance processes of the WFP.

The first section of the chapter outlines the WFP in its contemporary form, covering its functions, organizational characteristics and the formal structuring of its rules and regulations. While in some respects the WFP may appear like an NGO in its service functions, as the following sections show, it must be understood first and foremost as an intergovernmental organization – that is, it is state actors which are central to the WFP.

The feature of inclusion is the focus of the second section. When examining inclusion as an aspect of legitimacy, it is necessary to ask to what extent and under what terms actors are included or excluded. This is addressed in terms of three groups of actors. First, the state actors represented or potentially represented on the Executive Board, and, less formally, through such processes as staff recruitment. Second, the NGOs engaged in humanitarian relief and development work with whom the WFP works and, at times, competes. Lastly, the beneficiaries – those at risk of hunger and malnutrition, and in whose interests the WFP works.

While disparities in wealth and power interfere with inclusion in predictable ways, there is little evidence that the WFP suffers from egregious exclusionary practices in a manner that poses serious problems for IFAR or the WFP's legitimacy. However, the structuring of member-state representation through the Lists is starting to lag behind the shifting of some states into a transitional category between recipient and donor status. Non-state actors – primarily NGOs – have significant operational involvement with the WFP. However, NGO relationships, while extensive, are complex and heterogeneous. Where political differences exist between the WFP and NGOs they tend to be mediated through the member states more than by independent civil society style processes.

Inclusion of beneficiaries is more problematic due partly to their vulnerability, and partly to their lack of definition as actors (rather than subjects of aid or states) within the IFAR polity. This also raises problems for accountability – as noted in Chapter One, accountability and inclusion overlap as inclusion itself at least partially renders accountability through participation.

However, accountability involves more than just inclusion; it concerns more broadly the processes for constraining power, which connect to legitimizing that power. The Chapter's third section focuses on the feature of accountability, examined through three different facets. Firstly, the accountability of the secretariat to the EB (organizational accountability). Secondly, the accountability of the WFP to the beneficiaries (functional accountability). Thirdly, the accountability of the donor states (donor accountability). As with the analysis of inclusion, there are no discernible egregious failures of accountability in WFP, subject to the limitations inherent to intergovernmental organizations. Indeed, the institutional constraints the IFAR imposes through the feed-the-hungry norm provide some important accountability mechanisms in relation to the way in which wealthy states respond to the facet of global inequity represented by hunger.

Overall, this chapter will show that by and large WFP does not suffer from significant failings in legitimacy on account of the extent to which its governance is inclusive and accountable.

WFP organizational characteristics

As previously noted, since the start of the 1990s the WFP has been the largest of the UN operational agencies (Barrett and Maxwell 2005, 220), being the second largest source (globally) of development resources after the World Bank (Barrett and Maxwell 2005, 15) since 1983 (Charlton 1992, 637; WFP 2000, 12). In 2006 WFP total staff on contracts of one year or longer numbered 10,587 and 'direct' (operational) expenditures were US$2.9 billion (WFP 2007d). In 2008 in the context of the food crisis the WFP received incoming resources of more than US$5 billion. WFP accounts for 95 percent of multilateral food aid, and well over 50 per cent of all food aid (INTERFAIS/WFP 2008, xi; WFP 2007d, 39).

WFP functions and operations

Estimates of the number of people in the world who can be classed as suffering from hunger, both in its acute form and from chronic malnutrition, vary, and change over time. The FAO is generally regarded as the most authoritative source of such estimates; in its 2006 report State of Food Insecurity in the World the FAO gave an estimate of 854 million hungry over the period 2001-03 (FAO 2006c, 8), though this estimate has subsequently increased to over 1 billion as a consequence of the 2007-08 global food crisis (Blas 2009; World Summit on Food Security 2009). The WFP aims to feed these 'hungry poor' primarily through identifying and responding to famines and food crises with food aid – that is, aid in the form of food commodities. It provides a multilateral forum for obtaining and distributing food resources and related donations, both cash and in-kind, and logistical operational capacity to identify needs and send food resources to feed the hungry poor, mainly in emergency situations such as famines and refugee crises.

During 2006, WFP press releases began to add a paragraph at the bottom describing the organization. The precise form of description varies a little, with some versions having the WFP feeding 61 million hungry children each year (Al-Bawaba Reporters 2006b), others putting the figure at 58 million (Al-Bawaba Reporters 2006a). The following is the most detailed of such descriptions:

> ABOUT THE WFP
>
> The World Food Programme is the United Nations' frontline agency in the fight against hunger. As the largest humanitarian organization in the world, it feeds an average of 90 million people -- including 61 million hungry children -- every year in more than 80 countries. Working in the poorest, most remote regions of the world, WFP helps people whose lives have been affected by natural disaster and conflict as well as those, especially women and children, who suffer from hunger due to extreme poverty. WFP is funded entirely by voluntary contributions and when disaster strikes, WFP is among the first on the scene. Its food aid is often the only difference between life and death. (Giarraputo 2006)

The WFP's regional and country-based offices and information systems help it work with both recipient and donor countries, and over nearly 50 years of operations it has probably been able to prevent the imminent deaths from starvation of many millions. In 2003 the WFP estimated during its first forty years in operation that its food had reached 1.2 billion poor people (WFP 2006d). In particular, the WFP has made a significant reputation in logistical expertise in the context of significant relief operations in complex emergencies (Clay 2003).

As noted in earlier chapters, the WFP was established with what it refers to as the 'dual mandate' involving development work as well as emergency relief, though there has been a significant shift in balance between those two activities since the 1980s. Food aid for development is based on using food aid as a resource for development projects. This can include, for example, school feeding programs, or using food as payment for work on infrastructure such as roads and irrigation systems ('food for work'). In many such projects WFP works with or through relief and development NGOs (Ingram 2006; Shaw 2001; Westendorf 2006).

Apart from development projects and emergency operations (EMOPS), the WFP has two other kinds of activity. As refugee camps have developed into medium term institutions rather than purely emergency operations, the WFP has also developed Protracted Relief and Recovery Operations (PRROs), which sit between development work and emergency relief (OECD 2006, 22). However, they are often grouped with EMOPS for the purpose of categorising the aid involved – both are defined as 'relief' as opposed to development (WFP 2007d, 16, Table 4). Lastly, there are Special Operations, which involve generating transport and storage infrastructure (e.g. building roads and bridges, airfields) necessary to enable the delivery of food aid.

As the figures in Chart 1.1 showed, the distribution of resources between these different kinds of operations has seen the relief category (emergency operations and PRRO) dominate, albeit with considerable volatility, while development project expenditures have remained relatively stable in dollar terms. The proportion of resources devoted to development projects has varied given the volatility of relief resources from a low of 7.5 percent in 2003 (when relief resources spiked in connection with the Iraq war) to a high of 13.3 percent in 2004. The most significant part of development projects in recent years has been school feeding programs, accounting for approximately half of development project expenditures.

Strategic and management objectives

Since the mid-1990s WFP has used a Strategic Planning process to order and focus its work, in particular as a management tool. Each Plan is for four years, but reviewed and revised every two years. Thus, the Strategic Plan (2004–2007) adopted in 2003 was reviewed in 2005 and became the Strategic Plan (2006–2009). In adopting the Strategic Plan in 2005, the Executive Board (EB)

> ... **decided** that WFP should focus its operations on achieving the five Strategic Objectives:
>
> saving lives in crisis situations;
>
> protecting livelihoods in crisis situations and enhancing resilience to shocks;
>
> supporting improved nutritional health status of children, mothers and other vulnerable people;
>
> supporting access to education and reducing gender disparity in access to education and skills training; and
>
> strengthening the capacities of countries and regions to establish and manage food-assistance and hunger-reduction programmes;
>
> ... **noted** that these Strategic Objectives and the longer-term strategic direction will enable WFP to contribute to global efforts towards achieving the Millennium Development Goals and that they are within WFP's mandate and existing policy framework;
>
> ... **emphasized** the importance of working in close and complementary partnership with other agencies, funds and programmes of the United Nations system towards the achievement of the Millennium Development Goals; and
>
> ... **encouraged** the Secretariat to work towards the following Management Objectives in order to help achieve the Strategic Objectives:
>
> build strong partnerships with national governments, the United Nations, bilateral donors, other organizations, particularly NGOs, and the private sector;
>
> be the employer of choice for competent staff committed to ending hunger;
>
> achieve excellence in implementing efficient and effective programmes;

build and share knowledge on hunger to inform combined efforts to end hunger;

provide technical and operational infrastructure services to support effective operations;

be transparent, accountable and manage risk; and

raise resources to meet needs.
(WFP 2005, 1–2).

These strategic and management objectives make clear some important contemporary characteristics of the WFP. It has a primary emphasis on emergency relief; an ongoing emphasis on vulnerable children and women; and, implicitly on development through school feeding programs. Interestingly there is no explicit mention of a 'development' objective outside the 'Millennium Development Goals' (MDG) appellation, where its importance seems primarily to be linked to coordination with other parts of the UN. Lastly, there is the emphasis on 'partnerships' with both states and non-state actors, including other parts of the UN, NGOs and the corporate sector. The 2008-2011 Strategic Plan is based on five similar strategic objectives, with a similar emphasis on partnerships (WFP 2008).

The WFP has been typical of UN agencies in recent times in being part of two countervailing developments. On the one hand, there have been a number of attempts at improved coordination between different development and emergency relief organizations. New attempts to pilot better coordination structures in Africa (Natsios 2001), and in handling the Asian Tsunami through the UN Emergency Relief Coordinator Jan Egeland (Egeland 2008) have been prominent in recent years, and the WFP has been involved in all such processes along with other relevant agencies.

Yet, despite this work on coordination, attempts by the UNDP in the mid-1990s to resurrect its old role as the UN's coordinating agency for development and aid activities were resisted by UNICEF and the WFP (Murphy 2006, 290–5). This is partly because of the old coordinating role had often functioned ineffectively, creating a bureaucratic bottleneck for field operations, but also because various UN agencies have been working hard to establish their 'brands'. Given their reliance on donor funding, and the need for brand recognition to underpin fundraising – whether directly from individuals and corporations, or through public support for government funding, there has been a perception that the agency brand needs to be both linked to the UN and differentiated from it. This flows through a range of levels. At the simplest is Bertini's concern on taking over the WFP that the organization did not even have its own T-shirts or means of enabling its field staff to be easily identified (Bertini 2005b). More recently has been the hunt for celebrity 'ambassadors', and the care with which Hollywood films are cultivated as promotional tools (e.g. *The Constant Gardener*, 2005 and *Blood Diamond*, 2006 featured WFP promotional trailers, and prominent displays of the WFP logo on planes, trucks and other supplies within the film itself). Such branding exercises are related to the fundraising/advocacy nexus discussed further below.

WFP Finances

WFP operational expenditures only partially equate to cash resources. In 2005 and 2006 only 28 percent and 26.9 percent respectively of direct operational expenditures were spent on food purchases, totalling approximately half the tonnage of food aid distributed; the other half of the tonnage was made up of in-kind donations (WFP 2007d). Apart from procurement of food, the WFP spends cash on operational costs – direct and indirect. Indirect Support Costs (ISC) are used to fund its program support and related head office operations, as distinct from Direct Support Costs (DSC), related to transport, freight, logistics, storage and distribution costs.

The food aid resource base is notoriously uncertain, depending on commodity prices and the related variable of surplus availability, leading to a lot of volatility in resources for the WFP, and a strategic emphasis on trying to generate longer-term resource stability (WFP 2000).

The move away from a development to an emergency relief role has changed the relevance of resource stability in some ways, but in general there has been an ongoing shortage of cash with two significant effects. Firstly, a relatively small and unstable cash base has led to a longstanding leanness of HQ operations compared to other UN agencies with a basic guaranteed income from assessed state contributions (Bertini 2005b).

For example, in January 2007 the Secretariat forecast contributions of US$5.6 billion for the 2006-2007 biennium (i.e., averaging US$2.8 billion per annum in each of the years), 'split between US$5.248 billion for operational costs and US$352 million for ISC'. For the same period, the budget for Program Support and Administration (PSA – roughly equivalent to the ISC) was US$372 million (WFP 2007c, 10). Those figures put the PSA/ISC cost ratio at approximately 6.6 percent of overall resource contributions.

On the one hand this leanness has prevented the WFP from getting beyond basic operations into policy development and forms of advocacy. On the other hand, it has helped generate considerable respect for its operational efficiency and effectiveness.

Secondly, together with the volatility of food donations and reliance on the US as principal donor, the shortage of cash has led increasingly to attempts not only to increase funding, but to diversify the sources of funding. This has led the WFP to place greater emphasis on fundraising, along with what at times can appear a problematic link between fundraising and advocacy. Consequently there has been some recent political conflict with European NGOs over competition for private sector donations. Chapter Six will explore some of the consequences of this in more detail.

The FAO Resolution establishing the WFP called for a 'cash component of at least one-third of the total contributions' (see Appendix 1, 'Annex', para 2). Accordingly, the General Regulations of the WFP since its inception have required all donations to be accompanied with sufficient cash contributions to cover the (DSC and ISC) ancillary costs (Shaw 2001, 193) – what is now termed by the WFP as Full Cost Recovery (FCR):

> ...FCR means that public and private donors are required to meet their contribution's share of all associated costs, including external transport, landside transport, storage and handling (LTSH), other direct operational costs (ODOC) and indirect support costs (ISC).
>
> ...Some donors have the capacity to meet FCR; others do not. To determine whether a member state that cannot provide for FCR is eligible for special efforts and to ensure that objective criteria are applied, WFP proposes to use per capita gross national income (GNI) as the criterion. Countries eligible for assistance in meeting FCR will be least-developed countries, low-income and lower-middle income countries defined by the Organisation for Economic Co-operation and Development (OECD) Development Assistance Committee (DAC) as having a per capita GNI of US$2,975 or less ...
> (WFP 2004c, 7).

This definition comes from a policy document adopted by the EB in 2004, which moved away from assuming donors were member-states, defined as either traditional or non-traditional. The policy proposed to bring all member state donations together under the public donor category, albeit with allowance for different FCR arrangements for donations from poorer countries, while establishing the new category of 'private donor for individuals and corporations (WFP 2004c, 5). The policy stated that:

> WFP aspires to raise 10 percent of its resources from private donors by 2007, with modest growth beginning in 2003–2004, seeking cash and in-kind contributions from private donors that are aligned with its priority needs and can best serve its beneficiaries. Private contributions will not be a substitute for Member State funding. (WFP 2004c, 4).[1]

This ambitious target (equating to around US$300 million per annum) signalled the start of concerted attempts by the WFP to increase its private sector fundraising, and increased the importance of branding and associated marketing efforts. These efforts have since continued, though by the issue of the 2009 Annual Report the target had been modified significantly: 'By 2017, WFP envisions $200 million coming from the private sector through expanded partnerships and intensified fundraising efforts' (WFP 2009, 6). The year 2008 ended 'with companies and foundations giving $145 million in cash, 'including $66 million from the Bill & Melinda Gates Foundation' (WFP 2009, 41).

Fundraising and Advocacy

As noted in Chapter Four, both Ingram and Bertini were suspicious of the tendency for UN organizations to construct HQ empires out of touch with the field, and introduced policies which would encourage staff mobility between the field and HQ. Under ED James Morris (2002–2007), the strict staff mobility policy of Bertini appeared to have been relaxed somewhat, and there was some growth of HQ, especially in the fundraising area, with high level staff being employed to fundraise. Budget reprioritizations in early 2007 cut operational budgets across the board by 3.5 percent and staff travel and reassignments (i.e. the funds for staff mobility) by 20 percent, largely to fund an increase of more than US$6 million (15.6 percent) to the fundraising and communications department (FD) budget. On receiving this increase, which amounted to more than 70 percent of the reallocated money, the FD became easily the largest department in Rome after the Administration Department (that is, larger than the Operations Department and the Policy and External Affairs Department). (WFP 2007c, p6-7, Table 2).

The expansion of WFP fundraising has been closely linked to its 'advocacy', which it sees as equating to raising awareness (implicitly in wealthy countries) of the issue of global hunger, in order to motivate and organize the fight against hunger. There is a significant gap between the number of people who as the hungry poor need assistance (over 1 billion), and the number of people the WFP has sufficient resources to assist each year (approximately 100 million). In this context it is often difficult to separate out WFP advocacy on the issue of hunger from its concern with 'resource mobilization' (or fundraising) to cover this gap. At the same time, members of the Secretariat have endeavoured to separate the two things to avoid charges of advocacy being in the interests of the WFP organizationally, rather than for the hungry poor (Interview#16 2005).

The 2008-2011 Strategic Plan devotes a paragraph to advocacy as follows:

> **Advocacy.** Political awareness is the first step in the fight against hunger. WFP has long been confronted with this fact and has thus created a broad and successful variety of instruments to disseminate information on, explain, and mobilize resources to fight global hunger. Advocacy will continue to play a prominent part in WFP's activities at the field, regional and global levels, in order to reach the whole range of actors in the fight against hunger. Furthermore, WFP will use the impact of its advocacy in the pursuit of a variety of objectives – from fundraising for its operations to influence on broader policy issues, such as climate change – that are instrumental in affecting positively the fight against hunger. (WFP 2008, 31)

WFP advocacy generally follows a script along the following lines:

- We need to tell the (First) World about the problem of world hunger: The phrase 'raise awareness' is commonly used in WFP campaigns;
- This problem is defined largely in terms of the numbers of starving people (emphasising especially numbers of children), juxtaposed with the work of the WFP in assisting them;
- When people have had their awareness of the issue of world hunger raised, they will be motivated to do something about it. Not only does the WFP raise awareness, it offers a concrete means of addressing the issue; hence one of a number of concrete straightforward actions open to people concerned about hunger is to assist us in our work by donating to us.

One example of this script is the Tackle Hunger campaign linked to the 2007 Rugby World Cup, and endorsed by the International Rugby Board. On the WFP website, the Tackle Hunger homepage is headlined "RAISING AWARENESS OF WORLD HUNGER DURING THE RUGBY WORLD CUP 2007" (WFP 2007b), immediately followed by the subheading "Click to Donate Now".

Such a script with its emphasis on garnering donations echoes the operation of many international NGOs. In this context it is not surprising that Barrett and Maxwell group the WFP with NGOs as a service organization in their analysis of food aid (Barrett and Maxwell 2005, 219ff). As will be discussed further below, the relationship of the WFP to NGOs is a complex mixture of collaboration and competition. The competitive element of the relationship hints at the WFP being akin to an NGO in some respects, which is partly why the WFP Secretariat produced a study in 2003 explaining the differences between it and NGOs when it came to the efficiency of its indirect support costs:

> The study found that most donor decisions that were related to the apportionment of food aid resources between WFP and NGOs, and among NGOs, were made on programmatic and policy grounds rather than being based on a comparison of support costs. One reason for this is that WFP and NGOs are very different types of institutions—they are structured differently and therefore operate in different ways. (WFP 2003a, 3).

Nevertheless, as the formal constitution of the WFP shows, for all the hints of an NGO style to its work, it is first and foremost an intergovernmental organization.

WFP General Regulations and Rules

Formal governance of the WFP is codified in a single document containing the General Regulations and General Rules, along with WFP Financial Regulations and the Rules of Procedure of the Executive Board (WFP 2004a). These make clear the WFP's legal status as 'an autonomous joint subsidiary programme of the United Nations and FAO' (WFP 2004a, Article VIII.1, 13). It is these parent organizations through the UN General Assembly and FAO Conference respectively that made and can amend the General Regulations (WFP 2004a, Article XV, 26), though the WFP Executive Board may recommend amendments to the General Regulations 'through the Economic and Social Council and the Council of FAO' (WFP 2004a, 26). This process of the WFP governing body making recommendations for changes was followed in 1991 when the last major governance structure changes were made.

While the Executive Board must operate within General Regulations as set by the UN and FAO, it approves its own General Rules, though they must be submitted 'for information' to the Economic and Social Council and the Council of FAO. (WFP 2004a, General Rule XV.1, 26).[2] Articles VI and XIV of the General Regulations provide respectively for the EB to adopt its own Rules of Procedure, and to establish Financial Regulations. Article V of the General Regulations states that the Executive Board and the Secretariat comprise the 'organs of WFP' (WFP 2004a, 7). As such, they form the critical governance structures of the WFP.

Since 1996, the WFP has been governed by an Executive Board (EB), comprising 36 member-states, half elected by the UN Economic and Social Council (ECOSOC) and half elected by the FAO Council (WFP 2004a, Article V, 7). Article VI of the General Regulations sets out the powers and functions of the EB, broadly summarised in paragraph 1:

> The Board shall, within the framework of these General Regulations, be responsible for providing intergovernmental support and specific policy direction to and supervision of the activities of WFP in accordance with the overall policy guidance of the General Assembly of the United Nations, the FAO Conference, the Economic and Social Council and the Council of FAO, and for ensuring that WFP is responsive to the needs and priorities of recipient countries. The Board will be subject to the general authority of the Economic and Social Council and the Council of FAO. (WFP 2004a, 8).

A review of WFP Governance articulated the EB role in terms of four interrelated frameworks: Strategy, Policy, Accountability and Oversight (WFP Governance Group 2005).

The EB meets formally three times per year for between three and five days, with many non-member states, the European Commission, and various NGOs attending as observers. In addition, the Board undertakes field trips to observe WFP operations, and engages in 'informal consultations' out-of-session (WFP Governance Group 2005, 13, 19, Annex IV, 31).

At its first session each year the Board elects a Bureau comprising a President, Vice-President and three other members (WFP 2004a, Rule IV, 60). The Bureau has the primary function of facilitating 'the effective and efficient functioning of the Board' through planning, preparation and organization of Board meetings and 'the promotion of dialogue' (WFP 2004a, 61). The Vice-President position has been regarded as an important innovation,[3] created to groom the next President for a year before taking that position, and thereby assisting with succession planning.

Article VII of the General Regulations describes the 'organization and functions' of the Secretariat which 'shall be headed by an Executive Director, who shall be responsible and accountable to the Board for the administration of WFP and for the implementation of WFP program, projects and other activities' (WFP 2004a, 11). Apart from management and administration of WFP, and servicing the Board, the Executive Director (ED) is delegated specific authorities under General Rule VI.2 with regard to approving emergency and special operations under a certain size, and the revision of budgets and reallocation of resources within certain limits for other projects. Country Programs (in the form of agreements between WFP and a specific nation allocating funding and responsibilities across one or more specific projects) require EB approval. In any case, all exercise of delegated authority is reported to the EB as part of the extensive reporting it requires of the Secretariat through the ED.

Inclusion as a feature of WFP governance

> WFP has no formal membership, although countries that participate in its various activities are often informally referred to as "Member States". Participation in the governance of the Programme is open to any State Member of the United Nations, or Member Nation [of the FAO]. Any member of these organizations wishing to be elected to a seat on the governing body—the Executive Board—needs to be listed by the United Nations or FAO in one of the five, essentially geographic, electoral lists A-E ... (WFP Governance Group 2005, Annex II, 22).

Relationship of state members to the WFP

The most important of the structures linking states to the WFP is the EB. The states which are members of the EB include a mix of donor and recipient nations, with representation defined under a distribution of seats in Appendix B to the WFP General Regulations (WFP 2004a, 30). This governance structure is based on a UN General Assembly resolution in 1993 to establish identical Executive Boards for WFP, the

UN Development Program (UNDP), the UN International Children's Fund (UNICEF) and the UN Population Fund (UNFPA).

Appendix A to the General Regulations (WFP 2004a, 27–9) groups the states members of the United Nations and FAO into five regional and economic 'Lists'.

Lists A, B and C are termed 'Developing Countries': List A is composed of 53 African nations from which eight are elected to the EB. List B includes 54 Asian, Middle Eastern and Pacific nations from which seven are elected to the EB. List C comprises 33 Caribbean, Central and South American nations from which five are elected to the Board. There is one additional EB position rotated on a cycle of four terms through List A, List B, List A again, and List C (WFP 2004a, 30). Thus 21 of the 36 EB positions are allocated to developing countries.

Lists D and E are termed 'Economically Developed Countries.' List D contains 31 nations, including the richest and most developed economies, from which twelve are elected to the Board. List E contains 22 nations from central and Eastern Europe from which three are elected to the EB.

This distribution of rep.esentation was established in 1999 by resolutions of the FAO Conference (Res 6/99 of 13 November 1999) and UN General Assembly (Res. 53/223 of 23 April 1999), and is to be reviewed in 2010 (WFP 2004a, 30). Half of each List's representation is drawn from FAO Council and half from ECOSOC, with uneven numbered List representations splitting evenly in aggregate between them.

EB members are elected for three-year terms on a staggered basis, with one-third of the Board starting their term in 1 January each year. As a result, each year there are six EB member positions up for election in ECOSOC, usually in May, and six EB member positions up for election in FAO Council, usually in November. These elections usually result in a mix of newly-elected members and re-elected members via the complex politics of such intergovernmental processes (see below).

The significance of achieving or retaining EB membership for states cannot be articulated without reference to the specific nature of the state's relationship with the WFP. Formally, these relationships tend to be mediated through the Lists. For example, List meetings are held with the Secretariat to consult on policy issues (Interview #11 2005). However, the structure of the Lists does not entirely capture the three different state perspectives towards EB membership – donor, recipient and transitional.

Donor Nations

For the major 'traditional' donor nations (all of which are in List D – see Table 5.1), given the dependence of the WFP on their voluntary donations and their historical dominance of WFP governance, EB membership is an important means of, as it were, safeguarding their investment. As would seem logical, the largest and most significant IFAR donors historically (US, Canada, Japan, and Australia) have tended to maintain an EB representative position continuously. The position of many significant European donors is complicated by food aid donations being made through both national and European Union (EU) structures (see Chart 5.1); within List D, the EU creates a sub-list layer of politics regarding Board representation.

Over the decade ending in 2005, the European Commission (EC) contributed over 30% of WFP food aid donations from the European Union, with EU member states donations aggregated together making the balance of EU donations. The most significant European state donors include Germany, the Netherlands and the UK (each with over 10% of EU donations).

The position of the UK in 2005 helps demonstrate some of the complexities of donor state representation on the EB. At the June 2005 EB Annual Session the UK was one of more than 60 member states to attend the EB Annual Session in observer capacity, as at that time it was not a member of the Board. Indeed, the UK was the only one of the P5 (five permanent members of the UN Security Council) not to be an EB member continuously in recent years. Nevertheless, at the time of the June session the UK had already been elected by ECOSOC in April 2005 to its next term as a Board representative starting from 1 January 2006 (UN Economic and Social Council 2005, 12).

Even in an observer capacity, the UK representative participated more vigorously and effectively than many Board members, reflecting the real power of being a large donor with some of the strongest policy capacity through its Department for International Development (DFID), and involvement in the OECD Development Assistance Committee (DAC). In addition, at that same meeting, a former EB President, and UK permanent representative to the UN agencies in Rome, Anthony Beattie was present in his capacity as chair of the WFP Governance Steering Committee. UK involvement seemed little constrained by not having the formal status of Board membership during the meeting, and would seem to demonstrate the importance of the effects of wealth and capacity together with history and organizational culture[4] on the significance of formal EB membership.

Table 5.1: WFP top 5 donors by proportion of contributions, 2007-2008

2007		2008	
Donor	**%**	**Donor**	**%**
US	**38**	US	**41**
EU	**31**	EU	**25**
Canada	**7**	Saudi Arabia	**10**
Japan	**5**	Canada	**5.5**
Australia	**4**	Japan	**3.5**

Data sources: (INTERFAIS/WFP 2008, 10; WFP 2009, Annex 2, 50-1). Note – The EU figure for 2008 includes the EC (7% of contributions) and separate contributions from up to 26 member states. Five of the 10 countries that donated more than US$100 million that year were EU members: UK, Netherlands, Spain, Italy and Germany.

Twenty-eight of the member states attending had between two and five in their delegations. The two largest delegations in attendance at this meeting came from List D members - the United States (16 persons) and Switzerland (8 persons). However assessing the numbers from EU members is complicated by the presence of the third largest delegation - the European Commission (7 persons) – as observers in addition to national delegations. The European Commission has an interesting status as the first ranked amongst all observers in the speaking order, and both represents a significant bloc of donors (the various European Union member states, several of which are EB members in their own right), as well as the EU which is a donor in its own right.

Chart 5.1: EC and EU member shares of WFP contributions from the EU (by $US value), 1996-2005

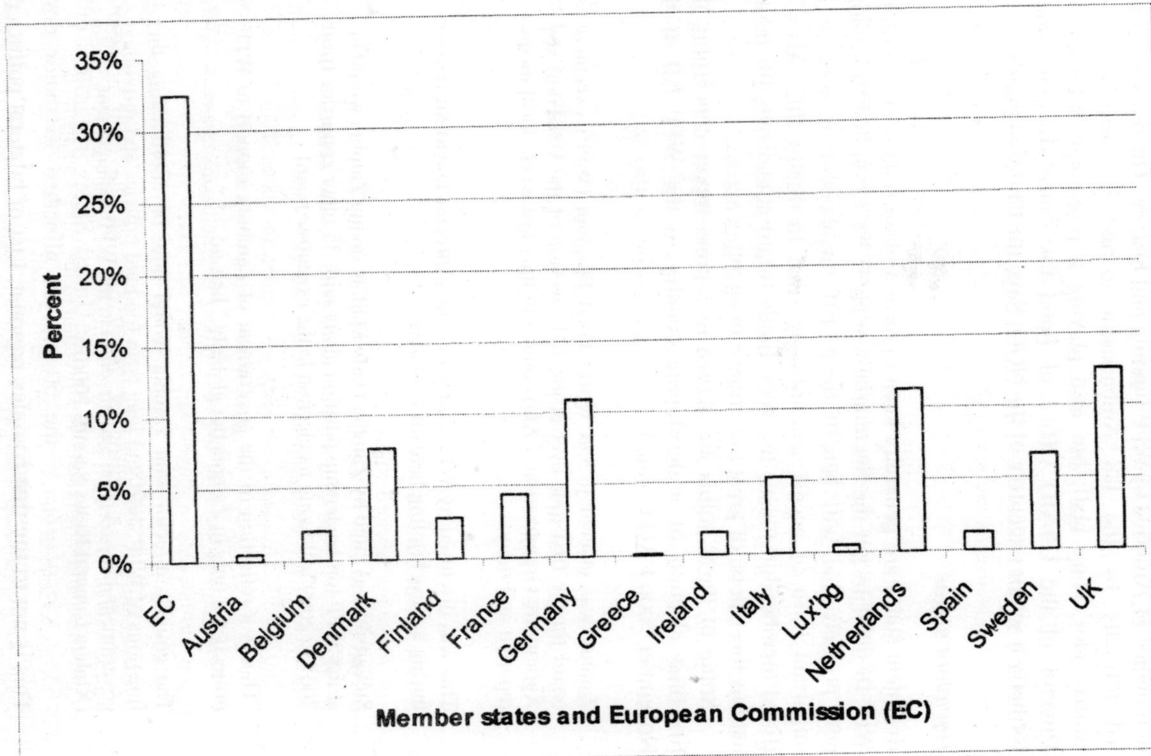

Data Source: (Hanrahan and Canada 2006, Appendix Table 2, 6).

The size of the American delegation was commensurate with the dominance of America in WFP funding and history. The delegation was led formally by the US Ambassador to the UN food agencies, Ambassador Tony Hall, but also playing a prominent role was the Director of the USAID Office of Food for Peace (Lauren Landis, formerly a senior executive of the NGO, Save the Children Fund).

Recipient states

Recipient states are generally keen to have a close relationship with the WFP in order to get the Secretariat's support for extending or creating new projects that will benefit them; EB membership is seen as an important form of access and influence that facilitates this. Also, as Board membership means the WFP funds Board attendance, for poorer nations this can be of great importance in enabling access.

Some of these points are shown in a press report concerning the first-time election of a developing country to the WFP EB at the November 2006 FAO Council:

> Zambia was elected to the World Food Program (WFP) executive board for the first time ever at the 131st session of the UN Food and Agriculture Organization (FAO) council in Italy last week, local media reported on Friday.
>
> This was disclosed by WFP Zambia country director David Stevenson during a press briefing here on Thursday.
>
> Stevenson was cited by Zambia Daily Mail as saying Zambia would be at the WFP top leadership position along with 35 other countries from 2007 to 2009 following its election to the executive board.
>
> "This is a reflection of the government of Zambia's support to WFP projects not only in Zambia but globally," he said.
>
> The country director said Zambia would now be coordinating the functions of WFP short and long term food aid policies and providing governmental supervision and direction to the WFP management. (Xinhua General News Service 2006).

This is not to say that complex regional, List or bilateral politics do not play a role amongst recipient countries as they do amongst donors. For example, EB positions at times are effectively 'traded' in the context of bilateral negotiations, as the text of this letter shows:

> The Embassy of the People's Democratic Republic of Algeria in Italy presents its compliments to the Embassy of the Gabonese Republic in its capacity as Chair of the Candidatures Committee for the Africa Region and has the honour to refer to the 131st Session of the Council of FAO from 20 to 25 November 2006, which will be called upon to elect six members of the WFP Executive Board for a term of office of three years.
>
> The Embassy recalls that, at the 130th Session of the Council of FAO held in November 2005, Algeria was elected to the WFP Executive Board for a period of three years from 2006 to 2008. However, following an agreement with the Sudan, it has undertaken to resign its seat in favour of that country for the remaining period of office, that is 2007-2008. Algeria accordingly stands down in favour of the Sudan for the years 2007 and 2008.
>
> The Embassy of the People's Democratic Republic of Algeria kindly requests the Embassy of the Gabonese Republic to inform the Secretary-General of the Council of this matter and avails itself of this opportunity to renew the assurance of its highest consideration.
> (FAO 2006b, 3).

Transitional states

In the last decade or so a number of nations have shifted from being recipients to also being donors. This reflects various interrelated factors. First, the real advances in reducing poverty by countries such as India and China (FAO 2006c; Ravallion 2004), and shifts in agricultural production and trade diversification (FAO 2007, 129). Second, a WFP policy desire to break down the donor/recipient barrier by trying to encourage this transition (Interview #11 2005). Third, a culture of development and the operation of national moral claims in the feed-the-hungry norm in which 'graduating' to donating food is seen as a sign of national success. For nations in this transitional category, acknowledgement of their development into donors becomes an important part of their EB membership, along with a desire to maximize agricultural export opportunities through WFP purchasing contracts.

For example, after his country won election to the WFP EB for the first time in November 2006, the Philippine Ambassador to Italy and Permanent Representative to the Food and Agriculture Organization, Philippe J. Lhuillier, saw two benefits to the Philippines from EB membership. One was participation in UN reform efforts, the other was the potential use of EB membership to generate commercial opportunities. It was the latter that attracted the most repeated, specific and concrete public explication:

> "This is a significant milestone for us for two reasons. We have never been a member of the WFP Executive Board and this gives us an opportunity to sell to the WFP rather than get aid form (sic) them and the WFP Executive Board will have a strategic role to play in the ongoing reforms of the United Nations," Lhuillier said in a report to Foreign Affairs Secretary Alberto Romulo.
>
> "Whenever people hear of WFP, they only think of emergency assistance. They never realize that it is also the world's biggest food buyer. Our Filipino food exporters can have this opportunity of selling to the WFP, products like canned sardines, dried fish, mungbeans, and even bottled water - items that are needed during an emergency," Lhuillier noted.
>
> ...
>
> He added that the Embassy campaigned hard for this election so that the Philippines can sell to the WFP rather than receive aid from it. (Asia Pulse 2006).

Lhuillier also stated this success was only after a four way battle for the two available List B positions in which Pakistan (30 votes) and the Philippines (29 votes) easily outpolled Iraq (12 votes) and incumbent Bangladesh (17 votes) (Asia Pulse 2006). This example demonstrates the diversity of recipient and transitional states within the developing country Lists, and how this can lead to vigorous electoral competition as well as horse-trading over EB positions.

A further example of this transitional perspective can be seen in the speech the President of Nigeria (and then Chairman of the African Union) Chief Olusegun Obasanjo gave to the EB on 10 June 2005. Chief Obasanjo commented that until recently the WFP had 'very limited contact' with the Nigerian government. This changed in 2004 with the visit of a High-Level WFP Mission to look at possible collaboration:

> The discussion centred on the prospects for *increased purchase of food commodities*, technical assistance to the Nigerian Emergency Management Agency (NEMA), collaboration with the National Special Programme for Food Security (NSPSF) and technical assistance to the Federal Ministry of Education on the design of a School Feeding Programme in Nigeria. (Obasanjo 2005, 1, emphasis added).

President Obasanjo went on to make clear the importance to Nigeria of the WFP as a purchaser of food, noting that the 'present disposition of WFP to source food to be used as aid in the African region from within the region is a welcome development' (Obasanjo 2005, 2).

> Nigeria will continue to support the World Food Programme either as a donor or as supplier of agricultural produce at very attractive and competitive prices.
>
> Let me therefore use this opportunity to urge the WFP to establish a befitting office that would drive its project in Nigeria rather than operate by proxy. We are ready to provide all possible support in this area.
> (Obasanjo 2005, 5).[5]

While Nigeria has still not been elected to the Executive Board, it seems likely that it would be interested in attaining a position on it in the near future for the same reasons as the Philippines.

In terms of the feed-the-hungry norm, transitional countries are able to start exercising the moral claim of surplus production countries; the alacrity and emphasis with which they do so is a powerful testament to the projection of power associated with that particular moral claim, as much as concern for commercial benefit. For example, in the speech cited from above, President Obasanjo of Nigeria also made a strong reference to the national moral claim of food surplus countries:

> I am pleased to state at this juncture that the World Food Programme (WFP) is among the few multilateral/donor agencies that have painted a good picture of Nigeria. It recognizes the efforts of the present civilian administration in providing food security and has objectively assessed and excluded Nigeria from the category of countries suffering from food deficits. In other words, Nigeria is confirmed to be producing enough basic food to meet local demand as well as producing surplus which can be sold or donated to food-deficit countries in other parts of the world. (Obasanjo 2005, 1).

A further example of the importance of this moral claim as an element in power projection is China. China in recent years has gone from being a recipient country to become the third largest global donor of food aid, though the bulk of this aid is given bilaterally (and mainly to North Korea) rather than through the WFP (Sui 2006; WFP 2006h).[6]

To summarise what has been a largely structural analysis of the EB so far, the following points have been made. Against the structural majority of the developing nations, there is the dependence on the donations from the wealthiest nations; participation in the EB is easier and more effective for the wealthier states with greater policy and personnel capacity. Donor, recipient and transitional states have different kinds of interests involved in Executive Board membership; though all engage in the usual horse trading for positions, such trading does not exclude out and out competitive votes; the Lists, reflecting the donor/recipient divide, largely structure and contain political conflicts amongst states.

The structural trade-off between the financial power of the donors and the numerical power of developing nations is also reflected in the long-standing tradition of the EB operating by consensus, noted in Chapter Four. This tradition means contentious decisions are generally deferred and either dropped or modified to find broad enough support to enable consensus adoption rather than put to a vote. Nevertheless, the transitional states do not fit within the current structure of the Lists which is based on a donor/recipient bifurcation as much as regional logic.

The roles of people and culture

Up to this point, the explication of WFP governance through Executive Board members has been largely structural; a further three points concerning the interaction of structures with people and culture need to be made to round out this analysis of state inclusion.

First, Ingram, writing of the 1980s notes that

> WFP's constituency was spread across several ministries in member states. In developed countries they were the overseas development department, the agriculture ministry and in some instances also the trade ministry, and foreign ministries which had oversight of UN system matters. Such a dispersed constituency was inherently weak but, worse still, the constituency was divided within itself. (Ingram 2006, 314).

While the sort of political conflicts involving the WFP that concerned Ingram have, to some extent, been left behind, there is still some relevance to his point about the diversity of the constituency when it comes to those involved in EB meetings. It does result in a particular complexity of domestic state policy making in relation to the WFP, with agricultural interests in donor countries having particular influence. Also, the mix of diplomatic, development and agricultural expertise has contributed to maintaining a culture which valorizes the technical along with the political.

Second, the actual physical representatives on the Board are individuals, not states. As noted above, many of these representatives may well have stronger links with their country's agricultural ministry than with its foreign service. Ingram notes the repetition of debates on the EB resulting from a reasonably frequent turnover in delegates (Ingram 2006, 60). At the same time, these individuals typically hold a specific Permanent Representative or Ambassadorial rank position to the UN agencies in Rome, including FAO and the International Fund for Agricultural Development (IFAD) as well as the WFP. This results in a different role from jetting in from elsewhere three times a year for EB meetings (though many members of the larger delegations do so). Rather, such representatives have an opportunity to develop ongoing relationship with each other, especially those in the same List, and with members of the WFP Secretariat. Also, they will tend to interconnect the WFP with the FAO and IFAD, rather than seeing it in isolation.

The impact of such things tends to be subtle. For example, in 2005 Australia was the only significant member state without a Rome-based permanent representative to the UN food agencies. On the one hand, Bertini suggests that this has meant Australia is 'out of the loop' to some degree (Bertini 2005b). On the other hand, the active engagement and effectiveness of the Australian representative to the OECD, based in Paris, who attended the June 2005 EB meeting as her country's representative seemed little constrained, though perhaps limited to the most significant issues. However, it is difficult from such limited observation to assess the deeper implications of not having a Permanent Representative for building relationships with the Secretariat or other country representatives outside of List D.

Inclusion and staffing

The third point about people and culture concerns the operation of staffing decisions. Within the UN system, the sharing of staff positions around the member states has long been seen as a proxy measure of inclusion. Periodically, states have demanded detailed reports on WFP staffing and their share of representation in it. Unlike organizations funded solely by assessments of members, voluntarily funded UN agencies do not apply quotas to staff recruitment to ensure equitable representation of member states. However they do pay some regard to such issues, as the WFP noted in a 2004 policy on the subject of staff recruitment and geographic representation (WFP 2004e, 6–7).

In the WFP, Bertini devised a methodology to manage this issue in 1998:

> The need to develop and apply an objective methodology was recognized in response to concerns expressed by members of the Executive Board. The purpose of the WFP methodology is to guide the Executive Director in establishing equitable levels of representation that reflect the contributions made to the Programme and the need for diversity among international professional staff ... [The ED's methodology] is tailored to the circumstances of WFP, taking into account the major sources of funding and endeavouring to ensure that all countries receive some level of representation.
>
> ... The methodology is referred to as the "WFP Informal Formula". It must be stressed that it is used only as guidance on staffing targets rather than to establish quotas to be filled.
>
> ... The Executive Director uses reports based on the methodology to review staffing trends and to make adjustments to maintain equitable geographical distribution and gender balance among international professional staff. The reports are not made public because to do so might imply the imposition of a quota system, which could discourage applications from the best qualified candidates, irrespective of nationality. Representatives of missions are welcome to inquire about the status of their countries in terms of the level of representation, and regularly do so.
> (WFP 2004e, 4).

In summary, the Informal WFP Formula:

- provided for 60 percent of the number of international professional staff to be allocated to major donor countries and the remaining 40 percent to all other countries;
- the target number of staff per major donor country is based on their contribution percentage calculated exclusive of US contributions;
- placed a ceiling of 20 percent on the total number of international staff for the United States, regardless of its proportion of the 60 percent allocated to major donor countries; and,
- no targets are set for the remaining countries; a country is considered to be adequately represented if at least three of its nationals are members of the staff.

Source: (WFP 2004e, 7-8).

The formula was applied to the elite international professional staff grades, rather than across total staffing, including contractors and locally appointed staff working on particular operations in the field. The international professional staff constituted approximately 9 percent of the total staff of WFP – at 31 December 2003, 979 positions (WFP 2004e) out of 10,790 (WFP 2004b, 3). Based on the formula, the US was under-represented, other major donors had a mix of over-representation, fair representation and under-representation (WFP 2004e, 12), though overall, other major donors were over-represented. Developing countries had 39.1 percent of international professional staff, just below the 40% target (WFP 2004e, 9).

Consistent with UN policy, which relates staffing representation to contributions (assessed or donated) the focus of the formula was on donors. No explicit reference was made to recipient countries, although arguably the particular perspectives of nationals of states receiving WFP food aid would enhance the diversity of staffing in accordance with the avowed UN principles. This is in contrast to the detailed accounting for relative amounts of donation and the creation of finely tuned staff number goals for donor countries. The disparity points to the donor bias in important mechanisms for inclusion such as staffing policy – although the bias derives largely out of the political reality that the WFP depends on donations for its operation.

Since 2004, there have not been any further reports on the operation of the Informal Formula to the EB, implying its use has declined in importance or ceased. Rather, a broad-brush approach simply groups countries in their Lists rather than in terms of the amounts of donations. Lists A, B and C are assumed to represent 'economically developing' countries for the purpose of the UN system goal of at least 40 percent of international professional staff appointments for nationals of such states (WFP 2006a; 2006b; 2007a).

Staff data from 31 December 2006 suggested an increase of more than 32 percent in international professional staff employed by WFP since three years earlier, to 1,295 (WFP 2007a, 3). Staff employment distributions amongst Lists since 2000 have not changed greatly, and developing country representation was then sitting at 40.4 percent (WFP 2007a, 3).

At 15.3 percent of international professional staff (WFP 2007a, 16), in 2006 the US still seemed under-represented in terms of the informal formula, though still the largest single national constituency amongst staff. However, the Executive Director position has considerably more significance than any others, and this is clearly defined as American.

The Executive Director position

The US is undoubtedly a special case amongst member states due to its dominance of donations, and this is reflected most prominently in its now entrenched control of the ED position. The ED position is the most significant and powerful position in the WFP; a two-term incumbent will run the organization for a decade.

The Executive Director is jointly appointed by the UN Secretary-General and the FAO Director-General, for a five year term. Bertini was replaced as ED by James Morris, an American national and former businessman, (2002–07). On 7 November 2006, the appointment of a new ED, Josette Sheeran, was announced, with effect from the expiry of the term of James Morris in March 2007. According to the announcement,

> Kofi Annan, secretary-general of the United Nations, and Jacques Diouf, director-general of the U.N. Food and Agriculture Organization (FAO), chose Sheeran in consultation with the WFP Executive Board.
>
> ...
>
> Sheeran was selected from a field of nearly 80 candidates, according to a letter from Annan to WFP Executive Board President Mirza Qamar Beg of Pakistan.
> (McConnell 2006)

Ms Sheeran is an American, who prior to her appointment served as US Under-Secretary of State for Economic, Business and Agricultural Affairs. By the end of her five-year term, the ED position will have been occupied by American citizens consecutively for 20 years. There now appears to be a widespread assumption that it is on the list of UN organizations to which the US has the presumptive right to nominate the head, though as noted in Chapter Four, Bertini was effectively the first American to run the WFP.

Sheeran's appointment generated some controversy with critics regarding it as an example of the Bush Administration obdurately insisting on the installation of 'their nominee' without regard to the merit or quality of alternatives, and despite concerns about Sheeran's past links with the controversial Unitarian Church. Criticism was prominent in Canada and Switzerland (there were front-running alternative candidates from both countries). Some critics also noted that the leading internal WFP candidate, an American, was apparently discounted because of perceived past connections to the Clinton

Administration. The State Department, on the other hand, emphasised the rigorous interviewing process and Sheeran's breadth of experience, including recent involvement on a UN review panel. State also highlighted the fact that the appointment had been made and announced by FAO D-G Jacques Diouf and UN Secretary-General Kofi Annan, after consultation with incoming Secretary-General Ban Ki-Moon and the WFP EB (Lederer 2006; Lynch 2006; McConnell 2006; Pisik 2006; Turner 2006). Nevertheless, it would clearly be difficult for the two formal decision-makers to appoint someone other than the person nominated by the US President. It is extremely unlikely that the EB would advise them that the nominee was not appropriate in view of the importance of American and allied donations to the viability of the WFP.

NGOs and inclusion

The WFP has extensive and complex relationships with NGOs. In the mid 1990s the WFP began working to more actively manage its relationship with NGOs. In 1995 Bertini instituted an annual round table meeting between the WFP and NGOs (WFP 1996), and formulated a model Memorandum of Understanding (MOU) to formalise WFP/NGO relationships (Bertini 2005b). By 2001 at least 16 MOUs with NGOs were in place (WFP 2001b, 3).

In both 1995 and 1998 the WFP/NGO field relationships were surveyed (Borione and Comergnat 1998, 3). The 1998 survey showed a large amount of collaboration between WFP country offices and NGOs – whether local, national or international. It found that more than 1,000 NGOs were involved with WFP field activities, across a range of functions, including distribution, data collection, needs assessment, project preparation and monitoring (Borione and Comergnat 1998, 4–6). A 2001 report to the EB proposing a partnership framework for NGO relationships noted approximately 1,100 NGO collaborations (WFP 2001b). This report was generated with considerable input from NGOs, reflected in recommendations to the EB 'put forward for consideration by WFP and its NGO partners' (WFP 2001b, 16). In each of 2007 and 2008, the WFP reported the number of NGOs with which it worked as exceeding 2,800 (WFP 2009, 9).

The heterogeneity of NGOs in size, scope of activity and type of collaboration with WFP makes it difficult to generalise about the nature of their participation in the polity of the IFAR, and suggests that some sort of generalised analysis based on NGOs representing 'international civil society' is not viable. Moreover, there is some evidence that many

NGOs ultimately regard their representation as stakeholders as occurring at least partly through their home states.

For example, in recent times there has been considerable criticism by European NGOs of the WFP's move to expand its fundraising from government donations to corporate and private individual sources (WFP 2004c). European NGOs see the WFP as competing (unfairly) with them by engaging in private sector fundraising (Interview #9 2005; Interview #12 2005; Bredholt 2005; European Food Security Group 2005; Schenkenberg 2005), rather than sticking to governmental funding. European NGOs are also critical of the WFP's excessive reliance on in-kind donations, and support its pursuit of broader objectives than emergency relief (European Food Security Group 2005). At the same time, as noted in Chapter Four, US NGOs are largely integrated in the domestic US food aid iron triangle. As a result, they largely favour status quo on these fronts, due to perceived risks of loss of resources if US in-kind donations were to decline, and desire to maintain their dominance over USAID development assistance.

The clear differences between European and US NGOs reflect (and contribute to) differences between the positions taken by their respective states (and trading blocs) in the IFAR and agricultural trade regime. NGOs in the IFAR polity are better understood as aligned with their states of origin, rather than joined together in a non-state actor collective. As was suggested by comments from a German NGO at the 2005 EB Annual meeting, where they disagree with actions of the WFP they ultimately expect to exert influence through political pressure on their government to withhold or constrain WFP donations (European Food Security Group 2005).

Nevertheless, it would not be accurate to view NGOs as mere ciphers of states. Some NGOs do attend EB meetings as observers; the annual roundtable meetings remain well attended – approximately 25 attended in 2004 for example (Schenkenberg 2005) – and, as noted above, there are broader attempts by the WFP to include them as partners – for example in consulting them about proposed strategic planning (European Food Security Group 2005).

One of the key ways in which NGO partners are of importance to the WFP is in providing mechanisms for including beneficiaries in project design and delivery (WFP 2001b; 2003a).

Beneficiaries and inclusion

The beneficiaries of the WFP are generally defined as the hungry poor who benefit from food aid and are the focus of the WFP's mission. Their inclusion in the IFAR polity generally works formally through states acting in a representational role. This is informally supplemented by NGOs and at times some other UN agencies such as UNICEF and UNHCR also playing a de facto representational role, together with the WFP's own operational processes.

Given the primary beneficiaries are an ever-changing group, varying between regions and countries over time, and defined by their vulnerability, and a position at the end of the supply chain, direct inclusion in a political sense is difficult and hindered by technical decision making. For example, it is widely agreed that targeting of the most needy is required for effective food aid policy. But this can lead to a difference in given locales between those who subjectively wish to get food aid (i.e., be accorded beneficiary status), and the generally smaller group which, from a technical point of a view, would be appropriate beneficiaries. Also, inadequate resources constantly plague WFP operations, meaning there is often insufficient food aid to go to all potentially eligible beneficiaries. In that context, targeting is also linked to the rationing of scarce resources, and the WFP also announces periodic ration cuts to cope with inadequate resources. In these situations, inclusion of the hungry poor in IFAR governance occurs largely via NGO, WFP and recipient government pleas for increased donations.

The role of recipient states is not always linked to inclusion of beneficiaries through representation. State interests in control of food aid resources can sometimes actively obstruct beneficiary inclusion in the sense of IFAR definitions. For example, the Democratic People's Republic of Korea has had a poor track record in its dealings with the WFP, consistently obstructing independent monitoring of food distribution and allocation. An External Auditor's Report to the EB in 2007 noted that:

> In 2005, we found evidence of the inadequacy of monitoring operations because of limitations imposed by DPRK authorities on WFP's access to beneficiaries. Audit observation of two food monitoring visits at a sub-office identified procedures that adversely affect the level of assurance available over the integrity of the monitoring operation:
>
> • The DPRK Government required advance notice of planned food monitoring visits;

- WFP monitors were not provided with unrestricted access to field operations, limiting the assurance obtained over the type of beneficiary and the quantities of food consumed; and

- Interviews were conducted by non-Korean speaking WFP staff through an interpreter in the presence of government officials.

(Bourn 2007, 15; see 16 for history of problems with monitoring going back to 1995; also Noland 2003).

As is suggested by the WFP's awareness of and work on such problems, it has provided an organizational capacity to at least partially overcome problems of beneficiary inclusion posed by state actions. The WFP has demonstrated a capacity to push and cajole governments to step back enough from sectional interests to allow it to focus assistance on appropriate beneficiaries. For example, since Bertini became ED, the WFP has had a strong focus on gender based inclusion, acknowledging the centrality of women to food management processes in families and communities, and the importance of beneficiary processes that work to include women and children as direct recipients of food aid.[7]

The EB provides an important public forum within which problems of beneficiary inclusion are regularly reported, and the IFAR feed-the-hungry norm can operate to constrain the more problematic behaviours of recipient states. Ultimately, however, beneficiary inclusion occurs most significantly through institutional means – that is, through the moral claim of the hungry within the feed-the-hungry norm.

Concluding remarks on inclusion

The above discussion on inclusion did not include all stakeholders. One group of growing importance is the Transnational Corporations (TNCs), with whom the WFP is seeking increasingly to partner (Giarraputo 2006; WFP 2004c; WFP 2009). Corporate partnerships in 2008 involved a range of companies, including Yum! Brands, Unilever, the Vodafone UN Foundation, TNT, and DSM, and involve in-kind assistance (e.g. with logistics or communication technology) as much as cash donations. The WFP obviously also has commercial relationships with shipping and other transport companies, and businesses from which it purchases food supplies or services. A detailed examination of these relationships, and their connections with states and other non-state actors would be of interest, but has been beyond the scope of my research.

As is evident from its governance and resource base, the WFP is best understood as an intergovernmental body – the most significant constituents that form its polity are states. The variations in capacity and interest that differentiate states are probably the most significant aspects of inclusion-related legitimacy in the IFAR. Additional stakeholder relationships with non-state actors - NGOs, beneficiaries, and TNCs – are secondary to and often mediated through WFP state-members.

Accountability

Examining the governance feature of accountability reveals more facets of the interrelationships between the WFP and its stakeholders. Accountability here refers to processes which constrain power, though this requires some more specific framing through definition of the attributional element of accountability: *who* is accountable *to whom* and for *what* (Ross 2000, Ch3). Three accountability scenarios are framed in Table 5.2.

Table 5.2: The WFP – three accountability scenarios defined by attribution

	Form of Accountability		
	Organizational	**Functional**	**Donor**
Who	WFP Secretariat/ ED	WFP	Traditional donor states
To Whom	EB; UN and FAO	Beneficiaries (primary, secondary, potential)	EB and Secretariat
For What	Organizational mission and operations	Assistance without creating dependency	Value, type and terms of contribution to Mission

Organizational accountability refers principally to the EB's role in relation to accountability and oversight. Specifically this means the accountability relationship of the Secretariat (and in particular the ED) to the Board and through it, to member states of the UN and FAO. Functional accountability refers to the relationship of the WFP to beneficiaries, though this also raises a crucial question about where producers and *potential* beneficiaries fit into accountability. Lastly, the most powerful actors within the IFAR remain the traditional donors; any consideration of accountability within the IFAR and the WFP must consider the constraints that operate on them. Donor accountability is largely constructed through the processes of the EB and Secretariat via the operation of the feed-the-hungry norm.

Organizational accountability

The Executive Board is composed of member state representatives elected by the governing bodies of the WFP's parent organizations, the UN and the FAO. It provides the main focus of accountability for the WFP organization – the place in which the ED reports on the work of the secretariat, and its performance in implementing the organizational mandate and achieving its mission. In practice, displeasure on the part of a donor with any particular WFP project proposal is likely to be expressed through a refusal to support it, while directing donations to other areas deemed more worthy of support (Landis 2005). In Hirschman's well known formulation, the EB provides member states with many viable options to use voice and at least partial exit strategies (Hirschman 1970). However, seeing the EB in terms of its accountability function requires consideration of structural, social and cultural factors beyond this formal description.

In structural terms, the different interests of different state members affect what they see as significant issues in the WFP's operation, and at times leads to political conflicts on the Board. These conflicts can distract from or distort the emphases placed on accountability of different aspects of the WFP's operations. For example, hostility between a donor member and a recipient state member may well affect the rigour applied to oversight of project proposals and reports. Ingram cites the case of a proposal for a project in Vietnam in the 1980s which encountered considerable hostility from the US, forcing delays and modification to the original proposal before something was eventually approved (Ingram 2006, 61–4). Such structural factors complicate the operation of organizational accountability, and are an important reminder that the consensual tradition does not equate to an absence of political conflict.

Apart from such structural conflicts, other social and cultural factors also have effects on the way in which the EB constrains the ED and Secretariat. The WFP is part of a broader UN culture which, at times problematically, blurs the boundary between governing bodies and secretariats. This is because of the not uncommon transition of government EB representatives into Secretariat staff roles. At first blush, such transitions might appear logical – after all, many governing body representatives are talented and well connected in their government. They can assist in building links between the Secretariat and its member-states, and from time on the body have valuable knowledge and understanding of the organization and its operations. On the other hand, such transitions create potential problems for accountability and pose conflicts of interest. How much is governing body oversight of the secretariat limited by the fact that some members on it are hoping to get (appropriately senior) positions in the secretariat when their term as representative is up? If you are hoping to be employed by an Executive Director, how likely are you to ask hard questions of that person about their discharge of duties?

From the other side of the coin, there has been much debate about dealing with the conflict between the political and merit principles of recruitment which has been an endemic problem for the UN: the merit principle within the UN tends to be undermined by the pressures from member states for appointing their nationals (Ingram 2006, 328-9). For example, Bertini tells of encountering several years of criticisms from a member-state on the Executive Board which she ascribed to her refusal to renew the contract of a national from that country on WFP staff (Bertini 2005b). Such problems appeared to stem more from the political connections of the individual involved than from a generalized concern that she was doing down the member state, but again would seem to work to valorize personal or political interests over the merit principle. Also, Ingram testifies to the at times petty and personalised politics encountered from individuals who happened to represent state members (Ingram 2006).

These factors all complicate the operation of organizational accountability, though arguably none of them is unique to the WFP amongst UN agencies. Indeed, overall it is important not to overstate the extent to which accountability is reduced or compromised by such factors in the WFP. The strength of the feed-the-hungry norm as a unifying force plays a role in enabling the EB to discharge a relatively focused accountability function.

Functional accountability

There are three groups of interest in relation to functional accountability. The first and most significant is the individual people defined as the hungry poor to whom WFP food aid is being directed. Apart from these primary beneficiaries, there is a secondary group of beneficiaries – those from whom the WFP procures food.[8] The last group can be termed the potential beneficiaries. Potential beneficiaries are not currently beneficiaries, but nevertheless are at sufficient risk of malnutrition and hunger that they would have some moral claim to becoming beneficiaries if WFP had sufficient resources, either now or in the near future.

When it comes to accountability in IFAR governance, primary beneficiaries are in a different position from member states. These differences were noted above with respect to inclusion – in broad terms, beneficiaries generally depend on indirect representation through member states, together with NGO advocacy and WFP operational processes.

Unlike states, primary beneficiaries are not a fixed and legally defined group of entities. They are a mutable, changing and complex array of people sustained or assisted in varying degrees by emergency, protracted relief, and development operations in a wide number of countries and regions. On the other hand, for all this apparent nebulousness, beneficiaries are consistently described by the WFP staff as the focus of its work (Interview #4 2005; Interview #11 2005; Interview #12 2005; Interview #14 2005; Interview #16 2005; Interview #17 2005; Interview #19 2005). To draw an analogy to corporations and 'customer focus' would not capture the strong moral element of this focus. Thus it is probably most accurate to describe functional accountability as operating through the organization's culture and norms – the imperative of the moral claim of the hungry is what holds WFP to its mission, and drives its operations to genuinely assist beneficiaries, albeit within terms set by the donor nations on the EB.

Secondary beneficiaries

> Currently, food procured in developing countries accounts for approximately 20 percent of global food aid. WFP has historically been the largest single procurer of food aid on a global scale. From 2001 to 2004, WFP bought an average of 1.25 million [metric tonnes] of food per annum (US$263 million) in developing countries. WFP's local purchases have also risen significantly, although they still account for only a third of its total food procurement and usually less than half of its procurement from developing countries. (WFP 2006e, 4).

Secondary beneficiaries are primarily those exercising the moral claim the IFAR feed-the-hungry norm grants producers from developing countries. However, the WFP policy on food procurement highlights the complexity of distinguishing this group from other primary and potential beneficiaries. This is because purchasing decisions by the WFP can disrupt and be damaging to agricultural markets in developing countries, due to irregular and inconsistent demands; also the driving up of prices from demand generated by WFP purchasing can lead to loss of access to food by poor people in the area (WFP 2006e, 15).

WFP notes potential trade offs between the needs of primary beneficiaries and the interests of secondary beneficiaries. This is because it is in the interests of primary beneficiaries that the quantity and quality of procured food is maximised and supply is reliable, yet local procurement may involve paying a premium or risking reduced quality or reliability of supply. If local procurement requires a price premium, for example due to seasonal variations in price, it reduces the amount that can be bought, and effectively shifts resource benefits from primary beneficiaries to secondary beneficiaries.

Attempting to purchase directly from farmers or farm associations is logistically difficult and has proven unreliable when tried. Case studies on Burkina Faso and Uganda

> found that WFP's experience of supporting farmers and farmers' groups has had mixed results. Farmers participating in groups have benefited from higher incomes, which many have invested in improving agricultural production. In addition, some of the groups were able to invest in storage and cleaning equipment, improving their food quality and thus the returns from traders. For WFP, however, the experience has generally been negative, resulting in higher prices paid, higher administrative costs because of having more contracts to monitor, and greater risk of default. As a result of higher prices paid, direct contracting has usually led to a transfer from WFP's beneficiaries to farmers supplying WFP, who are normally better off than WFP's beneficiaries. (WFP 2006e, 24).

It is perhaps a measure of clarity in functional accountability that the WFP has engaged in open analysis of these problems, and states a clear ranking of primary beneficiaries ahead of secondary beneficiaries in terms of to whom it owes accountability –

> WFP's current policy is to procure food in a manner that is cost-efficient, timely and appropriate to beneficiary needs, encouraging procurement from developing countries to the extent possible. When procuring from developing country food markets, WFP's procurement procedures aim to avoid causing negative effects on those markets, including price rises that would harm the food security of the poor. (WFP 2006e, 4).

It is in the interaction of these different objectives regarding primary and secondary beneficiaries that the interests of potential beneficiaries come into play. First, in seeking to maximise purchases through cost-efficient and timely processes, the WFP is attempting to maximise the resources it has to distribute, and thereby reach primary beneficiaries who would otherwise be relegated to potential beneficiary status. Second, in seeking to have constructive impacts on developing countries through procurement, while recognising the potential for negative impacts, the WFP is seeking to support development in ways that reduce the generation of more hunger amongst the poor, and thereby meet the needs of other potential beneficiaries.

This is not to suggest that the WFP is exempt from criticism in these areas. NGO staff sometimes argue that in the field the WFP generates dependency, and works against development by displacing local agricultural produce with imported food aid (Anon. 2005). However, to the extent they exist, such problems are often linked to the constraints on WFP operation posed by donor requirements, which brings us to the third facet of accountability under examination.

Donor state accountability

The operation of power in the IFAR has always fundamentally hinged around the traditional donor states, in particular the United States. Reflecting this, as one informant commented when asked about WFP accountability, it is perhaps too often equated as accountability to the donors (Interview #4 2005) – an issue highlighted above in the discussion on operational accountability. Yet what accountability mechanisms operate to constrain donor power?

Within the IFAR, donor power is expressed in complex ways. Most obviously, it comes in the form of control of the resources. This is reflected not only in the possibility that any actions from the WFP which threaten donor interests will result in their walking away; it is also in the form of 'directed' donations which effectively pick and choose which WFP work to support, and in the use of restrictions on donations (WFP 2000). These restrictions can take many forms. For example, the provision by the US of in-kind donations mostly shipped by American flagged ships is one form; another is the Canadian requirement that a proportion of its cash donations be used to procure food from the Canadian producers (Barrett and Maxwell 2005, 264, fn6). Restrictions have often been placed on donations from the European Community (OECD 2006), including, for example, a requirement to use local purchasing of commodities. While requirements for local purchasing may appear progressive, even here the exercise of power is problematic. The WFP's experience has shown

> the importance of flexible cash resources to optimize food procurement efficiency. WFP cannot always decide where to buy. Some cash donations are accompanied by a donor's conditions on procuring in a certain manner or area or for a particular destination, and this obligates the commodities to be procured as requested. In 2004, 23 percent of WFP purchases were made in developed countries because this was considered the best and most cost-effective procurement option. However, a further 8 percent of WFP's total purchases were made in developed countries because the donations were tied by donors to purchases in their own countries.
>
> Restrictions on the use of cash can lead to delays in the provision of food, and lower cost-efficiency. This can be especially true when cash is restricted exclusively to local purchases, as surpluses are not always available on local markets and procurement could lead to food price inflation, thereby reducing food access for poor households. WFP may therefore have to wait until new supplies appear on the market.[9]
>
> The provision of untied donor resources gives WFP the flexibility to procure food locally, regionally or internationally, in a way that optimizes cost-efficiency, timeliness and appropriateness for beneficiary needs.
> (WFP 2006c, 17).

Through case studies, policy debate, and sometimes pressure from NGOs or other member states, some accountability is placed on donor country behaviour. Donor states occasionally criticise each other over the problems with pursuit of their interests where it appears they conflict with the interests of beneficiaries, though this is usually in the context of conflict or competition between such states outside the IFAR. For example, the DAC Report on food aid (OECD 2006) was used to frame criticism of US in-kind donation policy at the June 2005 EB meeting by European states in the context of debates over agricultural trade policy in the Doha Round process.

Such criticism occurs as much or more within the FAO's Consultative Sub-committee on Surplus Disposal (CSSD – see Chapter Three) as it does in the EB or WFP context. For example, in its 2007 report to the FAO, the CSSD reported the following exchange on cash-based versus monetized in-kind donations:

> A recurring point of discussion was the issue of donations of domestically produced commodities from a government to a government of an importing country, or an intergovernmental organization or a private institution for distribution, by means of sale on the open market of the importing country (Type 2 transactions). In 2005 and 2006, all donations by the United States, except one, took this form. Several delegates repeatedly expressed concerns over this type of transaction. At the 458th meeting, the Australian delegate expressed concern about the mechanism by which a donation of 25 000 metric tonnes of wheat from the United States to Indonesia was to be monetized. He expressed the view it raised the prospect of displacing normal commercial activity within Indonesia. At the 458th and 460th meetings, the Canadian delegate responded to donations by the United States to the Philippines and Mauritania, respectively, for monetization by expressing Canada's view that monetized food aid often displaces local agricultural production and viable commercial trade, and rarely addresses genuine humanitarian need. At the 458th meeting, the delegate from Canada noted that on 22 September 2005 the government of Canada increased the amount of Canadian food aid that can be purchased (i.e. cash-based food aid) in least-developed and low-income developing countries from 10 to 50 percent. The United States delegate responded that for all proposed donations, the United States conducts its usual market assessment and for all donations, a food gap has been identified. The United States agreed that efficiency is important, but that what is more important is that the food actually gets there. At the 457th meeting, he noted that as the EC has moved from in-kind to cash-based donations its total level of donations has declined. Discussions were also held over comments made by United States Trade Representative Robert Portman at a Senate Agriculture Committee hearing (21 September 2005) that there was plenty of evidence that cash-based food aid donations were prone to corruption. (FAO Committee on Commodity Problems 2007, 3-4).

In the WFP context, the most significant mechanism for donor accountability is probably the way the WFP Secretariat pushes the EB (in particular its donor and potential donor nation members) to see itself as responsible to beneficiaries. At the heart of such efforts lies the feed-the-hungry norm. The WFP interest in expanding its donor base (WFP 2004c) is also a form of generating donor accountability in two senses. Firstly, if WFP dependence on the small number of traditional donors is reduced and spread amongst other nations, corporations and individuals, then this will in turn constrain the power of the traditional (and other) donors. Secondly, the call for more donors can be seen as an attempt to hold potential donors accountable for their capacity to donate.

The limits of these various ad hoc mechanisms for donor accountability are a testament to the power of donors in the IFAR. The most powerful are, by definition, the least constrained by accountability. Nevertheless, as discussed in earlier chapters, the international food aid regime has exerted some influence on American policy-making. Reform in multilateral food aid since its early days and the credibility of WFP in food aid policy circles suggest it is far more than a mere cipher for American interests, and in turn that donor power is subtly constrained and redirected institutionally through the IFAR.

Conclusion

This analysis of inclusion and accountability in the WFP and IFAR seems a little inconclusive. This is partly because these features are not absolute or simple concrete things, they are contextual and relational. Nevertheless using them to focus an analysis of the WFP has helped build a partial picture of the operation of power and legitimacy in that organization and the wider IFAR. The picture is incomplete largely because I have not yet considered the third analytical feature of effectiveness.

Nevertheless, for all that it is incomplete, the picture so far does illustrate how the member states effectively form the polity of the WFP/IFAR, mainly through complex interactions with each other and the WFP Secretariat. Important political conflicts, for example over private fundraising, or procurement decision making are largely dealt with by state actors on the EB. NGOs are more closely aligned to their national governments than with each other in a global alliance of civil society or non-state actors. While the European NGOs do tend to operate transnationally as a bloc, this can be seen as reflecting the quasi-state existence of the European Union, demonstrated by the role of the European Commission as the one (technically) non-state actor on the EB capable of acting as a mini-polity in its own right. More convincingly, it reflects the European logic of US – European differences on agricultural trade that flow over into the food aid regime. Here, the European NGOs share interests and perspectives with their national governments, which happen to be grouped in a bloc contra the US.[10]

Engagement in partnership with the WFP by transnational corporations is a relatively new development. As with the NGOs, the path for TNCs to take when there are problems with the relationship is most likely through the most relevant member state representatives on the EB. This is because the TNC national level political relationships are much stronger and deeper than anything on offer through the WFP or UN system, within which responsiveness is built around a member state polity.

This brings us to the other important part of any picture of WFP governance – the hegemonic role of the US. On the one hand, processes of inclusion can be seen as according appropriate weight to the role of the US, for example through giving it the right to nominate the ED, and through the presence of the largest of the EB delegations. On the other hand, the collective operation of the EB, through its strong tradition of consensus decision-making does dilute American power on that body, as does the functioning of the WFP Secretariat as a powerful player within the IFAR, largely independent of particular member states. The main form in which this power is exercised is over the definition and operational meanings given to the feed-the-hungry norm. As we have seen, the international regime version of this norm is for all their congruence, both different from and increasingly influential on, the American domestic variant.

Endnotes

[1] In 2006 private donations equated to approximately 2.1 percent of total contributions (not counting extraordinary gifts in-kind) - US$55.5m out of US$2.7b (WFP 2007d, 58). In 2008 this increased to 2.9% - US$145m out of US$5.01b (WFP 2009, 41).

[2] Each General Rule corresponds to a General Regulation, with the Rule bearing the same Roman numeral as the Regulation to which it corresponds.

[3] '...one of the features of WFP governance admired by the secretaries of the UNDP, UNICEF and UNFPA Boards when they came to Rome to observe WFP's Board in October 2003' (WFP Governance Group 2005, 20).

[4] These factors should not be overplayed as an element in decisions on which states go onto the EB; typically such decisions will be made in the form of strategic calculations by states in which WFP EB membership is used as a bargaining chip for other positions or issues in the UN system and beyond. I am not privy to the decision-making and tactics lying behind the UK's period of non-membership of the EB, but it would seem a fair assumption that it resulted from bargaining amongst EU member states.

[5] It is not, perhaps, surprising that the advent of Nigeria as a potential commercial provider of food commodities to WFP coincides with its adoption of agricultural subsidies typical of the major donor nations. 'On assumption of office, we introduced the *Buyer of Last Resort Programme* to ensure that there is a guaranteed market for agricultural produce for farmers if the traditional market failed to absorb their produce. This was to eliminate market disruptions that might lead to lower income from agricultural enterprise' (Obasanjo 2005, 5).

[6] China's use of aid is closely connected with its growing projection of power through aid assistance and trade (e.g. Zafar 2007)), though its food assistance to North Korea is probably also concerned with reducing refugee flows, and other more immediate strategic concerns.

[7] This process occurred in parallel with measures to achieve the UN target of 50% women in the international professional staff grade. By 2004, with women making up more than 38% of international professional staff the WFP had gone from being a male dominated logistical agency to having 'one of the highest' rates of senior female employment in the UN system (WFP 2004e, 8-9 and Annex V, 15).

[8] There are also those from whom WFP purchases services, however they do not have the political significance of the food providers.

[9] See also WFP (2006e, 17): 'In some countries, particularly in Africa, infrastructure weaknesses and insecurity result in trading patterns being regional rather than internally integrated. For example, sorghum in northern Ethiopia can competitively supply southern Sudan, but would be too costly to move into southern Ethiopia. Thus, regional linkages are sometimes more important to market development and food security than local food market development.'

[10] The impacts of the North American Free Trade Agreement (NAFTA) on Mexico and Canada with respect to agricultural trade and food aid have not demonstrated the potential for an equivalent North American bloc so far. This is probably due to factors such as the US dominance of that grouping, which makes comparison to Europe difficult.

6
Effectiveness

Effectiveness, as much as accountability and inclusion, brings with it a connotation of legitimacy – an effective organization is surely as much to be welcomed as an inclusive and accountable one. As noted in Chapter One, effectiveness is being treated here as a form of 'output legitimacy', to use Scharpf's categorisation (Scharpf 1999). This Chapter considers the extent to which the WFP and, by extension the IFAR, can be considered effective and hence attaining legitimacy, at least in the output sense.

As effectiveness speaks to ends more than means, embedded within the idea of effectiveness are the inherently political notions of intentions, aims and goals. The first section of the chapter considers criteria against which the effectiveness of WFP can be judged, and proposes two forms of effectiveness against which it can be assessed. *Relative effectiveness* takes account of the nature of the organization and its institutional context as a UN agency, and the year by year work of the WFP under its mandate. *Absolute effectiveness* refers to more absolute standards with reference to the problems of global hunger and poverty.

The most pertinent analytical question about effectiveness is best framed as *how* effective, rather than simply *whether* effective. 'How effective?' has some ambiguity as a question. It can be read either as 'to what extent effective?', or 'by what means effective?' Both questions are important. In approaching these questions, firstly, the chapter's second section considers the evidence against the argument that the WFP is an effective agency in both relative and absolute senses. Specifically, this involves considering the types of criticism to which the WFP is subject, and the extent to which such criticism has substance. There has been impressively little direct criticism of the organization itself, though debates over the merits of food aid do involve indirect criticism of its mandate. This implies that, in broad terms, the WFP is relatively effective as a UN agency. The latter part of this section then considers the characteristics of the WFP that have helped it to become one of the most effective UN agencies. These include the advantages of US support, its physical location, voluntary funding base, logistical expertise and use of depoliticised management strategies. These characteristics are integrated via the feed-the-hungry norm.

The last section of the chapter considers the ways in which the very strengths of the WFP that have enabled it to evolve into such a respected organization, also make it incapable of being effective in a more absolute sense. After examining conceptual approaches to the causes of global hunger, the section focuses on the WFP's development operations and advocacy as areas in which it could potentially address global hunger more at the causal level, and details the limitations of its operations in that regard. Ultimately, however, though it is difficult to argue that the WFP is effective in the absolute sense, it is not entirely fair to judge the WFP in such terms. When it comes to output legitimacy, the WFP's relative effectiveness is of greatest significance.

Effectiveness in the international food aid regime

In order to consider the effectiveness of the WFP it is necessary to first define the criteria against which its effectiveness can be assessed. In some regards, this is where effectiveness overlaps with the other analytical features of legitimacy: inclusiveness and accountability are themselves potentially criteria for effectiveness. Given that terrain has been covered already in Chapter Five, effectiveness for the purposes of this chapter is framed by considering the extent to which the WFP achieves what it has been established for.

During its life, the conception of what the WFP is for has changed. From the 1950s and 1960s, there was a view that the deployment of development resources would enable the poorer countries in Asia, Africa, Latin America and the Middle East to grow sufficiently to raise the living standards of their populations towards those of the developed countries. In that context, there was a view of hunger as a problem based on inadequate production of food, and resolvable through technical advice and technological development. This view accorded the FAO a prominent role in dealing with the agricultural development that was the crucial means for combating hunger.

As we have seen in Chapter Three, the FAO view that food aid had some role to play in development dovetailed with the problem of agricultural surpluses in the US, leading to the establishment of the WFP. This recognised that successful agricultural production in the technologically advanced Western nations implied that given appropriate development, in particular in technologies of agricultural production, the poorer nations would themselves be able to produce sufficient food to feed their hungry. As a testament to this confidence, the WFP was established on an implicitly temporary basis – it was a necessary means to help redistribute some of the badly apportioned global food supply in the service of development; but the development itself would eliminate the need for food aid within a decade or so (FAO 1961).

There are echoes of this conceptual frame in the explosion of domestic emergency food relief organizations in the United States from the early 1980s noted in Chapter Four. A quarter of a century later, these organizations are thoroughly institutionalised, but at the time were seen as purely temporary responses to an 'emergency' situation (Poppendieck 1998, 102ff). Congress established the Temporary Emergency Food Assistance Program (TEFAP) in 1983; in 1990 the 'T' in TEFAP was changed from standing for 'Temporary' to standing for 'The' (Poppendieck 1998, 141).

The world food crisis came just over 10 years after President Kennedy had announced the 'Decade of Development', and was an undeniable signal that existing development approaches were insufficient or inadequate to dealing with the problem of hunger. Part of the response was to establish the International Fund for Agricultural Development (IFAD), as a mechanism for getting some of the OPEC wealth deployed into agricultural development. Other changes such as the creation of the IEFR and the establishment of a new WFP governing body – the CFA – with broad responsibility for food aid issues are best summed up as an increasing institutionalisation of international food aid, and important steps in the evolution of an international food aid regime with stronger capacities to respond to emergencies.

The 1980s saw increased importance in the roles of the International Monetary Fund (IMF) and World Bank in supplying finance for development (or even just state viability), albeit in return for the implementation of 'Washington Consensus' reforms in developing countries via 'structural adjustment' (Woods 2006, 47-64). It was at this point, as discussed in Chapter Four, that the WFP began to shift its organizational model from a development to a relief focus. While the 1990s saw the GATT/WTO join the other Bretton Woods institutions in establishing global neoliberal policy settings (Stiglitz 2003, Ch9), some backlash against the (by now) clear failures of 1980s policy also saw a shift into a stronger focus for the UN system on development. These shifts came together by the end of the twentieth century in the adoption by the UN of the Millennium Development Goals (MDGs). The eight MDGs are summarised as follows:

Goal 1 - Eradicate extreme poverty and hunger*
Goal 2 - Achieve universal primary education
Goal 3 - Promote gender equality and empower women
Goal 4 - Reduce child mortality
Goal 5 - Improve maternal health
Goal 6 - Combat HIV/AIDS, malaria and other diseases
Goal 7 - Ensure environmental sustainability
Goal 8 - Develop a global partnership for development
(UN 2000).

*Specifically this translates to: 'By 2015: Reduce by half the proportion of people living on less than a dollar a day. Reduce by half the proportion of people who suffer from hunger' (UN 2000).

The MDGs originated in part from commitments made at the World Food Summit of 1996. However, the original Summit goal of halving global poverty and hunger by 2015 was significantly modified in 2000 by adjusting it to refer only to the *proportion* of the global population affected by hunger and poverty, and backdating the starting reference point from 1996 to 1990 (FAO 2006c, 8). These changes had the effect of including a period of significant growth in China, and lowered the bar a long way from the original commitments made in 1996 (Pogge 2007). As the FAO notes, thanks to population growth, the raw number of people suffering from hunger may stay the same or even increase, while the proportion of the population who are hungry declines (FAO 2006c, 8).

The WFP is most clearly connected to the first of these MDGs, though it has some explicit program emphasis on many of the others, for example through designing projects to target women in general, pregnant women, mothers and children as beneficiaries. The 2009 Annual Report lists data on WFP activities in relation to all eight MDGs (WFP 2009, 8-9), though this is dominated by reference to MDG 1.

Despite the importance in recent years of the MDGs, however, the clearest exposition of the WFP mandate can be found in the WFP Mission Statement. The Mission Statement (see Appendix 4 for full statement) is a product of the Bertini period, originating in 1994. It expresses a consensual EB view of what the WFP is setting out to achieve both strategically and tactically. As noted in Chapter Five, a recommendation of the WFP Governance Group in 2000 that the Mission Statement be revised was rejected due to the conflicts this would raise in the EB.

The Statement is rather long - more than 1,000 words in full. Much of its content is concerned with articulating what constitutes effective multilateral food aid. A pertinent overview of the WFP mission, however, is expressed in the opening paragraph:

> WFP is the food aid arm of the United Nations system. Food aid is one of the many instruments that can help to promote food security, which is defined as access of all people at all times to the food needed for an active and healthy life. The policies governing the use of World Food Programme food aid must be oriented towards the objective of eradicating hunger and poverty. The ultimate objective of food aid should be the elimination of the need for food aid.
> (WFP 2007e; for the full Mission Statement see Appendix 4).

The two halves of this paragraph neatly encapsulate the two versions of effectiveness which can be applied to the WFP -- relative and absolute.

Relative effectiveness

The WFP is 'the food aid arm of the UN system' and food aid is 'one of…many instruments' for promoting food security. These characteristics indicate a wider institutional context within which the WFP operates, and its role as just one part of a system working for food security. In this context, its effectiveness must be understood as a relative concept. If the WFP is effective, this refers to the specific work it does within that larger context, and in relation to its own particular role. It means, implicitly, relatively effective within the UN system. As is noted later in the mission statement,

> No single agency has either the resources or the capacity to deal with all the problems of hunger and underdevelopment. Hence the importance WFP attaches to collaboration with other agencies, particularly with its parent bodies, the United Nations and FAO…(WFP 2007e).

Assessment of this effectiveness occurs primarily with reference to the WFP's operations. Thus relative effectiveness refers to the targeting of food aid, the garnering, transportation and delivery of it to (mainly) emergencies; the supplementing of this with deployment of food aid in a manner which aids social and economic development, maintaining asset bases and other important elements of improving food security. It is to such elements of operational effectiveness that much of the Mission

Statement speaks. It is to such operational effectiveness that Barrett and Maxwell or Clay (Barrett and Maxwell 2005; Clay 2003) refer when they speak of the WFP as a respected and successful agency.

Not all the goals of the WFP referred to in the Mission Statement are purely operational in the narrow sense of identifying the hungry poor and getting food to them in a manner consistent with a mix of short- (emergency) and long- (sustainable development) term goals of the recipient country. The Mission Statement also refers to some more broadly stated aims which legitimise functions *indirectly* associated with the immediate feeding of the hungry such as advocacy and fundraising:

> WFP will play its part as an active member of the United Nations system to bring the issue of hunger to the centre of the international agenda. In its dialogue with recipient governments and the aid community, WFP will advocate policies, strategies and operations that directly benefit the poor and hungry. (WFP 2007e).

Apart from referring to the broader institutional context within which the WFP operates, this statement makes reference to all the analytical features of legitimacy. The dialogue referred to speaks to the *inclusion* of donor state aid bureaucracies, NGOs and recipient states. The aim to advocate for 'policies, strategies and operations that directly benefit the poor and hungry speaks to the functional form of *accountability* (to primary and potential beneficiaries); direct benefit to the poor and hungry is implied as a concrete basis for assessing effectiveness.

Yet there are limits to the focus on the poor and hungry in the phrasing of this statement. Rather, 'the issue of hunger' seems itself to be the focus. This is consistent with the forms of 'advocacy' in which the WFP engages. Rather than advocacy *for* the hungry poor, the WFP sees its advocacy as *against* hunger. Paragraph 68 of the WFP's 2008-2011 Strategic Plan states the WFP view of the role of advocacy as follows:

> **Advocacy.** Political awareness is the first step in the fight against hunger. WFP has long been confronted with this fact and has thus created a broad and successful variety of instruments to disseminate information on, explain, and mobilize resources to fight global hunger. Advocacy will continue to play a prominent part in WFP's activities at the field, regional and global levels, in order to reach the whole range of actors in the fight against hunger. Furthermore, WFP will use the impact of its advocacy in the pursuit of a variety of objectives – from fundraising for its operations to influence on broader policy issues,

> such as climate change – that are instrumental in affecting positively the fight against hunger. (WFP 2008, 31).

Thus, the WFP tends to view advocacy in a relatively abstract way – in the Mission Statement it is referred to as advocacy for 'policies, strategies and operations'; elsewhere as 'raising awareness of hunger'. In light of this, it could be said that the problem on which WFP advocacy is focused is cast as a normative one - the lack of attention paid by wealthy countries to the existence of 'hunger', rather than the more concrete problem of improving the lot of the hungry poor themselves.

As with the WFP's avoidance of the Right to Food debate (discussed further below), this tendency to advocate for abstractions rather than people reflects the compromises necessary to maintain EB consensus. It is important not to confuse such rhetorical manoeuvres with a lack of real focus on directly benefiting the hungry poor which is strongly part of the WFP culture, but in that case such a concrete focus can itself run the risk of being too narrow. If the fundamental measure of effectiveness is limited to the provision of direct benefits to the poor and hungry this could imply a co-dependence with their ongoing presence. The second half of the Mission Statement's opening paragraph addresses this problem.

Absolute effectiveness

The statement that 'The ultimate objective of food aid should be the elimination of the need for food aid' is first and foremost a reflection on the trap of institutionalisation embedded in too narrow a focus on relative effectiveness. Poppendieck points to the problems posed for domestic US food aid organizations, which by dint of the processes of institutionalisation have come to rely on the hungry as a part of their reason for existing (Poppendieck 1998; Riches 1997b). An important means of avoiding this trap of institutionalisation lies in not losing sight of an absolute measure of effectiveness – 'the objective of eradicating hunger and poverty'. The first MDG reiterates this objective with a target of halving the proportion of the global population who are hungry by 2015.

Looking at effectiveness in such absolute terms can redirect our attention to some degree away from the specifics of WFP food aid operations towards the things it does to prevent hunger from remaining as a systemic global problem. Traditionally, this role has been seen as part of the WFP's development mandate, through which the WFP seeks to attack the underdevelopment which is seen as the root cause of hunger and poverty. Although an advocacy role which highlighted and criticised the global economic systems which maintain and intensify hunger and poverty could also be defined as relevant to absolute effectiveness, and indeed is undertaken by the UN Special Rapporteur on the Right to Food (see e.g. Ziegler 2005), the WFP's definition of advocacy is cut from a much narrower cloth as noted above.

The ways in which the WFP attempts to be effective in the wider, absolute sense are subject to significant limits which point to the compromises and constraints posed by the nature of legitimacy in the IFAR. This point will be developed in more detail later in the chapter.

The absolute/relative effectiveness distinction has tended to be codified in food aid by the development/emergency dichotomy. To use the well known rhetorical questions – is it better to give a fish to a starving man, or teach him how to fish; is it better to run an ambulance to the bottom of a cliff or build a fence? The answer from the WFP is, given that many are too hungry to lift a fishing rod, or are well past the bounds of any future fence, that the WFP must try and do both, through its dual mandate.

The development/emergency relief dichotomy both calls up real differences, for example when it is used to differentiate different kinds of WFP operations, and simplifies a more complex reality. The aid community and practitioners within the WFP, NGOs and government agencies are constantly attempting to blur the differences – to make emergency assistance as congruent with and similar to development assistance as possible; to organize operations so that they shift seamlessly from one mode to another, as noted in Chapter Four. Barrett and Maxwell argue that the greatest potential for innovative use of food aid is probably in the 'blurry' area between project and emergency use (Barrett and Maxwell 2005, 122; also Singer 2001). Indeed, they critique an argument for the WFP to become the lead UN agency on all emergency response as such a proposal does not deal with the fuzzy boundaries and linkages between emergency operations and development projects (Barrett and Maxwell 2005, 220).

Similarly, the distinction between relative and absolute effectiveness is analytically useful, but it is important not to lose sight of the complex interconnections between the two. Both are implicit elements of the WFP Mission Statement, which in its structure attempts to incorporate them in a single approach. While it might be possible to distinguish between absolute and relative efficiency analytically, they are not opposed to each other. It is their interrelationship that ultimately constructs an overall sense of the WFP's legitimacy as it relates to its effectiveness in achieving its mission.

Assessing the relative effectiveness of the WFP

We turn now to look at criticisms of the WFP and what they suggest about its effectiveness.

On the whole, the WFP seems in remarkably good standing for a UN organization. Good standing is certainly implied by donor behaviour - as Webb notes, 'from 1994 to 2001 the donor response to WFP's food aid request within the United Nations consolidated appeals process was on average 85 percent, compared with only 58 percent for all other sectors combined' (Webb 2003, 10, fn8). The leading food aid expert Edward Clay describes WFP as 'unquestionably a success story with the UN system' (Clay 2003, 707); a claim echoed by a range of others (Barrett and Maxwell 2005; Bertini 2005a; Clay 2003; Singer 2001), even including vociferous UN critics such as former Australian Foreign Minister Alexander Downer (Smiles 2008).

In the context of extensive criticisms of the UN system, its agencies and operational failings (Bolton 2008; Esty 2002; Hancock 1989; Judt 2007; Klingebiel 1999; Maren 1997), the relative lack of serious and significant criticism of the WFP in recent years also implies it is a relatively effective agency. However, there is some applicable criticism that should be considered in relation to WFP's claims for effectiveness.

Critique of the WFP

Criticism of the WFP can be loosely grouped into four different categories: indirect via critique of food aid; direct through failings of specific projects or field activities; concern that it is too close to member states (donor or recipient); or, that it competes inappropriately for funds.

The first category - indirect criticism based on a broader critique of food aid - has taken various forms relating to the alleged benefits for rich nations, the costs to poor nations, and depending on whether it refers to development or emergency relief forms of aid.

Food aid has long been criticised for its links with disposal of rich nation surplus agricultural produce (Cathie 1982; George 1991; Rothschild 1993) and the potential for disrupting local agricultural markets and creating food aid dependency in recipients (Schultz 1993; Shaw and Clay 1993, 1). These criticisms largely refer to the development uses of food aid, regarding it as an inherently limited or flawed form of development aid that is more about serving donor interests than recipient interests or the interests of hungry people. These critiques highlight the problems with food aid due to the marginal and uncertain nature of the resources involved. Food aid has been notoriously volatile (OECD 2006) and pro-cyclical - least available when stocks are low and commodity prices high, which is just when it is most needed (Barrett and Maxwell 2005; Clay 2003; OECD 2006). These characteristics tend to work against the interests of recipients and for the interests of donors, implying food aid is inherently regressive. However, these problems are most significant in relation to bilateral and development forms of food aid, and tend to be minimised by multilateral and emergency relief modes (Barrett and Maxwell 2005; OECD 2006).

Another critique of food aid is that it changes consumption patterns and increases dependency – for example by beneficiaries developing a taste for the aid commodities instead of their indigenous foods. Uvin argues that food aid forms only a small part of the systems which create tastes and consumption patterns (Uvin 1994, 171-2), and notes that the main indication that food aid has this effect comes from donor rhetoric pitched to domestic interests about the development of markets (Uvin 1992). Barrett and Maxwell discuss the record of food aid and changes in recipient consumption behaviors and conclude there is some evidence that poorly targeted food aid can have deleterious impacts by disrupting or changing local consumption patterns (Barrett and Maxwell 2005, 181-2), though poor targeting again tends to be minimized by multilateral and emergency relief modes.

The view of a legitimate role for food aid in development expressed by Hopkins and Uvin in the early 1990s (Hopkins 1992; Uvin 1994) has been echoed more recently by Barrett and Maxwell and the OECD DAC. This work seems relatively convincing in that it has drawn on considerable empirical research and not hesitated to criticise food aid as problematic when not used appropriately (Barrett and Maxwell 2005; OECD 2006). In any event, the shift from development food aid to a focus on emergency relief by the WFP has largely neutralised the application of these indirect criticisms to it. In such debates on food aid, the WFP benefits both from its multilateral status in a context where criticisms tend to focus on problematic bilateral food aid programs (Barrett and Maxwell 2005, 63), and from its status as an operational agency, which tends to get it put into the same category as operational relief NGOs (Barrett and Maxwell 2005, 219ff).

The use of food aid in emergency relief has generally been acknowledged as beneficial (Barrett and Maxwell 2005; OECD 2006; Uvin 1994, 172), provided that it is appropriately targeted and controlled. However, the use of food aid for emergency relief, though less controversial, has still been the subject of some criticism. Such food aid can be vulnerable to a number of problems, such as donor delays, corruption and misuse (Uvin 1994, 158–60). George, for example, argued that food aid (both development and emergency) helps 'shore up repressive client states' (George 1991, xiv). Similarly, de Waal argues that the development of UN relief work had led to the internationalization of responsibility for famines, resulting in a 'retreat from domestic accountability in famine-vulnerable countries' (de Waal 1997, 70).

Although, as Uvin argues, there might not be much clear evidence of such a structural impact of food aid on state accountability, there is considerable evidence of recipient governments using food aid to buy-off groups, such as the military or urban middle class in Bangladesh (Sen 1981, Ch9) or Sudan (Uvin 1994, 165–71; also de Waal 1997, Ch5). In the case of North Korea, Jean Ziegler and various NGOs have accused the WFP and other agencies of effective complicity with the regime by allowing food aid to be controlled and used to the benefit of the military and elite, rather than those at most risk of disease and death from starvation (Noland 2003, 7, 11).

Similarly, there is evidence of emergency relief food aid, along with other types of aid (Terry 2000), becoming a resource which is deployed by belligerents in armed conflict. For example, Maren interviewed a leader in the Somali Salvation Democratic Front (SSDF), Mohamed Abshir Waldo in Nairobi in 1995. In the interview, Waldo explained why 'SSDF had turned down food aid from the UN' when they were offered it in 1992, (despite being in a region not affected by famine):

> 'If 10,000 tons of food arrives it will be sold on the black market and the proceeds used to buy arms,' he said. 'It becomes an arms race. It means war. If food comes we lose our ability to control the peace and the stability of the region. Everybody will want to have a share, but that's not possible. It's been three years since there was any food aid and three years since there was the hijacking of a truck. The only trucks that are hijacked are the ones carrying food aid. No private truck with private cargo has been hijacked.' (Maren 1997, 103).

Waldo also noted the regional economy was functioning with trade and production, but food aid would have disrupted all this – for example through the nomads leaving their animals to get it. However, commenting on why, in the end food aid was accepted, he depicted a situation far removed from the normal evaluations of food aid projects:

> 'On the other hand, we could not say we did not want food. We wanted the food to buy arms. The donors were giving food to our enemies and they were buying arms. We did not even dare not to protest very loudly for aid because otherwise the population would say, why are we not getting our share of the food? And secondly, what do you do about the liquidity that the food will bring in, the selling of the food, realizing money, and then buying arms?'
>
> 'It's like a mini arms race fueled with food. If your enemy does not buy arms you don't have to be armed yourself. Or if they rearm and get the finance and so on, then you need to rearm also, to balance. Just like the big powers were doing.'
>
> 'So we decided to minimize the damage. What we actually did - why we had peace - was to give 90 percent of the food straight to the militias. That was not what the donors intended, but the donors were giving it to our enemy. What would you do?'
> (Maren 1997, 104).

Maren further notes the way that emergency food aid disrupts traditional barter and exchange systems of coping with famine by bringing recipients into camps, and also exposes them to greater risks from disease (Maren 1997, 21).

As well as documenting ways in which the application of food aid to an 'emergency' can expand and intensify that emergency and institutionalize conflict and dependency, Maren also documents the biases within the system against recognising and mitigating these impacts. His critique applies broadly to NGOs, government and UN agencies, all of whom ignored evidence of problems:

> Document after document said that the entire [Somali relief] operation was a wasteful fraud. I'd sat on a cold cement floor [at UNHCR] for two days searching through thousands of papers and not one of them was a positive independent report about people's lives being saved or of children being provided with a brighter future. Every document and confidential memo over a nine-year period concerned the politics of the relief operation, showing that everyone involved at every level knew it was a politically driven fiasco pushing Somalia to the edge of anarchy.
>
> Yet through all of this, the UN agencies, CARE, and other NGOs stayed in Somalia. They stayed for the contracts. They stayed for the money. They were, in every sense of the word, mercenaries.
> (Maren 1997, 135).

This amounts to one of the most powerful indictments of the work of the WFP to be found, though it is framed only in an indirect manner, by including WFP in a wide list of culpable actors. Maren's critique is echoed by de Waal (de Waal 1997, 159-78), who bluntly states that 'the UN specialized agencies failed in Somalia throughout' (de Waal 1997, 172). De Waal documents in particular the relative failures of the WFP and CARE compared to a more successful food aid operation by the International Committee of the Red Cross (de Waal 1997, 169, 174-5, 182).

More recently, a UN inquiry appears to have uncovered deep and chronic problems with WFP's food aid distributions in Somalia, involving diversion of aid from targeted recipients to armed belligerents and corrupt individuals (Gettleman and Ibrahim 2010; Gettleman and MacFarquhar 2010). The report of the Monitoring Group on Somalia pursuant to Security Council Resolution 1853 (2008) (Bryden, Laloum, et al. 2010) details the significance of the WFP to the UN's humanitarian work in Somalia, where it accounted for almost 60% of the UN's $850 million assistance budget for 2009 (Bryden, Laloum, et al. 2010, 60). Worth approximately $200 million in 2009, 'WFP transportation contracts to Somali businessmen constitute the greatest single source of revenue in Somalia and just three contractors receive 80 per cent of this business.' (Bryden, Laloum, et al. 2010, 60). The same three contractors also owned and controlled local NGO 'implementing partners' responsible for certifying that the food aid being transported has been delivered – a situation in which diversion of food aid from its intended recipients increases dramatically. Moreover,

> Since WFP requires Somali businessmen to arrange for their own protection when delivering food aid to those in need, transporters have built the costs of protection into their contracts. The provision of food aid has thus become a militarized business, with businessmen maintaining their own militias in order to protect their warehouses, convoys and distribution points. Not surprisingly, WFP contractors have maintained some of the largest private militias in southern Somalia.

The report notes,

> As in other conflict zones around the world, the high volume of food deliveries to a disoriented population in a zone of contested military control makes it a conducive environment for diversion. Access to some camps is effectively controlled by armed groups, who oversee food distribution in order to take credit for aiding the people under

> their control. The families of combatants are routinely registered as internally displaced persons in order to receive rations, inflating the numbers of those in need.
> (Bryden, Laloum, et al. 2010, 61).

Most prominently reported were claims that up to 50% of food aid was being diverted from the intended recipients. The report claimed that 'Percentages vary, but sources interviewed by the Monitoring Group describe an approximate division of 30 per cent for the implementing partner and local WFP personnel, 10 per cent for the ground transporter, and 5 to 10 per cent for the armed group in control of the area.... The remainder of the consignment is distributed to the recipient population.'

The WFP rejected the report's claims as based on hearsay and lacking evidence, and invited an inquiry to establish facts about food aid diversion in Somalia. Others in the aid and development sector pointed to inevitable problems with corruption and diversion that arose when operating in complex, militarized and poorly governed contexts (Bailey 2010). While the politics of aid in Somalia since the 1980s have arguably been distinctively bad; it is not clear that the problems Maren, de Waal and the Monitoring Group document are necessarily typical of or broadly applicable to WFP operations.

NGO criticisms of WFP's complicity with oppressive regimes or belligerents are also made more broadly of other UN agencies and some NGOs (Terry 2000), as part of a wider debate about engagement or withdrawal characterised by complex moral and political considerations. Similarly, de Waal's critique is part of a larger argument querying the institutionalization of humanitarian work and its failings in terms of absolute effectiveness. His argument has fewer implications for relative effectiveness as it is mainly concerned with the ways in which NGOs, governments and intergovernmental organizations all operate systemically to perpetuate famines. As such, it will be considered in more detail in the discussion of absolute effectiveness below.

The criticisms of the WFP in Somalia, while forming part of a wider critique of institutionalized emergency food aid, also fall in the second category of criticism – that of the failings of specific WFP projects or field actions. This category of criticism largely takes the form of anecdotes from the field, implying that the WFP is variously overly bureaucratic, insufficiently responsive to recipient needs, overly responsive to rich donors, unable to address the political or economic bases of malnutrition, and destructive of fragile agricultural markets or social systems in recipient countries (Anon. 2005; de Waal 1997, 174–5). Also in this category, in 1994 an evaluation sponsored by three WFP

EB member-states – Canada, the Netherlands and Norway (Chr. Michelsen Institute 1994) – contributed to the shift away from development projects with criticisms of the effectiveness of a number of WFP projects (Barrett and Maxwell 2005, 62; Clay 2003, 700; Shaw 2001, 245–6). Leaving aside this internal critique, it is, perhaps, only to be expected that an organization such as the WFP will suffer from bureaucracy, insensitivity and similar faults leading to such criticism. Perhaps of more interest in the context of its relative efficiency is whether such criticisms occur frequently and with such vehemence as to suggest systemic governance problems. They do not appear to.

The third category of criticisms relates to the WFP's multilateral character. On the one hand, the WFP's closeness to, even dependence on, the US as by far its most significant donor also leads to concern about its multilateral credentials at times (Barrett and Maxwell 2005, 220; Clay 2003). The IFAR is a regime in which the US has been the hegemonic actor, though the extent of US dominance has waxed and waned to various degrees since the early years of the international food aid regime in the early 1960s when the US share of world food aid was in the order of 95 percent (Hopkins 1992, 231). More generally, the WFP is criticised for being excessively oriented towards its donors, rather than its intended beneficiaries, through the control they exercise in volunteering and directing donations. While this criticism is in many ways accurate, it relates to structural characteristics of power in the IFAR, and more broadly within the global system. These structural issues relate most significantly to the systems which maintain global hunger as a problem, and hence to the WFP's absolute effectiveness. The implications of the role of donors for WFP's relative effectiveness are discussed further below.

On the other hand, recipient governments can be complicit in creating problems of conflict, displacement and hunger amongst their populations; well documented examples have included Ethiopia and Sudan (Clay and Holcomb 1986; de Waal 1997; Meredith 2005), North Korea (Noland 2003) or more recently Zimbabwe (Commonweal 2007). As an intergovernmental organization and part of the UN system, the WFP works through governments and must do so ahead of concerns with actions or inaction which led to the hunger crisis, though there are some limits placed on involvements where imminent death from starvation is no longer a likelihood in accordance with wider UN policy (Bertini 2005b). As a consequence, at times NGOs have accused it of being too close to such regimes (Interview #9 2005). Such criticisms reflect the structural difference between NGOs and intergovernmental organizations, and are of more significance to absolute rather than relative effectiveness.

The last category of criticism is that the WFP is competing inappropriately for funds. As noted in Chapter Five, this criticism has come from European NGOs who see the WFP as competing (unfairly) with them by engaging in private sector fundraising (Interview #9 2005; Interview #12 2005; Bredholt 2005; Schenkenberg 2005). While the fear of the NGOs is that the WFP may prove too effective in its pursuit of private sector support (and thereby crowd them out), the other side of the private fundraising coin is its distorting effect on WFP's operations, and the prospect that the costs may outweigh the benefits. For example, the following anecdote suggests some problems with the branding and competitive aspects of fundraising:

> 'At 3 p.m. the first relief flight appeared over the newly-liberated airport. It was a UN World Food Programme flight: the first for weeks to arrive at Mogadishu international airport. It circled for over half an hour to give Mitchell, the WFP man on the ground, time to ensure that all the television cameras were trained on the aircraft's WFP insignia. It landed. It slowly edgea its way along the tarmac. It taxied for 20 minutes. It usually takes five minutes to maneuver from the runway to the airport apron but the UN had to get its publicity just like everybody else. Mr Mitchell was heard saying with elation how he had secured more live television broadcasts for WFP than his "rival" UN agency, UNICEF.' (Mark Huband reporting for *The Guardian* cited in Maren 1997, 203).

More recently, in February 2005 the WFP instituted a Walk the World fundraising (and awareness raising) event, establishing a Division to organize the event. In Walk the World, on a specified day local supporters in cities around the world undertake a publicly organized walk, led by associated celebrities and ambassadors. A review in January 2007 noted that the WFP Management Plan for 2006-07 had allocated US$2.6 million to fund the costs of the 2006 Walk, 'as an advance in the expectation that it would be recovered from sponsorship and the proceeds of the walk'. However, receipts

> directly attributable to the 2006 walk and related events were US$1.872 million - US$1.7 million in donations to WFP child hunger projects and US$172,000 in sponsorship income…
>
> … More than 60 private companies contributed cash in support of one or more local walks, but only US$10,000 was received from corporate sponsors for overheads. (WFP 2007c, 8).

As a result of this shortfall, the WFP was forced to cover the Walk the World income deficit of US$2.6 million from its General Fund. (WFP 2007c, 8). In other words, the WFP spent $2.6 million to raise $1.7 million for child hunger projects, along with some (unquantifiable) awareness. In the context of a Program Support biennial budget of some $370 million, and overall resource deployment of $5.6 billion these amounts of money are negligible, but it is not good for their credibility when service organizations spend more money on fundraising than they actually raise. A critic might point to an uncomfortable statistic not provided to the people donating whereby for every 17 cents donated, the WFP had notionally spent 26 cents generating the donation.

In such matters, the WFP is not very different from UNICEF (which established the model for UN private fundraising), or from many NGOs, which perceive a need to play to a donor audience and invest in their brand so that they can garner donations. For critics such as Maren[1] and de Waal, the distortions to the actual humanitarian work necessitated by these processes too often come at the cost of those meant to benefit from the aid. On the other hand, the WFP would argue that by publicizing its work it is informing the audiences (predominantly in Western countries) about the problem of hunger, motivating those people to do something about a problem that it would otherwise be very easy for them to ignore. This means that the actual direct raising of money is not necessarily the primary aim of such work. It can, for example, help build and maintain a constituency of support for government donations to the WFP, or government allocations to aid more generally, and may increase contributions to or involvement with NGOs working to address the problem of hunger. Moreover, while other UN agencies and NGOs are promoting their work and actively seeking donations, the WFP must compete in such activities or risk losing any capacity to broaden its funding base, which is already heavily reliant on one country.

Concluding comments on WFP critique

Clearly the WFP is potentially or actually subject to a range of criticisms. However many such criticisms are not unique to the organization, but tend to be generic to other humanitarian organizations, or other intergovernmental organizations. Also, specific criticisms of food aid tend to be less applicable to the WFP than to other state or NGO actors. While no organization as big and complex as the WFP is without faults, poor practice and error, an argument that the WFP is generally regarded with respect as a relatively effective UN agency can be sustained. In the following subsection the reasons for this are examined in more detail.

Factors in WFP (relative) effectiveness

To argue that the WFP is, in relative terms, successful and effective as an intergovernmental organization is to say that it manages and uses its resources responsibly and accountably in attempting to achieve its mandate, and is regarded as a credible, (and ultimately legitimate) organization by member states and their citizenry. The following discussion examines five interrelated organizational and structural factors contributing to this effectiveness - leadership, location, focus, donor processes, and hegemonic support. The feed-the-hungry norm provides a normative core enabling these factors to interact in a fashion which ameliorates the problems for legitimacy posed by the double-edged nature of many of them.

Leadership

The role of leadership in the WFP's effectiveness has been discussed to some extent already in Chapters Four and Five. Ingram and Bertini were both capable Executive Directors who reformed and renewed the WFP and built on its strengths. While different in many ways, each had a combination of administrative and political skills that enabled them both to oversee effective operational management, and the building of a constructive intergovernmental governance culture around the IFAR feed-the-hungry norm. Having survived a bruising struggle over FAO control under Ingram's leadership, under Catherine Bertini the WFP became seen as an exemplar for managerial reform within the UN system. Reflecting the respect for her leadership of the WFP, Bertini was appointed Under Secretary-General for Management in the UN on completion of her second term as WFP ED in 2002.[2]

Central to the effectiveness of this leadership model was its entwining of the political and administrative around the feed-the-hungry norm in a manner that emphasised technical competence, minimised corruption and, lastly, depoliticized governance. Of course, governance is a fundamentally political process; here 'depoliticized' refers to the absence of a layer of conflict over different state interests with only tangential relevance to the WFP mandate. Such conflict (such as competition between Cold War superpowers, or Middle Eastern states) has all too often complicated the governance of intergovernmental organizations (Talbot 1990).

The effective management of WFP governance politics, together with competent management of operational systems and an organizational focus on technical and logistical problems contributed to creating a self-image from the EB down of the WFP as that classically depoliticized entity: the service organization.

Focus

A number of interviewees made comments on the way in which feeding hungry people is not political and lends itself to clear measurement and accountability (Bertini 2005b; Interview #12 2005). These advantages derive much more from emergency relief than from development projects, emphasising the way in which a shift to an emergency relief emphasis fitted closely with managerial reform. The shift to an emergency relief emphasis arguably has simplified operational and management tasks, enabling them to be discharged efficiently and effectively. Also, other UN leaders apparently regard WFP as advantaged by its 'focus' on food and emergency relief (Bertini 2005b).

It should be noted, however, that this focus is not necessarily all advantageous. The other side of the coin to this focus is the narrowness of the resource base – food. This has also led to problems with resourcing of the work of the WFP, and limits to its attempts to maintain a development aspect to its mandate.

Location

A further factor in WFP effectiveness is the location of its headquarters in Rome. A number of informants commented on the advantage the WFP has in being located in Rome, rather than New York. In their view this removed a layer of politicking from its governance which tends to be a problem for New York based UN organizations (Interview #4 2005; Interview #12 2005; Bertini 2005a; Bertini 2005b). In turn, this has assisted considerably in its managerial reforms and distanced the WFP from some of the morale problems afflicting other parts of the UN. The Rome location also seems to have a subtle effect undercutting expectations or perceptions of American dominance and control both on the part of the US itself, and on the part of other state and non-state actors.

Rome has not always been an advantageous location. Arguably during its battle for autonomy from FAO during the 1980s, the geographic closeness to FAO and distance from the UN in New York weakened the WFP's position at times; however, since the resolution of that issue in 1992 the WFP has been organizationally advantaged by distance from New York.

Donor Processes

The donation process by which WFP garners its funding allows effective tying and directing of aid by the donors.

Tied aid can be meant in different senses. Commonly it refers to aid which requires something of the recipient agency or country to the benefit of the donor (Kanbur 2003, 6) – for example, the employment or use of donor national companies to provide aid related services (OECD 2006). A notorious example in food aid is the legislated requirement to use US national ships to transport at least 75 percent of US food aid (Barrett and Maxwell 2005, Ch5).

In a multilateral context tying can also be taken to refer to what Barrett and Maxwell call 'earmarking', or directing – where the precise recipient and purpose for the aid are specified when (and if) it is donated. This means donors can pick and choose to some degree which emergencies (or development projects) they will donate to and under what circumstances. The WFP's 'genuine' multilateral aid – aid that is donated to it to use as a multilateral organization without specific member-state strings attached – is relatively small. Barrett and Maxwell recently estimated that the proportion of WFP resources not earmarked had fallen to 20 percent (Barrett and Maxwell 2005, 64, Fig.3.2), although this 'bilateralization' through WFP has operated in some form for many years (Ingram 2005b; Uvin 1994). More recently there has been some fluctuation, with the proportion of non-earmarked resources falling to 9.5 percent in 2007 before increasing to 18 percent in 2008 (WFP 2009, 37).

Assessing the extent to which donations are directed is complicated by the difference between pledged amounts of aid and actual amounts when adding in additional emergency aid provision. For example, US pledges amounted to $200 million in 2005, of which an estimated $40 million was not directed, but the actual provision was in the region of $1 billion when other emergency funding (all directed, in the sense that it is allocated for a specific purpose) is added in (Landis 2005).

While bilateralization is seen as a problem by the WFP, and would appear to undermine its multilateral nature and capacity, it also results in relatively high levels of donor satisfaction with the WFP, and arguably could be said to strengthen its capacity in other ways. For example, the wealthy donor nations (grouped in List D) are generally positive about the WFP, regard it as relatively accountable, and are not engaged in power struggles with the numerically larger numbers of recipient nations on the EB. The significance of this can be seen in the centrality Bertini gives to instituting donations as the basis for UN resources as an essential element of UN reform (Bertini 2005a), though, as noted in

Chapter Five, it also leads to some criticism of the WFP as being more oriented to accountability to donors than to recipients.

Also, it should be noted that the dynamics of donor control are complicated by the capacity of the WFP secretariat to work up proposals for projects with one or more recipient countries, lobby for support amongst EB member-states (and NGOs who it may well contract with to deliver the aid), and put forward a proposal at the Board. The Board dynamics are such that donors are usually reluctant to be seen to be opposing well-prepared project proposals, and it would be a mistake to equate donor power with control over WFP activities.

These comments on donor processes illustrate the interactions between the posited legitimacy features of accountability, inclusion and effectiveness, and underline the need for care in assuming the distinctions between them are of more than limited analytical use.

Hegemonic support

Pre-eminent amongst the wealthy donor countries is the US, which has never provided less than one third of WFP resources, and in many years has provided close to half – that is, as much as the rest of the world put together (see Table 5.1; Chart 6.1). The convention of the US nominating the Executive Director has been noted in Chapter Five. Strong US support has been crucial to resourcing the WFP at levels that have enabled it to be effective. Simply put, without this support, the WFP would be a shadow of itself – a relatively insignificant organization whose worth would almost certainly be under question.

Clay and the WFP itself (Clay 2003; WFP 2004c) suggest that this American dominance poses risks for the WFP by diminishing its multilateral credentials. Also, though more within the international trade regime than the IFAR, there is considerable criticism of US agricultural protection and links with its food aid policies (Clapp 2004). At the 2005 EB Annual meeting these criticisms spilled over into the most significant debate and controversy of the meeting.

In the draft strategic plan under discussion at this meeting, the WFP Secretariat flagged the Doha Round agricultural trade reform debate as potentially involving a risk to food aid resources. From an EU perspective (Clapp 2004), US bilateral concessional grants and export credits (which the US classifies as food aid) are disruptive to free trade in agriculture. From the US perspective, the EU position on reducing US agricultural trade protections amounted to an attack on food aid and therefore ultimately on the world's hungry poor. This reflects the view of the domestic US food aid lobby which sees the whole food aid

Chart 6.1: US contributions as a percentage of total WFP contributions, 1996-2005

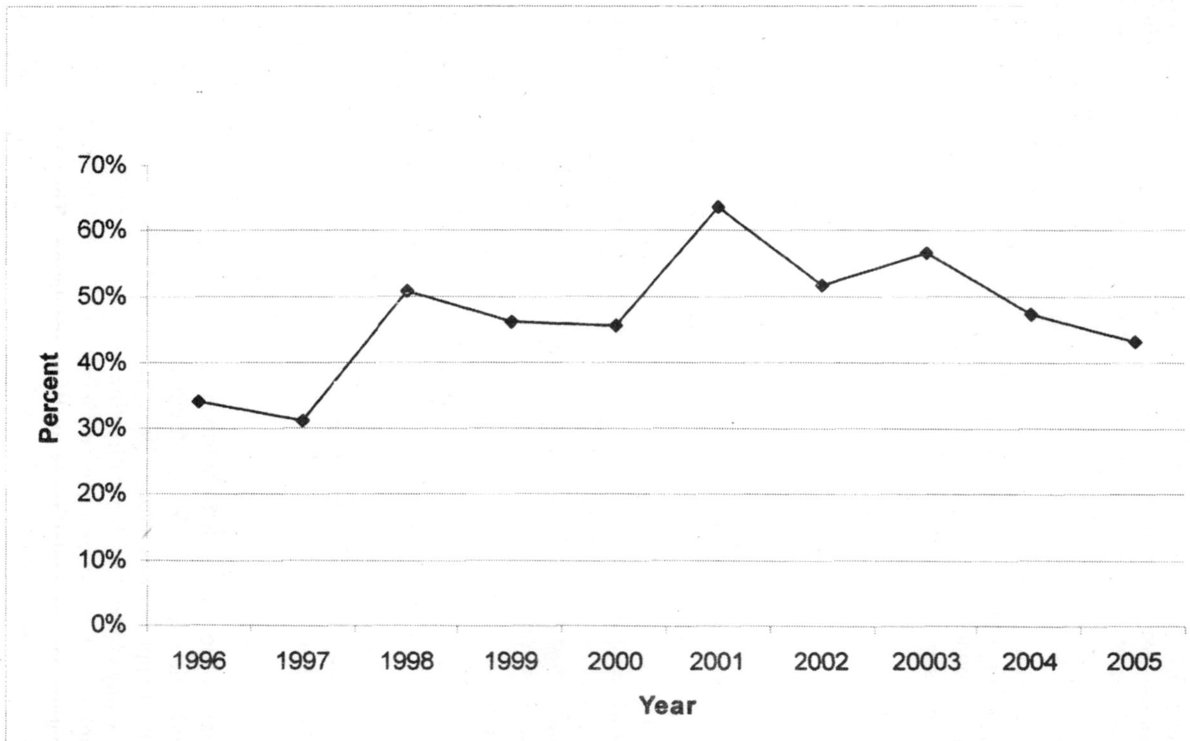

Data Source: (Hanrahan and Canada 2006, Appendix Table 2, 6).

apparatus as built on a coalition of interests and support, and being placed at risk if any part of it – such as export credits, or the use predominantly of in-kind aid, or monetization – is removed (Zeigler 2005). At the meeting, the EU response was a blunt rejection of any strategic plan containing a statement that agricultural trade reform posed a risk to food aid. In turn, the US delegation insisted that it was a true statement of a risk and could not be deleted. The compromise outcome brokered by the (Danish) EB President was to leave the statement of risk in but to acknowledge it simply as the view of the Executive Director.

The complexity of the US relationship with the WFP is reflected in decision making about projects involving recipients about whom there are US sensitivities. Thus, on the one hand Uvin noted a tendency of '[c]ertain donors, and especially the US' to use the pledging process to 'delay or block food aid for particular countries or projects - even if they have formally approved these uses of food aid in the CFA'. Yet Uvin also noted 'on the other hand, all through the 1980s, the WFP has given food aid to countries such as Cuba, Vietnam, Nicaragua and Iran, against explicit US desires' (Uvin 1994, 149).

Consistent with the expression of such desires, there has been a history of periodic American criticism, at least within the EB, over WFP emphasis and direction undercutting any charge of WFP being a mere client of or cipher for the US (Bertini 2005b; Hopkins 1990, 186ff; Ingram 2005b; Landis 2005). The experiences of Bertini and Ingram also suggest that it is important not to overestimate the coherence and co-ordination of American policy in relation to food aid, beyond a strong Congressional constituency for it in domestic, bilateral and multilateral forms. On balance, notwithstanding concerns about the potential for American dominance to undermine its multilateral credentials, there is a general perception that the WFP does good work and helps deploy US resources constructively.

Concluding comments on factors in effectiveness

Many of the factors that contribute to the WFP's relative effectiveness are double edged. The WFP's focus can also be viewed as a narrow and limited approach; its strong US support can also be seen as dependence on a single resource; donor direction of resources can be seen as further display of donor power and politicization of multilateral assistance. Its location can be isolating as well as insulating. The WFP's relative effectiveness can therefore appear as occurring almost in spite of its organizational characteristics, as well as because of them. The most significant criticisms of the WFP point to precisely the negative implications of these characteristics.

Given this, the WFP's relative effectiveness must be seen as contingent and historical; more a conjunction of circumstances than the result of a careful plan originating in the early 1960s. Consistent with this, Clay attributes WFP success primarily to its adaptability and piecemeal and ad hoc reforms rather than to any 'grand design' (Clay 2003, 707).

Nevertheless, Clay emphasizes the risks posed to the organization by two important tensions: an increase in American donations and decline in EU contributions leading to an erosion of WFP's 'multilateral character'; and the almost complete displacement of development work with relief work leading to a disjunction with WFP's mandate which still assumes a considerable role in development work. It is to the implications of these tensions as the source of significant limits to WFP effectiveness in a more absolute sense that we now turn.

Limitations of WFP effectiveness

> ...Worldwide 850 million people around the world continue to suffer from chronic hunger and the number is actually rising by 4 million a year. That is hard to understand, especially when our planet is wealthier than ever, and produces more than enough food to feed everyone.
>
> James Morris, WFP Executive Director, 2 November 2006 (WFP 2006h).

The WFP enjoys relatively high levels of legitimacy in its exercise of global governance. It is respected as capably undertaking worthwhile work. There is no doubt that the WFP has fed starving people facing death and disease in their millions over the course of its history. If US food aid policy has been regressive in many instances, and remains so in some of its uses, the WFP has given at least a proportion of it a more progressive role. Critiques of the WFP being dominated by the US or providing food aid in ways which sometimes undermine development, for all that they have elements of truth to them, tend to be rendered carping by its achievements.

Even before the global food crisis of 2007-08, while the proportion of the global population suffering hunger or malnutrition had declined from 20 percent to 17 percent over twenty years (FAO 2006c, 8), in raw numbers the trend in that time had not been encouraging:

> The number of undernourished people in the developing world declined from 960 million in 1969–71 to 830 million in 2002–04, but almost all of the decline occurred before 1990–92, and, in fact, the number rose from 1995–97 to 2002–04... In the period 1990–92 to 2001–03, the only significant progress towards reducing the number of undernourished people was concentrated in very few, but populous, countries and subregions: China, Southeast Asia and South America...(FAO 2007, 130).

The next Chapter will discuss the impact of the food crisis in more detail, but in the wake of the severe increases in food prices, peaking in mid-2008, the numbers of hungrry across the globe are now more than 1 billion, eclipsing earlier FAO concerns that the food crisis would cause the number to exceed 900 million (FAO 2008).

As with the related issue of global poverty, much of the decrease in pre-food crisis proportional terms of the hungry poor can be attributed to economic growth and development in Asia, in particular India and China. Africa, and in particular sub-Saharan Africa, saw increases in hunger and poverty during the period since the 1980s (FAO 2007; Meredith 2005).

On current measures, it is difficult to point with any confidence to any significant improvement in the numbers of people suffering chronic or acute hunger at the global level, even before adding in the growing impact of climate change (Pauchari 2007). Thus, apart from the substantive work the WFP does in alleviating human suffering, and its valiant attempts to keep operating with some longer term development projects despite the overwhelming demand for emergency relief, questions remain over the extent to which it is providing more than stop-gap assistance.

Barrett and Maxwell comment that '[f]ood aid, almost by definition, addresses acute *symptoms* of poverty and food insecurity, it rarely tackles underlying *causes*. Indeed, food aid may, in some cases, contribute to them' (Barrett and Maxwell 2005, 114). As this implies, any consideration of WFP effectiveness in the absolute sense must start with clarifying how to conceptualise the nature of global hunger (and poverty) and their underlying causes.

Conceptualizing global hunger

The most well known and influential mode of thinking about hunger and starvation until the 1980s was Malthusianism (Barrett and Maxwell 2005; de Waal 1997; George 1979; Sen 1981; Uvin 1994) derived from the works of the late eighteenth and early nineteenth century English economist Malthus (Malthus 1992). Malthus argued that hunger and famine resulted when the human population exceeded the food production capacity of a society's agriculture, and predicted periodic famines as inevitable processes which would cull the numbers of people when they became excessive. In a Malthusian analysis, hunger is principally a problem of insufficient supply of food, generally linked to failures in production, or possibly failure to control population growth. In its simplest and most compelling form, the neo-Malthusian conceptualization of hunger is based on the proposition that people starve when there is not enough food.

In the period following the Second World War, this conceptualization, linked to undeniable differences in national agricultural production capacities, led to the technical focus of the FAO on addressing hunger through focusing on improvements in agriculture. Uvin (1994, 75ff) points out the co-existence of neo-Malthusian thinking with a more political notion linking hunger to poverty in much of the proceedings of the Hot Springs Conference in 1943 and the 1974 World Food Conference (see also Barrett and Maxwell 2005, 108).

The Green Revolution of the 1960s in agricultural production (Fogel 2004; George 1979; Sen 1981) was inspired by the prospect of resolving such supply problems more or less permanently, and indeed until recently it had generally been taken as having succeeded. Since at least the 1960s, the global food supply has exceeded the food needs of the planet's population, and increases in production have more than kept pace with growth in population (Fogel 2004), although it mainly succeeded in Asia and is now seen as having failed in Africa (Gregory 2009). However, there is some debate over the environmental sustainability of Green Revolution technologies given their reliance on fertilization and pesticides (George 1979; Patel 2007). Also, the capital intensive nature of the technologies has played a role in generating debt amongst poor farmers, contributing to poverty and other poverty-and-hunger-linked shifts such as urban migration and changes from subsistence and domestic food production to growth of export crops (Patel 2007). These debates are being further played out as various governments and philanthropic foundations embrace the idea of a second Green Revolution in Africa (Annan 2010; Baxter 2010). Also, on top of endemic problems with distribution and access to the food being so effectively produced at the global level, there are increasing signs that the rate of food production increase is falling behind the rate of population increase.

Neo-Malthusianism continues to be influential in food aid policy because of the temptation to view hunger and starvation as related to global level distribution failures linked to problems with regional level supply of food – a view implicit in much emergency food relief, if only reflecting operational experiences.

Sen describes this neo-Malthusian mode of thinking deployed to analyse famine as *food availability decline* (FAD), and regards it as dangerously misleading and narrow in the analysis and explanation of famines. As he shows, 'some of the worst famines have taken place with no significant decline in food availability per head' (Sen 1981, 7). This is because a sudden collapse of access can occur for a section of a community, even against a rising trend for the community overall (Sen 1981, 43). Sen's studies of famines in Bengal (1943), Ethiopia (1974), the Sahel region of Africa (1972), and Bangladesh (1974) showed the insufficiency of the FAD analysis:

> Even in those cases in which a famine *is* accompanied by a reduction in the amount of food available per head, the causal mechanism precipitating starvation has to bring in many variables other than the general availability of food...The FAD approach gives little clue to the causal mechanism of starvation, since it does not go into the *relationship* of people to food." (Sen 1981, p154, emphasis in original).

Sen's 1981 essay, which 'revolutionized' the analysis of hunger and food insecurity (Barrett and Maxwell 2005, 108), proposes that rather than FAD, analysis be based on the concept of exchange entitlement. This could be applied to individuals and groups (such as occupational categories, e.g. rural laborers), and focuses on analyzing the resources, whether in the form of capital, assets or labor that given subjects control, and their capacity to exchange them for access to food (Sen 1981, Ch5).

Sen is careful to distinguish the entitlement approach from a focus on income. Income gives only a partial picture of entitlements:

> People died because they didn't have the income to buy food, but how come they didn't have the income? What they can earn depends on what they can sell and at what price, and starting off with incomes leaves out that part of the entitlement picture. (Sen 1981, 155–6).

Also, Sen notes examples of food being *exported* from an affected region in famine, such as the nineteenth century Irish famine, and the Wollo (Ethiopia) and Bangladesh famines of the 1970s (Sen 1981, 161).[3] These examples are echoed more recently in people dying of starvation in Brazil while soy beans grown locally are exported to feed intensively farmed poultry in Europe (Uvin 1994, 91, fn103; Wagenhofer 2005). McGovern notes another example from Peru –

> ...although large numbers of Peruvians suffer from protein deficiencies, much of the fish caught in Peru's rich Pacific waters goes to North America for pet food. Why? Because American pet owners can pay higher prices to feed their dogs and cats than Peruvian parents can pay to feed their children. (McGovern 2001, 150–1).

These are not examples of market failure, they are examples of market functioning:

> Viewed from the entitlement angle, there is nothing extraordinary in the market mechanism taking food away from famine-stricken areas to elsewhere. Market demands are not reflections of biological needs or psychological desires, but choices based on exchange entitlement relations. If one doesn't have much to exchange, one can't demand very much, and may thus lose out in competition with others whose needs may be a good deal less acute, but whose entitlements are stronger. (Sen 1981, 161).

Echoing this analysis, Poppendieck notes that in the 1930s Depression in America the 'contrast of overproduction and underconsumption was given a name: It was called "the paradox of want amid plenty" or "the paradox of scarcity and abundance" or simply "the paradox"' (Poppendieck 1986, xii). But Poppendieck questions the appropriateness of the term:

> Technically, a paradox is a statement that contains a contradiction or a statement that seems false but is in fact true. In common usage, it carries connotations of absurdity and abnormality. But the so-called paradox that evoked federal food assistance was not, in fact, a paradox; it was the normal, predictable working of the economy rendered extreme by the Depression. (Poppendieck 1986, xiii).

It is only through neo-Malthusian assumptions that starvation amidst plenty seems paradoxical. An exchange entitlement analysis shows it to be, unfortunately, quite unsurprising.

Poppendieck documents how the responses to 'the paradox' in 1930s America resulted in a focus on dealing with the overproduction part of the paradox, and left in place the political economy that allowed widespread hunger to continue to occur. Implicitly, if production was controlled and prices stabilized so that no further destruction of surplus commodities was required, this would resolve the paradox, even while large numbers of people remained hungry. Thus the food assistance programs of both the Hoover and Roosevelt administrations were addressed 'to the paradox, rather than to the simple hunger of the poor people or the nutritional inadequacy of their diets' (Poppendieck 1986, xiii). This example suggests that food aid is limited, at best, to symptomatic relief when constructed with as much an eye on the moral claim of producers as the moral claims of the hungry. More than that, though, it raises the possibility that food aid is a political strategy that props up a fundamentally inequitable system of economic relations that makes hunger an inevitable function of inequality.

The problem in the IFAR context, as Uvin poses it, is that linking hunger to poverty is a political proposition difficult for intergovernmental organizations to pursue:

> The Malthusian principle, on the other hand, is easy to understand to [sic] most of the experts that man the development community: engineers, agronomists, economists, medical doctors and the like. It allows them and the institutions they work for to do research and consulting funded by the many international development agencies, while being politically neutral, not offending the sensibilities of elites and governments in donor or recipient countries. (Uvin 1994, 79).

These comments suggest a particular context for the WFP strategy of technical, non-political management. It may have brought relatively high organizational effectiveness, and even in some senses enhanced inclusion and accountability, but has it been at the cost of effectiveness in more absolute terms?[4] After all, although the WFP now has a heavy emphasis on emergency relief and recovery operations, some 90 percent of global hunger is chronic rather than stemming from emergency situations such as war or famine (WFP 2004d, 4). To answer this question it is necessary to examine the efforts of the WFP to address global hunger at a causal rather than symptomatic level.

The WFP and the causes of global hunger

Two aspects of WFP work could be said to create some opportunity to try to take on the problem of global hunger and poverty at a causal, rather than symptomatic level: the development part of the dual mandate; and the role of advocacy. Both these elements of WFP's work are delimited by practical and political boundaries to the point that it is probably not capable of having a wider impact on the absolute measures of the number of hungry poor at the global level. In fact, even if boosting the development or advocacy elements of WFP operations were possible, such change would most probably be counterproductive in terms of its relative effectiveness, as the discussion below outlines. This reflects the fact that these limitations are inherent to the normative underpinnings of global governance in the IFAR.

The WFP development mandate

As noted earlier, the proportion of WFP operations devoted to development rather than emergency work is now very small, albeit with the proviso that the distinctions between the two are blurred as much as possible (Russo, Luzot et al. 2005, 5). The blurring of the distinctions largely refers to the operation of the WFP Enabling Development Policy (Russo, Luzot et al. 2005; WFP 1999; 2002) on emergency assistance which requires it to be structured as much as possible to, if not support development, at least to minimise negative longer-term effects such as dependency and loss of self-supporting skills or assets.

A two year external evaluation of the Enabling Development Policy (EDP)[5] found that it had succeeded in making the WFP's emergency and recovery operations more relevant to beneficiaries (Russo, Luzot et al. 2005, 40), largely achieving the overarching goal of the policy – to enable 'marginalised people to take part in the development process and to benefit from it' (Russo, Luzot et al. 2005, 44).

The philosophy underpinning the EDP draws on much deeper appreciation of the humanity of the beneficiaries than a simple technocratic approach would suggest. Its adoption resulted, in part, from the Tripartite Evaluation of the WFP in the early 1990s (Chr. Michelsen Institute 1994). This report, in criticising WFP effectiveness in development projects had implicitly raised a question about the dual mandate.

> However, far from concluding that development activities should be phased out from WFP activities, the Tripartite Evaluation was of the opinion that, for compelling equity reasons, WFP was to *"maintain some level of development activities if it improves its performance"*. Though an external document to the WFP system, the Tripartite Evaluation Report was taken very seriously by WFP's Executive Board and its management endeavoured to implement its recommendations, amongst others through the Country Programme system and in large measure through the EDP. (Russo, Luzot et al. 2005, 7, emphasis in original).

The WFP development mandate refers to the use of food aid not just to feed hungry people in an immediate sense, but as a resource to help development which will enable the beneficiaries to improve their chances of avoiding hunger and malnutrition in the future. This can be done through human resource development projects such as maternal and child nutrition, or school feeding; alternatively there are projects which aim to provide a safety net protecting assets (for example, enabling poor rural families to avoid having to sell livestock to get money for food), or food for work projects supporting the building of public infrastructure such as roads through providing food in return for labour.

The evidence is mixed on the efficacy of using food aid in such projects to achieve longer-term development aims which could be said to contribute to longer-term systemic reductions in poverty and hunger.

Barrett and Maxwell comment that, in general, food-based safety nets 'really only protect food security and nutritional status (or other assets) in the short term... safety nets are not themselves investments in households' (Barrett and Maxwell 2005, 128). On the other hand, there is some evidentiary support for maternal and child health supplementary feeding programs resulting in 'long-term investment in human capital accumulation' (Barrett and Maxwell 2005, 129). With specific reference to WFP projects, the EDP Evaluation found that the

> Evidence on results for strategic objective 1 (*to enable young children and expectant and nursing mothers to meet their special nutritional and nutrition-related health needs*) was less convincing ... In practice ... food seems to have played a more important role as an incentive to attend health services than as food in its own right. (Russo, Luzot et al. 2005, 40).

This finding hints at the complexity of assessing and evaluating the effects of such projects.

When it comes to food for education (as school feeding projects are described), there is some evidence of positive outcomes, but

> school feeding may not always address the limiting factors, especially the quality of education. There are also questions about whether food is the appropriate resource. Similar cash-based programs in Latin America have achieved the same goals, with recipients expressing a preference for cash over food resources (Barrett and Maxwell 2005, 130-1).

Again, the EDP Evaluation of WFP projects in this area was not unequivocally positive. On the one hand,

> Results were particularly positive for school feeding projects which consistently showed an increased level of attendance, whilst lower repetition rates and increased attention during lessons were also reported. Particularly encouraging are the increased school enrolments by girls...(Russo, Luzot et al. 2005, 40).

On the other hand,

> Increased school attendance levels have rarely reflected increased quality of the education systems, and the potential benefits of food aid assistance in school feeding projects have therefore not always been fully exploited. (Russo, Luzot et al. 2005, 41).

This latter point raises a significant problem for the WFP in development work. As Barrett and Maxwell note, it is 'the only UN agency with both humanitarian and developmental mandates but essentially a single resource: food' (Barrett and Maxwell 2005, 220). It is this narrowness in its resource base that appears to be the most significant impediment to the WFP's capacity to run larger scale, credible development projects. Most unbiased evaluations of food aid consistently point to its problematic nature when used for development work outside of relatively narrow boundaries, while regarding it as genuinely positive when used for emergency relief. Barrett and Maxwell thoroughly survey empirical studies of food aid and conclude that 'food aid is probably overused as a tool for development, although there are some roles in which food aid can be a useful resource to support development efforts' (Barrett and Maxwell 2005, 129). The evaluation of the EDP, while pointing to some successes with development projects, also consistently referred to chronic problems with the level and reliability of cash resourcing to support projects, noting that cash resources needed to be proportionally greater in development projects than in emergency or recovery operations (Russo, Luzot et al. 2005, 36, 39).

In view of the mixed and uncertain outcomes documented in evaluation of development food aid, it is difficult to see how any significant expansion of the WFP's development work would actually enhance its effectiveness in an absolute sense, even if it were possible in the face of donor non-interest. This raises the question of why the WFP persists in attempting to maintain the development part of its dual mandate, given 'some degree of reluctance on the use of food aid in a development context is common to a large number of donors' (Russo, Luzot et al. 2005, 7), and the strategic benefits of a simpler focus on emergency relief operations.

Politics of the WFP dual mandate

The building of political consensus between the Member states in the EB and the Secretariat has revolved around the construction of a compromise over different ways of interpreting the feed-the-hungry norm. The delicacy of this compromise is hinted at by the concerns noted in Chapter Five that if the EB adopted the Governance Group recommendation to revise the Mission Statement it would create dissension and conflict in the EB. It is in the Mission Statement that the compromises in how to interpret the feed-the-hungry norm are apparent.

Two interpretations of the norm are held in tension via the dual mandate. The first is a literal reading – feeding hungry people in an immediate sense. The second is a more symbolic reading of doing what can be done to attack the systemic causes of hunger – this is the reading on which the agenda for development food aid is largely based.[6]

The political support for the symbolic reading stems from a mix of different sources.

Partly it can be ascribed to recipient nations and some NGOs, seeking to maximise the amount of resources in aid, if only through maximising the routes by which the aid can arrive. Partly it derives from WFP's history as a development agency and institutional inertia. Partly it derives from human motivation to get beyond bandaid solutions: a theme which emerged from interviews with organizational personnel was a suspicion that too narrow a focus on emergencies would deprive it of important opportunities to work for change to the very mechanisms which create those emergencies, and condemn the WFP to a reactive role. Hence to 'give up on' development is perceived as likely to lead to a debilitating effect on the confidence and forward looking capacity of the organization and Secretariat. There is also a respectable argument that the very tension in the dual mandate is itself productive, for example through the EDP being applied to making emergency relief operations look beyond the immediate future and take a more active account of beneficiary interests.

Adding weight to the sympathy for development projects is the fact that, despite the problems with using food aid in development, there *are* some successes and worthwhile projects.[7] Thus the WFP continues to maintain at least some development operations, while attempting to generate as much longer-term thinking as possible about its relief operations.

The WFP and advocacy

As discussed earlier in the chapter, the WFP tends to strategically interpret advocacy in abstract terms – against hunger rather than for the hungry – even while its specific advocacy tactics seek to humanise the brutality of hunger, both as an ethical necessity and to mobilise support. This derives mainly from two interrelated processes. Firstly, the need to have a politically neutral approach to advocacy which will not offend the donor nations, in particular the United States; secondly the focus on emergency relief, which tends to render less relevant broader causal factors underlying chronic hunger and food insecurity. Also important in the political calculus on advocacy are the agribusinesses, with strong political connections in the US in particular, which are the main beneficiaries of global systems of production and markets that help create endemic global hunger, and important commercial stakeholders in the food aid system (Patel 2007; Ziegler 2005). Raising awareness of hunger is an aim with impeccable credentials to keep happy the powerful actors who benefit from the systems that help create and maintain large-scale malnutrition.

In contrast to the interpretation of advocacy as the raising of awareness is rights-based advocacy. Rights-based advocacy 'means holding other actors (often, but not necessarily, state actors) accountable to their obligations to respect, protect, and fulfil human rights' (Barrett and Maxwell 2005, 113). In this, it poses a fundamentally political analysis of problems, as opposed to the tendency of what de Waal describes as a technocratic food policy/famine elite to work on the basis of hunger as a technical problem (de Waal 1997, 24-5).

The Right to Food

> 'If hunger is a moral issue, what about WFP's position on the Right to Food?'
>
> -question raised by WFP staff in 2004 Global (WFP Staff) Meeting (WFP 2004d, 20).

In terms of the feed-the-hungry norm, rights-based advocacy reifies the moral claim of the hungry into a quasi-legal claim of a right – the Right to Food.[8] Yet, echoing the distinguishing of food aid from financial assistance, the IFAR feed-the-hungry norm has also been sharply distinguished from rights-based norms.

The Right to Food has long been established as a principle in international legal instruments (see for example, Article 25 in the Universal Declaration of Human Rights, and Article 11 of the International Covenant on Economic, Social and Cultural Rights; Barrett and Maxwell 2005, 111). Consistent with these instruments, the 1974

World Food Conference report included a Universal Declaration on the Eradication of Hunger and Malnutrition (UN General Assembly 1974).

In the context of the 1996 World Food Summit, and developments in the international human rights regime, in 1997 the UN Commission on Human Rights (UNCHR) adopted the first of a series of resolutions on the Right to Food (UN Commission on Human Rights 1997). In 2000 the UNCHR resolved to appoint a Special Rapporteur on the Right to Food (UN Commission on Human Rights 2000), and similar resolutions on the right to food have since been adopted by the UN General Assembly in 2001 (UN General Assembly 2001) and more recently in 2005. The first UN Special Rapporteur on the Right to Food, Jean Ziegler, was a prominent advocate for the hungry poor, pointing to the roles of globalization and corporate interests in agricultural production as a significant contributing factor to global hunger (Accardo and O'Neall 2005; Leahy 2007; Wagenhofer 2005; Ziegler 2005).

Despite what would seem to be an obvious relationship between the UN Right to Food campaign and its fight against hunger, the WFP has no presence in the UN right to food discourse, although the FAO does (see e.g. Robinson 2002). This absence is mirrored by an effective EB prohibition on WFP engagement with the debate over rights-based development (Barrett and Maxwell 2005, 114; Schenkenberg 2005). The source of this separation of WFP from the Right to Food discourse in the UN is to be found in US policy, demonstrating the hegemonic role of the US in the international food aid regime.

US antagonism to defining certain types of rights in international regimes dates back to debates over the Universal Declaration of Human Rights in the 1940s (Evans 1996; Thakur 2001). In the context of conflict with communist regimes, the US supported codifying international civil and political rights (free speech, the right to vote) linked to democratic and liberal norms, but opposed codifying international economic rights – for example, the right to employment or income – linked to materialist ideology. The concern was the latter could be taken to imply an imperative to change or limit the character of capitalism, and hence to be inconsistent with liberal democratic ideology valorising freedom ahead of equality. Given this historical context, and the vigorous critique of corporate agribusiness and US policy in which Ziegler and other Right to Food advocates engage, it is not surprising that the US has been hostile to the Right to Food discourse and its associated concept of 'food sovereignty' (Suppan 2002, 2). For example, at the 'World Food Summit – *five years later*' Conference held in June 2002, the US opposed a resolution supporting the right to food, arguing instead for greater trade liberalisation and a bigger role for the private sector and biotechnology to improve food security (Barrett and Maxwell 2005, 114).

This issue and its connection to the WFP was implicitly raised by a member of staff at a WFP global staff meeting in Dublin, 2004, during a panel discussion involving then USAID Administrator Andrew Natsios:

> Mr Natsios was asked to explain the USA's position on the concept of the Right to Food. He replied that the USA did not believe that food was something to which a right could be assigned. He feared that the Right to Food diverted attention from the operational side, which he thought should be the focus. (WFP 2004d, 6).

Interestingly, the same meeting was later addressed by Ziegler. In his talk Ziegler 'laid out the juridical status and definitions of the Right to Food and listed the practical measures he was allowed to use in the fight against hunger' (WFP 2004d, 7).[9] However, his participation was only as part of a panel with two journalists and Senator McGovern on 'Communicating the Right to Food: how to put hunger higher on the public agenda.' There is no record of the other panel members in this session saying anything on the Right to Food; there is no indication of Ziegler's contribution having any relationship to the other sessions at the meeting devoted variously to NGO, UN and private sector partnerships, or the work of the UN Secretary General's Hunger Task Force. More recently, the 2008-2011 Strategic Plan lists 9 'core principles' guiding the WFP, the third of which states that the WFP will be 'responsive to the principles related to the right to food, and based on the practical wisdom and needs of local populations wherever possible' (WFP 2008, 7).

When taken in context, these few references to the Right to Food are akin to damming the notion with faint praise. Although it is not correct to argue that the Right to Food issue is completely absent from WFP planning and thinking, it is not anywhere near the normative or conceptual heart of the organization, even in the form of a subject of debate.

In the context of general US hostility to international rights-based discourse, this can be portrayed as a case of the use of hegemonic power to neuter WFP's engagement with an important human rights issue in its field of operations. As a consequence, according to this interpretation, the WFP has had its advocacy role limited so that it is devoid of any capacity to argue for change to the systemic causes of global hunger.

It is possible, however, to make a different, and more nuanced and convincing analysis of the disjunction between the WFP and the Right to

Food discourse. This analysis amounts to a defence of the WFP and its avoidance of a more political version of advocacy, as a trade off in return for which it has maintained its formidable record for relative effectiveness. This analysis argues that the WFP, in avoiding the Right to Food debate, has quarantined itself from some of the most politically contentious debates in the UN system over human rights issues – something which has assisted its operational credibility and effectiveness. It is easy to see how WFP participation in the Right to Food advocacy could have caused bitter political struggles on the EB, and almost certainly a decline in US support (both governmentally, and in its domestic US political standing as it became a political target of anti-UN rhetoric). It is much harder to see how it would have contributed to an improvement in the problem of global hunger at either a symptomatic or causative level.

Conclusion

The limitations to the WFP's effectiveness in absolute terms are deeply connected to its capacity to maintain relative effectiveness, and the operation of the IFAR feed-the-hungry norm. A multilateral food aid organization dependent on food donations, largely directed by donors, and with limited cash supplementations, quite simply lacks a capacity to do much in an obvious, macro level way about the systemic causes of global hunger.

However, through a continuing attempt to articulate a development ethos along with logistical capacity to deliver food in a timely manner to people at risk of death and disease from malnutrition, the WFP does make a positive difference to many lives. Also, in subtle ways, in the process of undertaking and evaluating its operations, and discussing the nature of hunger as a problem in human societies, the WFP keeps open opportunities for efforts at both micro and macro levels to address hunger in a deeper way than simply providing food to hungry people.

The non-debate over the Right to Food points the distinctiveness of the IFAR's central norm. The feed-the-hungry norm is *not* fundamentally based on the usual international law underpinning of international regime norms. The legal principles that underpin most of the norms of international regimes – that is, that they are part of a rules-based system – have much less purchase in the WFP, because they do not underpin the feed-the-hungry norm. This is important because the WFP's effectiveness is so closely connected to US support, and this support derives at least partly from a normative congruence with domestic US norms, which themselves are antagonistic to quasi-legal compulsion in relation to material rights. In these terms, the US plays a hegemonic role in the IFAR.

The IFAR normative connection with the US is significant, not only because it reflects a congruence between international and US domestic feed-the-hungry norms, but also because it avoids the politically damaging (apparent) compulsion of a norm based on international law.

Endnotes

[1] Maren is particularly critical of Save the Children Fund (Maren 1997, Ch8).

[2] Her tenure in that role was for only three years, and ended with Bertini expressing some frustration with the obstacles to UN reform built into its politico-bureaucratic structures (Bertini 2005a).

[3] More recently O'Grada (O'Grada 2009) has identified some faults in Sen's classic case study of the Bengal famine of the 1940s (Sen 1981,Ch. 6), and suggested it is important not to downplay actual failures in food production and supply as key triggers for famines. That is, both systems of production and distribution play a role in causing or averting famine.

[4] This argument is made at some risk of oversimplifying complex developments in the conceptualising of chronic hunger and malnutrition (which is far from being only about famine). Barrett and Maxwell note the centrality of 'food security' as a means of addressing the problem, which combines elements of availability and access, while '[f]urther refinements in the late 1980s and 1990s added the issue of utilization of food as well, creating the availability-access-utilization triad most popularly used today in policy discussions of food aid." (Barrett and Maxwell 2005, 110); see also USAID Office of Food for Peace 2005). Also, concepts such as risk, vulnerability, and coping mechanisms are now prominent in literature on food and livelihood security (Barrett and Maxwell 2005, 110). Interestingly, Poppendieck suggests that in the late 1980s, domestic food aid advocates in the US adopted the food security concept from the international discourse (Poppendieck 1998, 79).

[5] Sponsored by seven different donor states – US, Canada, Denmark, France, Germany, Japan, Italy – and conducted by a consortium of NGO research organizations 2003–05 (Russo, Luzot et al. 2005).

[6] In the wider IFAR, the dual mandate is referred to as the 'twin track' approach – as the Deputy Director-General of FAO put it in 2007: 'FAO, IFAD and WFP advocate a twin track approach to reducing hunger. The first track focuses on policies and investment in rural areas and agriculture to improve the productivity of smallholders and to create employment opportunities for the rural poor. The second is the direct and immediate access to food for the most vulnerable groups.' (FAO Committee on World Food Security 2007, 15).

[7] Assessing this is complicated by the existence of strong incentives for proponents to claim success for development projects to justify the investments in them, even where such claims may not be reliable. Such claims of success are made all the easier by the difficulties of measuring the effects of development work. For example, the defence of food aid monetization by US

NGOs (Alliance for Food Aid 2007a; 2007b; Shaw and McKay 2006) illustrates how easily and convincingly a case can be made for development food aid, even in circumstances where the most credible independent analyses demonstrate regressive overall effects.

[8] Rights-based advocacy also impinges on WFP in relation to the principles used in responding to humanitarian emergencies (see Barrett and Maxwell 2005, 114-6 for details of various codes of conduct and principles). For the most part these principles have not been deeply problematic for WFP, but have contributed to its relative effectiveness.

[9]These were: 'general reports to the Commission on Human Rights and to the UN General Assembly'; 'field visits to initiate collab. with gov's & identify/report violations of the Right to Food'; and 'urgent condemnations in cases of violations of the Right to Food.' Also, 'Mr Ziegler gave examples from India, South Africa and Nigeria where the Right to Food had brought about positive changes by appeals to the legal system.' (WFP 2004d, 7).

7
Feeding the Hungry

The WFP is a UN agency that is generally well regarded across the spectrum. This is surprising given the regressive tendencies of food aid in development, the dominance of the US as founder and main donor, and the trenchantly criticised US agricultural protection policies so closely linked with American food aid policies. Why and how this came to be are important questions to ask, because their answers may point to some useful lessons in what may make global governance better in both normative and functional terms.

The institutional setting within which the WFP is established, and on which it is a major influence, is central to understanding the politics of WFP governance. The feed-the-hungry norm sets the basis for the consensual decision making and strong US support that form the basis for its legitimacy as an organisation. This concluding chapter explores the implications of this portrayal of the WFP as a legitimate and successful actor in global governance.

In the first section, I consider the prospects for the WFP's legitimacy in the near future. While the corollary of the WFP improving its legitimacy over time is that it may also lose legitimacy over time, there is reason for some cautious optimism about its capacity to maintain its current levels of legitimacy.

That said, the futures of the food aid regime and the WFP cannot be considered in isolation from the aftermath of the 2007-08 global food crisis, and the near certainty of further such crises in the near future. In the second section of this chapter, following a brief description of the crisis I consider the responses to it at the global level, which seem predicated on the normalization of large scale global hunger, and how they relate to the international food aid regime.

While in an immediate sense food aid is no longer a central part of the debates over how to address the problem of global hunger, this issue brings us back to broader issues to do with global governance, framed as it is around the Millennium Development Goals (MDGs). Although the circumstances of the WFP's legitimacy are too specific to provide a simple 'recipe for success' in global governance, it does suggest the direction in which we should look for more viable international organizations that can contribute to making the world a better place.

In particular, the international relations discipline can contribute to the search for improved global governance through developing a deeper understanding of the interactions between great power interests and norms in the evolution of robust and legitimate international institutions.

The future of IFAR global governance

A number of past and present UN officers spoken to in the course of my research used the wave metaphor for organizational success. According to this metaphor, organizations might be riding up a wave, peaking at the crest of a wave (being seen as at the top of their game), or falling from the top of the wave. There was a consistent view that the WFP was at the crest of the wave, and had been since around the mid to late 1990s. Yet this metaphor implies that the WFP's effectiveness and legitimacy can only decline from here. So, how sustainable is the legitimacy enjoyed by WFP?

Trends in Food Aid

Over the half century since multilateral food aid through the WFP began, some long-term trends in food aid have become discernible. Food aid has declined steadily and significantly as a proportion of Official Development Assistance (ODA) since the early 1960s. From constituting 22% of ODA in 1965 (Webb 2003, 2), and still over 13% of ODA in 1971, since 1995 it has averaged less than 2% of ODA (Barrett and Maxwell 2005, 6–7).

Similarly, viewed as a proportion of agricultural trade, food aid has shrunk steadily over the last forty years. Table 7.1 shows that cereal food aid deliveries as a percentage of annual world cereal production and imports in the last five years have averaged less than half the proportions of the early 1990s.

Table 7.1: Cereal food aid deliveries as percentage of world cereal production and world cereal imports – annual averages, three five year periods

Period	% of Imports	% of Production
1991-1995	0.62	5.9
1997-2002	0.47	3.9
2003-2007	0.3	2.62

Data Sources: (INTERFAIS/WFP 2008, xi; WFP 1996, 27;WFP 2003b, Annex 1, 34).
Note, Barrett and Maxwell argue that looking at cereals rather than all commodities tends to overstate food aid as proportion of agricultural production and trade. Nevertheless they acknowledge the proportions are very small either way, and the trend has been clearly one of decline (Barrett and Maxwell 2005, 260, fn6).

Food aid data is complicated by the fact that it may be presented based on two different measures – by value (usually $US); and by volume (usually metric tons). Given the volatility of agricultural prices, dollar values can fluctuate considerably when translated into volumes, so care should be taken when reading statistical charts as to the measure being used. As food aid has moved away from in-kind donations to cash donations, increasingly food aid measurement has moved towards a focus on dollar value and away from volume measures. Nevertheless, from the perspective of recipients, it is the actual volume that arrives that matters more than how much (or little) donors have given to enable its purchase. The price/volume relationship generates relatively little concern during periods of sustained surpluses and low global prices. However in the context of recent significant price increases in wheat, maize and rice – the major coarse grain commodities in food aid – the WFP has found its purchasing capacity reduced commensurately. Logically, if the prices double, it can only purchase half the volume for a given dollar amount.[1] The converse also holds: Following the decline in food prices from their mid-2008 peak, WFP noted that although 'only 8 percent less food was procured in 2009 than in 2008, the total cost dropped by nearly 32 percent.' (WFP 2010b, 5).

When looked at on the basis of volumes, overall global food aid has been steadily declining (Chart 7.1). Record commodity prices in 2007-2008 impacted on food aid, reducing the volumes available for given dollar allocations, on top of which transport and handling costs increased significantly. Thus, despite record levels of income in 2008 for the WFP, the volume of food aid delivered by the WFP increased by only 18%. Overall global food aid in that year was barely more than in 2007, even in the midst of the global food crisis.

These facts put together with other data canvassed earlier can be summarized as follows:

- Food aid as a proportion of aid overall has declined as volumes have shrunk, the dollar value of food aid overall in real terms has declined, and as Official Development Assistance (ODA) has increased.
- Multilateral food aid (which virtually amounts to the WFP's food aid) has become the most significant channel for food aid.
- Multilateral food aid has the greatest emphasis on procuring commodities from developing countries.
- Multilateral food aid is predominantly concerned with relief rather than development.
- The US is still easily and by far the largest food aid donor, as well as the largest donor to the WFP, though its proportion of the WFP's donations is averaging around 40%, considerably less than in the early years of the WFP.

Potential challenges for WFP governance

In this context, organizational change to the WFP with negative effects on its legitimacy could come from four different directions. First, the maintenance of the development part of the dual mandate has been relatively robust in the face of limited resources for development work, but increased demands from emergencies and a reduction of donor contributions, for example due to a shift from in-kind to cash donation by the US, could still result in effective collapse in that element of the WFP's operations. The pressures from the food crisis, and disasters such as the earthquakes in Haiti and Chile and floods in Pakistan are likely to continue to place pressure on the WFP's development operations as inadequate resources are allocated to an expanding array of emergency and recovery situations.

Second, an ever present risk for UN agencies is management failure, resulting in inefficiency if not corruption, scandal and subsequent credibility and fund raising problems. The WFP has remained relatively free of serious problems in this area, (though as noted earlier, some problems have emerged in its Somalian operations). It is always possible

Chart 7.1: Gobal food aid by volume, 1988-2008

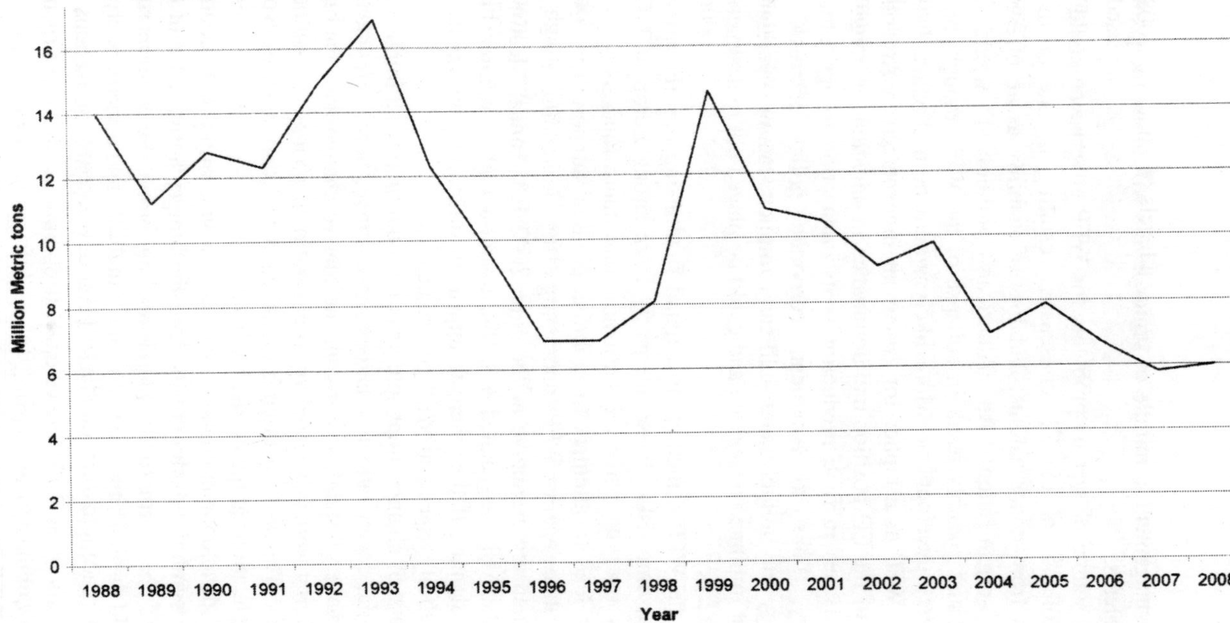

Data source: INTERFAIS (www.wfp.org/fais/). Note the spike in 1999 came because of large increases in program (government to government aid) from the US to Russia in the context of an economic crisis in the latter country, and grain surpluses in the former (Barrett and Maxwell 2005, 28–31; Webb 2003).

that inept management at middle or senior levels will allow the growth of such problems.

A third source of serious problems for WFP governance could be from the collapse of the EB consensus, resulting in one or more withdrawals from donor nations, and loss of viability as an effective multilateral organization. An American withdrawal would be catastrophic and possibly result in collapse of the WFP, though this is the least likely development. More likely would be a slippage into a view of the WFP as a cipher for American interests given American nomination of the ED position and dominance in donations. A range of contentious issues in food production – its connection to agricultural trade policy, links to American corporate policy interests in biotechnology and biofuel issues – all carry implicit state or sovereignty conflicts that impinge on food aid and could be played out to destructive effect on the EB.

Lastly, the WFP's attempts to expand fundraising into the private sector poses some risks. These are partly from strong European NGO antagonisms over its perceived intrusion into their fundraising turf, which could lead to attempts to mobilise political support from their polities and states against WFP fundraising efforts (something hinted at by the German representative at the June 2005 EB Annual Meeting). There are also risks associated with the development of relationships with private donors, if they were to appear to undermine the inclusion and accountability aspects of WFP governance.

In the face of changes to people, resources and policy all implicated in the potential organizational changes listed above, norms provide an important source of stability; however, normative change does happen, both influencing and influenced by organizational change, as well as external shifts. The possible organizational changes listed above all have different implications at the normative level.

Loss of development mandate capacity would imply a failure to maintain the symbolic reading of the feed-the-hungry norm, reflecting a narrowing of the norm to its literal reading alone. Such normative change would diminish the inclusion, accountability and effectiveness of WFP and the legitimacy of the IFAR. However, despite the increasing resource pressures on WFP's development operations, it is hard to see the political circumstances existing for a shift in the norm leading to cessation of WFP development operations.

Management failures, were they to occur to a significant degree, may see loss of credibility on the part of the WFP, and could lead to conflicts on the EB as various versions of blame shifting began to be used. They could also imply a failure of the US nominated ED, and hence imply a loss of legitimacy for the WFP as a US dominated organization. The fall-out could result in the Secretariat losing its credibility and hence its legitimacy as the accepted arbiter of how the feed-the-hungry norm is to be made operational; then state differences over interpreting and applying the feed-the-hungry norm could well expand into disputes within the EB, or the wider UN over the future of the IFAR. In other words, serious management failures could upset the balancing of interests and interpretations of the feed-the-hungry norm and thereby create a legitimacy crisis for the IFAR.

EB consensus could also be lost in circumstances not associated with management failure, but as a consequence of state conflicts – either within the IFAR, or spilling over into the regime from other issue areas. An important element of the IFAR's legitimacy can be ascribed to its historical capacity to keep functioning without being excessively drawn into conflicts in the international relations system. While other UN bodies have periodically been drawn by proxy into Cold War or Middle Eastern conflicts, the WFP has managed to stay largely apart from such distractions. If one or more such conflicts were to overwhelm the EB, this situation would be linked to the norm losing its status as transcending such politics. For this to happen there would need to be one or more inter-state issues which themselves were capable of transcending the feed-the-hungry norm – perhaps not a complete impossibility in the context of the war on terror and climate change.

Risks from fundraising go largely to the issue of state roles and responsibilities within the multilateral system. The implication of private fundraising can be taken as shifting the process of global governance from one based on a polity of states to something more complex, mixing states, corporations and individuals together as members of the IFAR polity. For example, while stating that '[g]overnance and policy will remain the sole purview of WFP Member States' (WFP 2004c, 11), in 2004 the WFP identified the need to establish a Business Advisory Council. This is 'a global network of chief executive officers and corporate leaders to discuss management issues with WFP executive management on an advisory basis...' (WFP 2004c, 12), and has the effect of making such donors part of its polity through including them in governance processes. The normative implications of these changes are not immediately obvious, though there is some shift implied by a move away from the idea that the moral claims in the feed-the-hungry norm are the primary responsibility of states and the intergovernmental community. Arguably this shift has nevertheless already occurred by dint of neoliberal policy reforms in liberal democracies over the last few decades.

To summarise this discussion, while there are clearly many pressures on and risks to the functionality and legitimacy of the IFAR, the extent to which they are able to diminish the quality of the governance in which it is engaged is limited by the extent to which these pressures are connected to a weakening or narrowing of the feed-the-hungry norm. It is difficult to detect strong signs that this is likely in the near term. That said, it is a well established critique of historical institutionalism that it tends to overestimate the continuities and resistance to change of existing institutions (Blyth 2002, Ch2; Schmidt 2010). Given the approach in this book is based partly on an institutional history of the IFAR, such a criticism may well have some application to the argument being made here. For that reason, while there is cause for some guarded optimism about the continued prospects for IFAR to remain legitimate through inclusive, accountable and relatively effective governance, it would be wise not to overstate the case for it. Interestingly, the WFP has resolved to relabel itself as a 'food assistance' , rather than food aid, agency (WFP 2009, 4). It is too early to judge the implications of such a change for the food aid regime, though it may be that by 2020, regime analysis in this issue area focuses on an international food assistance regime.

Whether it is seen as a food aid or food assistance agency, these propositions about the WFP's legitimacy raise a more fundamental issue about how such legitimacy fits into the wider canvas of significant, continuing and even worsening global hunger. Consideration of this issue requires us to consider the implications of the 2007-08 global food crisis for the politics of global hunger.

The Global Food Crisis

As I completed the research on which this book is based in 2008, the front pages of papers and magazines were temporarily dominated by references to a shocking catastrophe termed the global food crisis.

The proximate cause of the crisis came from a spike in food prices. In turn, this derived from spiralling prices for grains and oil, and hence of food (Chart 7.1).

At the global level the crisis led to a significant jump in the estimates of the numbers of people suffering from hunger, from 850 million to over 1 billion, along with concomitant increases in the numbers of people in poverty, or at increased risk of poverty and malnutrition. The food crisis also saw, in 2008, riots and destabilization of governments in a range of countries (Adam 2008; Doyle 2008). While the spike in prices peaked in mid-2008, the FAO's medium term projections are for agricultural food commodity prices to remain at higher levels than those prevailing since the mid- 1970s, due to increasing demand based on growing population and a range of pressures on production. While it remains to be seen what will happen to the numbers of people suffering from or at risk of malnutrition, it seems likely to be some time before they fall to the levels of the mid-2000s, let alone to lower than that.

Contributory factors

Like the world food crisis of the early 1970s, the global food crisis was the result of the complex interplay of a range of factors (Horton 2009). While there is some debate about the relative significance of these, there is a consensus that biofuels subsidies in Europe and the US were probably the most important (Headey and Fan 2008). These subsidies diverted corn supplies into fuel rather than food production, and also diverted other grain production into corn production, hence reducing supply and increasing the price of key grain commodities.

Increases in the price of oil due to concerns about declining reserves, environmental issues and Middle-East conflicts also played a role. As noted above, oil and food prices tend to be closely associated, given the role of oil in production as a source ingredient for fertilizers, and to run farm machinery, and in transport of food. Moreover, increases in the price of oil helped boost the economic viability of ethanol as a substitute, thereby boosting the increase in grains going to biofuels (Headey and Fan 2008).

Some commentary has highlighted declines in global stocks as contributing to the crisis, but serious analysis suggests this is not such a significant issue, as most of the decline in global stocks is accounted for by shrinkage in Chinese domestic food stores that would have had little impact on the wider global movement of prices (Dawe 2009; Headey and Fan 2008).

Changing consumption patterns are a further factor identified in the food crisis:

Chart 7.2: Food and oil commodity price indices, 2000-2009 (2005 = 100)

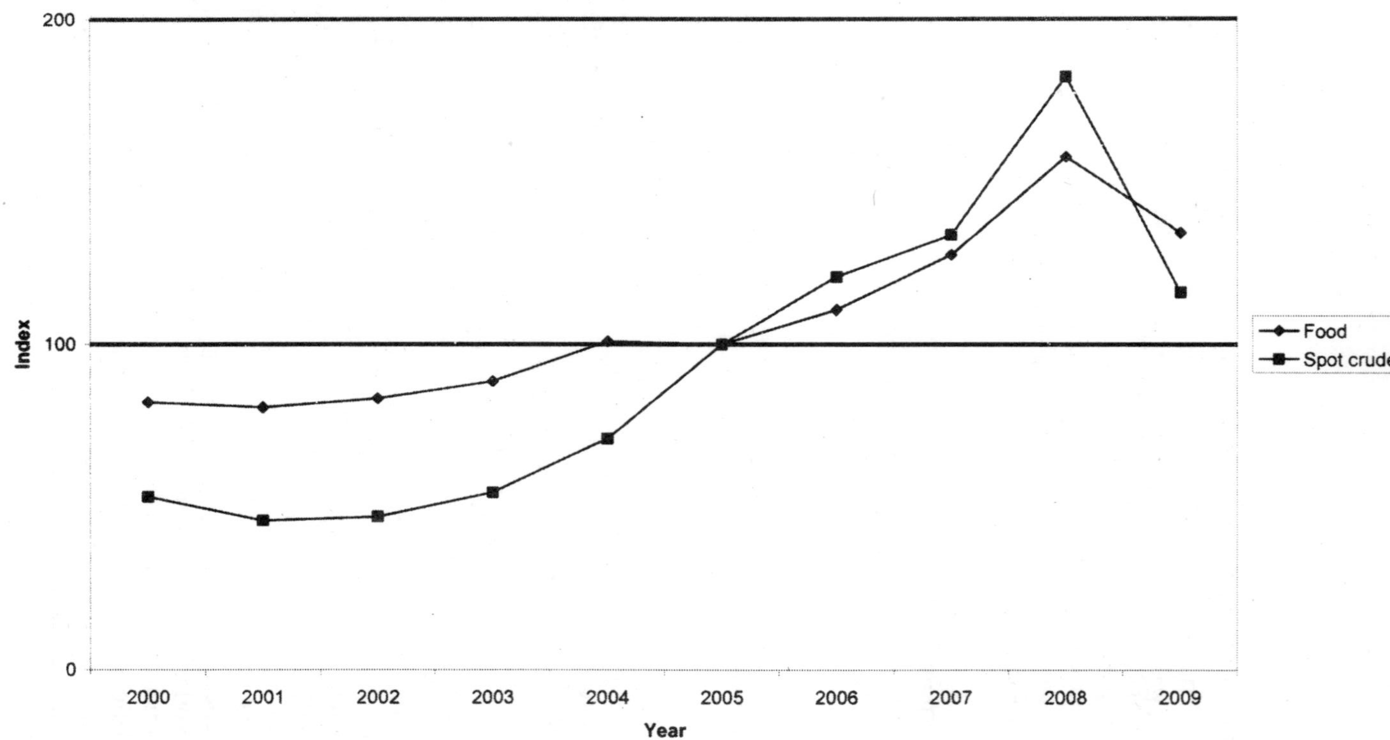

Data Source: IMF 2010

> The world's total meat supply was 71 million tons in 1961. In 2007, it was estimated to be 284 million tons. Per capita consumption has more than doubled over that period. (In the developing world, it rose twice as fast, doubling in the last 20 years.) World meat consumption is expected to double again by 2050, which one expert, Henning Steinfeld of the United Nations, says is resulting in a "relentless growth in livestock production." (Bittman 2008)

The problem for food prices is that production of livestock for food purposes requires the diversion of considerable amounts of grain away from the human food cycle. Two to five times as much grain is needed to produce meat calories equivalent to calories from direct grain consumption (Bittman 2008). This means the meat production process depends on high grain consumption, increasing demand for and reducing supply of grains. Meanwhile, while the meat it produces provides fewer calories than used in the production process, and is also more expensive and less accessible to the hungry poor than grain.

Another longer-term factor contributing to the food crisis has been diminished agricultural development linked to the loss of dedicated investment into agricultural development in developing countries (Bertini and Glickman 2009). By 2006, only 3.8% of Official Development Assistance (ODA) was going to agriculture, compared with 19% in 1980 (World Summit on Food Security 2009: 7).

This decline in investment coincided with the WFP's exit from development assistance discussed in earlier chapters. However the WFP's shift from development assistance to emergency relief was more symptom than cause of this trend. The redeployment of development assistance away from agricultural development is linked to the dominance of the World Bank in development financing for the last thirty years, and a model of development which valorised industrial development, urbanization, technology, and service industries ahead of rural and agricultural development. Another facet of this shift away from agriculture in development financing has been the emphasis of both the World Bank and International Monetary Fund on macro-economic and structural reforms (reducing the size of the public sector, addressing deficits on the current account and balance of payments; use of financing and the repayment of loans). Consequently, many poor countries, especially in Africa, have relatively unproductive agricultural sectors, depend on food imports, lack independent access to food supply, and are highly vulnerable to price fluctuations in agricultural commodities (Oxfam International 2008).

Apart from the lack of investment in agricultural development, there are some other broader structural economic issues that have contributed to the food crisis. As is implied by the biofuels issue, there has been continued failure to achieve agricultural trade reform, leaving in place subsidies and other national policy systems that helped fuel food price rises. A number of grain exporting countries - Demeke, Pangrazio et al. list 25 cases (2008, 6) - arguably worsened the crisis by responding to increasing prices with the imposition of export bans that further fuelled price rises, especially in the relatively thinly traded rice market (Demeke, Pangrazio et al. 2008, 9).

Despite the lack of reform to agricultural trade there have been significant long-term changes to global agricultural production chains. Agricultural production has increasingly been subject to industrial style intensification. This leads to large areas being devoted to monoculture production such as, for example, the case of Brazil's soybean production. Advocates for developing country farmers query the adoption of capital intensive agricultural technologies and economic processes which require the use of debt to finance, and have led to the impoverishment of small hold farmers not able to generate industrial style economies of scale (Patel 2007). There is considerable controversy over the attempts of agribusiness to use intellectual property (IP) rights to gain commercial control over plant breeding rights, using genetic modification (GM) technologies to leverage such IP strategies. A small number of agribusiness corporations such as Cargill and Archer Daniels Midland increasingly dominate commodity production and transportation.

These structural developments amount to the development of a globally integrated agricultural production chain which is capable of significant commodity production but is also vulnerable to failures and bottlenecks, and drives resources according to market logic. In the context of wealth disparities, this market logic tends to intensify distribution inequities. Moreover, in the least developed countries, the lack of developed infrastructure limits the capacity of people in many regions to participate in production and consumption processes in a way that can ensure they receive the benefits of market processes, for example, higher prices for their produce. The FAO gives the experience of Mozambique as an example, where

> high food prices were felt strongly at the consumer level but the size and the geography of the country limited price transmission to farmers. With a fractured agricultural market and poor infrastructure hindering trade, there are limited opportunities for agricultural producers to

> capitalize on the relatively high and growing incomes in the urban areas. The price of maize imported from Argentina to the market in Maputo, the capital, is the same as the price of maize transported internally from the northern part of the country. This means that domestic production is more likely to be traded within nearby rural communities or to rural areas of neighbouring countries such as Malawi or Zambia that face similar market infrastructure constraints. (FAO Committee on Commodity Problems 2010, 9-10)

Integrated and interlinked production chains have also contributed to good information flows about production, but this has also enabled some problematic market operation. Together with lack of regulation of derivative trading, and the financial services bubble, commodity price fluctuations have been intensified by processes of market speculation.[2] The US Commodity Futures Trading Commission has been loosening the rules governing agricultural futures trading since the early 2000s. This has enabled a significant increase in the trading of agricultural derivatives as more and more financial players outside the agricultural sector look for profit making opportunities (Irwin, Scott H. et al. 2007). This change has been linked to changes in price movements in grains at the Chicago Board of Trade since 2005 that have defied standard economic explanation (Henriques 2008).

The presence of speculation has led to some hyperbole. In April 2008, the then UN Special Rapporteur on the Right to Food Jean Ziegler, stated that speculation on international markets was behind 30 percent of the increase in food prices (Environmental News Service 2008) – a claim for which there is little credible evidence. More moderately, 184 NGOs in a joint letter to President Barack Obama argued that:

> A significant part of last year's [commodity] price fluctuations were the result of exccessive speculation in the commodities markets by the very hedge funds and investment banks that helped create the current economic meltdown … it is clear that excessive speculation in the U.S. commodity futures market dramatically exacerbated the volatility of world food prices. It was more than simple supply and demand issues that led to the 2008 food crisis. (Food Speculation Coalition 2009)

On the other hand, the problems for market stability posed by hedge funds and derivatives did not exist in the same way in the early 1970s, yet we still saw large price fluctuations in commodity prices cause a world food crisis at that time. In the case of the global food crisis, it seems likely that speculation did have some effect on agricultural commodity prices, however it is very difficult to quantify those effects.

Speculators undoubtedly make things worse, but the operation of markets, even without rampant speculation, can intensify supply and demand imbalances into larger price fluctuations than would seem warranted on actual levels of production.

Lastly, Headey and Fan (2008) note that there is an historical relationship between the value of the US dollar (USD), functioning both as the international reserve currency, and the currency of the world's largest agricultural exporter, and commodity prices. Because of this association, they consider it is possible that the long-term decline in the value of the USD since the mid-2000s may have also contributed to long run increases in commodity prices, although it will have also had complex macroeconomic impacts on the balance of trade of other countries too.

Other factors in the price spike of 2007-2008 can be brought in as well (for example uncertainty and declining production linked to climate change), but the above list is sufficient to demonstrate the complex interplay of production, policy, and economic structures that led to the global food crisis.

As we have seen in Chapter Three, the previous world food crisis resulted in changes to international organizations of some significance to the IFAR. The response to this more recent crisis, however, is difficult to regard as having the same impact on the regime.

Response to the food crisis

It is telling that, as opposed to the financial crisis in which powerful states have sidestepped the UN and organized and controlled the global response through the Group of 8 (G8) and Group of 20 (G20), it is the UN bureaucracy that has led the global response to the food crisis. Thus, the Secretary-General's creation in April 2008 of a High Level Task Force on the Global Food Security Crisis involved a list of 13 different UN system organizations as participants. Powerful states seem much more skeptical of the capacity of international cooperation to change the systems of poverty and malnutrition that underpin the food crisis – at least without unacceptable political costs to their own position – than they did in the early 1970s. Indeed, unlike the world food crisis in the 1970s, there has been little sense of a galvanising shock, and more of a reaction consistent with the normalization of high levels of widespread hunger at the global level. That is, the global food crisis appears to be viewed by states as a (temporary and regrettable) change in degree but not in kind of a pre-existing chronic problem. In this there are echoes of the institutionalization of America's domestic 'emergency' food relief measures.

The key mode of international response to food issues since the mid-1990s is the high level summit. The 1996 World Food Summit was followed in 2001 by 'WFS, *Five Years Later.*' These Summits were important as key processes contributing towards the Millennium Development Goals (MDGs), and trying to develop plans to achieve them within the rubric of specialist development and relief expertise. Since the advent of the food crisis, however, we have seen largely more of the same in a response – which itself speaks to a view of the food crisis as 'more of the same.'

An initial high level summit responding to the food crisis in Rome in June 2008 was followed by another 'high level conference' in Madrid in January 2009, at the end of which FAO Director-General Jacques Diouf began lobbying publicly for acceptance of the FAO's decision to call a high level summit on food security in Rome in November 2009 (Drago 2009). The G8 meeting at L'Aquila in July 2009 then issued a statement on food security acknowledging the crisis and pledging, rather vaguely, to 'aim at substantially increasing aid to agriculture and food security including through multiyear resource commitments' in the context of commitments by states 'towards a goal of mobilizing $20 billion over three years.' (G8 2009)

The vagueness of these commitments followed skepticism about the bona fides of the G8's 2008 commitment of $10 billion to support increased agricultural production in developing countries. 'Despite the media glitz ... this was not any new money, but a mere adding up of aid already pledged' (Mittal 2009)

The G8 engagement with the food crisis appears to have largely begun and ended with L'Aquila, though this is probably related to the G8 itself being displaced by the G20 as the key grouping responding to the global financial crisis, which by mid-2009 was perceived as the biggest crisis issue confronting states at the global level.

The G20 meeting in September 2009 in response to the global financial crisis produced a communiqué with a 9 paragraph section on fighting poverty. This communiqué noted that:

> The poorest countries have little economic cushion to protect vulnerable populations from calamity, particularly as the financial crisis followed close on the heels of a global spike in food prices. (G20 2009)

The G20 pledged to continue to support the MDGs, but focused mainly on lending and access to finance for developing countries in the context of the financial crisis, noting that sustained 'funding and targeted investments are urgently needed to improve long-term food security,' and asking

> the World Bank, the African Development Bank, UN, Food and Agriculture Organization (FAO), International Fund for Agricultural Development (IFAD), World Food Programme (WFP) and other stakeholders to coordinate their efforts, including through country-led mechanisms, in order to complement and reinforce other existing multilateral and bilateral efforts to tackle food insecurity. (G20 2009)

The FAO-initiated World Food Summit was held November 16-18, 2009 in Rome, and involved 60 government leaders, many from poor and developing nations, including marginal or illegitimate leaders such as Zimbabwe's Robert Mugabe and Fiji's Frank Bainimarama. The host country's Prime Minister and Summit Chairperson, Silvio Berlusconi was the only G8 leader in attendance. Apart from the Italian Prime Minister, only two other G20 member heads of state (Brazil and Turkey) attended. Britain sent two junior ministers (Squires 2009) and the United States head of delegation was the acting administrator of the US Agency for International Development (Institute for Agriculture and Trade Policy et al. 2009) – that is, below cabinet level. Australia's most senior representative at the summit was the Minister for Agriculture, Forestry and Fisheries, Tony Burke. Many other countries were represented by similar officials.

An initial proposal to specify 2025 as the year by which there would be eradication of global hunger was 'watered down' (in the view of food sovereignty activists) to the final Summit Declaration that: 'We will reinforce all our efforts to meet by 2015 the targets of Millennium Development Goal 1 and the World Food Summits. We commit to take action towards sustainably eradicating hunger at the earliest possible date.' (World Summit on Food Security 2009:1).

Compared to the Global Financial Crisis, and the climate change issue, the global food crisis is very much a second order issue for the most powerful states. A mark of the weakness of the response to the food crisis is the leadership role of the FAO, despite its relatively insignificant status within the UN system, and isolation from key decision making. The FAO was a much more important part of the UN system until the first World Food Crisis, which, as I noted in Chapter Three, many member-states took as representing a failure of the FAO.

Consequently the World Food Conference was not convened by the FAO but by the UN. If this process in the first world food crisis sidelined the FAO, this time around, replacing a UN convened World Food Conference with an FAO convened World Summit on Food Security represents a relative sidelining of the global food crisis. Placing the FAO at the forefront of co-ordinating the food crisis response has largely guaranteed its construction as primarily a technical problem related to improving agricultural development and production, with some political content in the form of advocacy for increases in Official Development Assistance (ODA) supporting agriculture.

Principle 3 of the Declaration of the World Summit on Food restates the dual mandate approach:

> Strive for a comprehensive twin-track approach to food security that consists of: 1) direct action to immediately tackle hunger for the most vulnerable and 2) medium and long-term sustainable agricultural, food security, nutrition and rural development programmes to eliminate the root causes of hunger and poverty, including through the progressive realization of the right to adequate food. (World Summit on Food Security 2009, 3)

However, the bulk of the declaration is concerned with agricultural and market development, with only one short paragraph explicitly contemplating emergency relief:

> We continue to be committed to the provision of, and the unhindered access to, safe emergency food and humanitarian assistance and support for the most vulnerable populations. We recognize the value of local purchase of food supplies, which supports local markets. We will remove food export restrictions or extraordinary taxes for food purchased for non-commercial humanitarian purposes, and will consult and notify in advance before imposing any such new restrictions. (World Summit on Food Security 2009, 4)

This brief mention is consistent with the fact that the impacts on the international food aid regime from the global food crisis have been largely limited to a short-run boost in funding for the WFP. Following a record level of resourcing in 2008 of $US5.1 billion, the WFP estimates its incoming resources for 2009 at $US4 billion – a drop of more than 20%; and predicts resourcing at an average of $US3.75 billion for 2010 and 2011 (WFP 2010). By the same token, this is all consistent with high levels of legitimacy in the regime, and the stability of the international feed-the-hungry norm.

Nevertheless, a niggling question remains: what does it profit the world to have a stable, legitimate international food aid regime if the need for it keeps expanding, rather than diminishing?

Global hunger as a systemic problem

A 'Peoples' Food Sovereignty Forum' was held in parallel with the World Summit on Food Security in Rome in November 2009, involving NGOs and small-scale producers from developing countries (Zaccaro 2009) along with protests, and submissions via NGO input to the Food Summit. Since the first World Food Conference in 1974, Susan George, and more recently writers such as Patel and Bello have mounted important critiques of the political economy of food chains and the role of agribusiness. The activist approach focuses on defending and advocating for small landholders against big agribusiness; local rather than transnational supply chains; traditional rather than industrial or genetic technologies of production; and equity in land distribution. Conceptually they argue for the right to food, and food sovereignty, and can therefore be seen as part of the wider rights based development discourse.

Much of the critical literature focusing on global hunger takes a structural approach to its analysis, starting with George whose first edition of *How the Other Half Dies* was published in 1976 (George 1991), and Frances Moore Lappé and Joseph Collins (1977; 1998). More recently Patel (2007) and Bello (2009) have produced similar types of analysis. These analyses place emphasis on the operation of the capitalist system, driven by corporate and national interests in generating disparities in wealth, agricultural development, production and trade, and ultimately access to food. Against these systemic problems are set the work of activists and NGOs (and sometimes UN agencies) in attempting to empower and feed the hungry poor, and expose the behaviour of Western and developing country elites. Central to these efforts are advocates of 'food sovereignty' like La Via Campesina, self-described as:

> …the international movement of peasants, small- and medium-sized producers, landless, rural women, indigenous people, rural youth and agricultural workers. We defend the values and the basic interests of our members. We are an autonomous, pluralist and multicultural movement, independent of any political, economic, or other type of

affiliation. Our 148 members are from 69 countries from Asia, Africa, Europe, and the Americas. (La Via Campesina 2010)

On the other hand, those such as Collier (Collier 2008) insist that only privately owned, high tech., large-scale, integrated production and distribution processes can feed the world. The role of the Green Revolution, as an example of Western technological innovation in agriculture that successfully boosted food production to levels sufficient to feed the global population is central to these claims.

In this debate there is clearly merit on both sides. As Collier's critics point out, he has been too quick to deride the capacity of small holder production, and too quick to dismiss the environmental costs of modern agricultural technologies (Aal, Jarosz et al. 2009), as well as the economic and social instabilities created by the international political economy of agriculture. Yet while it would worsen some significant problems to have a small number of agribusinesses increase further their dominance of food systems given their reliance on carbon intensive production, monocultures and destructive social and political impacts, the world cannot afford to lose their productive heft either.

I see two major problems with the dynamic of the debate about hunger between the mainstream intergovernmental position (strongly influenced by agribusiness interests via the US and international financial institutions), and food sovereignty activists. First, while there are significant structural problems with global food chains that are likely to result in further global food crises, serious critique has been relegated to the fringe, with limited political impact (much as their arguments might deserve more consideration). Second, for all the merits of the critiques of these structures, the challenge of sustainably producing sufficient food to feed the world' population, and distributing that food as part of sustainable food chain processes is going to need to work with the reality of mixed production – both large-scale industrial and small-scale. Zero-sum game positions, whether for or against transnational agribusiness corporations are not helpful in figuring out how to develop politically and economically viable models of sustainable agricultural production.

Where is the WFP in these debates? As discussed in Chapter Six, it has generally avoided them, consistent with the institutional premium placed on avoiding political conflicts. But does my portrayal of this as a key trade off for a strongly functional form of legitimacy in the institutional politics of food aid really let them off the hook?

Critics of my approach may well argue that it is too generous to the WFP and the US, and too complacent about the need to reform food systems that are implicated in the suffering of millions. After all, they can be seen as complicit to varying degrees in the structures that make global food crises inevitable. The US, in particular, bears culpability as a hegemonic actor determined to maintain the inequitable structures at the heart of global hunger.

Certainly, the portrayal of the US in this book can be read as 'benign' (cf Ross 2007). Yet, it would be a mistake to read my argument as a kind of apologia for, or defence of, American policy. In fact, as I hope this discussion makes clear, I recognise that the US has done much that is harmful in both agricultural systems of production and trade, and in transfers of wealth that effectively increase hunger and food insecurity globally and within its own borders. The trouble is not only that these points have been made repeatedly by others, but that to stop there is to end up with an overly static, simplistic, and ultimately unproductive analysis. There are some aspects of American policy making that have been broadly beneficial, and it is important to grasp a more nuanced sense of the ways US policy interacts with international politics in the food issue area than has been on offer so far. That is not to say that the good outweighs the bad overall in US actions, but to try and end up with an overall good or bad rating of the US seems to me to be beside the point. My hope is that this analysis can help create opportunities for more constructive interactions between US policy makers and their critics.

Conclusion – Lessons for legitimate global governance

In absolute terms, the WFP appears to have had limited impact on the problem of global hunger, with raw numbers of malnourished people not reducing but increasing over its 45 years of operations. Superficially this would seem to follow from dominance of donor interests in the WFP, reflected in an avoidance of any 'politicization' of food aid and inherent support for the global status quo. Such an argument might emphasise that the US has worked to narrow the scope of the WFP away from the more strategic use of development projects or advocacy linked to political ideas such, as the Right to Food, which might threaten to change the power relationships which make mass hunger possible, making the WFP complicit in a regressive system which causes starvation.

This is too systemic and overly deterministic as an analysis, though, for two reasons. Firstly, because it does not appreciate the fact that the role of food aid in development has tended to be regressive. Thus, the apparent narrowing of WFP's work away from long-term development to shorter-term emergency relief is also in fact a shift to focus food aid on the kind of work for which it is relatively and uncontroversially good. Secondly, because it does not take into account the ways that the operation of a multilateral organization, through its influence on international and domestic feed-the-hungry norms and related policy, has made possible the development of more progressive utilization of food aid, even starting to influence shifts in American policy. The WFP has created an organizational forum for testing and assessing ways of improving global governance in the food aid regime. This has resulted in more progressive policies being adopted by state and non-state actors as well as the WFP itself. This is most clearly demonstrated in the promotion of the moral claims of producers in poor countries ahead of rich country producers whose moral claims had been dominant in its early years.

Yet the linkage between food aid and donor (producer) interests in both bilateral and multilateral contexts is changing very slowly, and slowest of all in respect of the US, where the political alliances of domestic interest groups involved with food aid have so far blocked reforms, notwithstanding some normative and political pressure for change in procurement arrangements. The serial collapses (in July 2006 and then again in July 2008) of the Doha Round of trade talks on liberalising agricultural trade highlight the sensitivities of nations when it comes to agricultural trade. These failures also point to the structural difficulties confronting longer-term change to global politics, even when the numbers of the hungry poor are not declining. The 2007-08 global food crisis re-emphasizes the apparently intractable nature of global hunger in the international political economy as currently constituted.

In relative terms, the case of WFP shows us that international organizations within the UN system can evolve and adapt into successful, effective organizations (though there are no guarantees that such qualities will continue), given the right confluence of factors. Probably of most importance amongst these is the existence of stable hegemonic leadership based on credible inclusion, accountability and effectiveness creating legitimacy. Yet it is difficult to see how such leadership can emerge without a deep congruence between international regime norm(s) and norms within the hegemonic power's domestic polity. It is this congruence that may make it possible to diminish the tensions created by the paradox of hegemony to the point that genuinely legitimate global governance is possible.

At the same time, normative congruence does not occur in isolation from the operation of relevant interests, whether economic, humanitarian or strategic. The norm/interest pattern in a given issue area will be historically contingent and context specific. Failed attempts to reduce the predominance of in-kind food aid donations from the US point to the limits of international norm diffusion where a local norm and interests hold political sway. Nevertheless, understanding the interaction of norms and interests can assist in generating politically effective lobbying for change, as Barrett and Maxwell demonstrated when they successfully convinced CARE to stop monetizing food aid.

The international food aid regime provides a classic demonstration of hegemony, in the sense of a material dominance functioning in a politically legitimate domain. The central organization in the IFAR, the WFP, has emerged from a tawdry display of apparent benevolence driven by rich country self-interest to become one of the UN's most significant and respected operational agencies. It demonstrates American power, while at the same time garnering considerable international credibility. These characteristics suggest it is important to understand the extent to which WFP is actually engaged in legitimate (effective, inclusive and accountable) governance, and how it got to that point. In undertaking this task, this book has also been implicitly endeavouring to expand our understanding of global politics and the conditions in which intergovernmental organizations can function with relative success.

At the core of the WFP's high level of legitimacy is the fact that the number of hungry poor, and especially the number of fatally malnourished, is considerably less than it otherwise would be thanks to the work of that organization. More broadly, apart from its effectiveness, the WFP's legitimacy is also derived from reasonable levels of inclusion and accountability. All these characteristics incorporate some tensions and potentially negative aspects, but the institutional environment operates through the feed-the-hungry norm to harmonize and resolve such tensions. Although the international variant of the feed-the-hungry norm has diverged from the US domestic variant, there is still sufficient congruence between them to help the WFP garner strong support from the US, and there are even signs that the US domestic interests preventing improvements in US food aid policy may yet be constrained by the influence of the international norm.

Yet the form of global governance in which the WFP is engaged is not capable of changing the structures that ensure widespread malnutrition and food insecurity. The WFP is relatively effective, but not in terms of more absolute measures. This should not be surprising. Given the heterogeneous and fragmented nature of international regimes, regime-based global governance, even at its best, tends to be effective only in the relative sense, though a bad situation would surely be worse without such global governance.

The Millennium Development Goals (MDGs) are an expression of aspiration for a form of global governance which can make a real difference to substantial global problems. No one single regime is capable of solving a complex political problem of the order of global hunger by itself, as the framing of the MDGs attests. Thus, in providing measures of absolute rather than relative effectiveness, the MDGs have been consciously structured to try and bring together various international regimes around specific shared goals.

But what are the kinds of political circumstances that would be most propitious for achieving these goals? This examination of legitimacy in the IFAR and the WFP sheds some light on this issue because it illustrates the beneficial, yet constraining implications of US hegemony, and also the kind of confluence of factors by which constructive engagement of the US as hegemonic power can occur. The WFP's legitimacy stems from a normative underpinning that has enabled a peculiarly constructive, if limited, form of intergovernmental political consensus to emerge. This normative context also suggests that soft normative power can, in certain circumstances, be a path to effectiveness in international relations, despite the tendency for effectiveness to be seen as linked to hard, rule-based (legal) normative power.

If we can take away one important insight about global governance from the case of the WFP it is the importance of generating a genuine normative congruence between the international and the domestic. Such congruence can avoid too much reliance on the formulation of international law, which, all too often, lacks political salience at the domestic level. It is this congruence that can motivate action and deployment of resources by the most powerful nations, but on a shared international basis of understanding within the framework of an international regime. The story of the WFP suggests that such congruence can develop even in the most unlikely of circumstances.

Endnotes

[1] See the discussion in INTERFAIS/WFP 2008, 19 for these effects in recent years.

[2] Horton (2009, 36) argues that speculation on commodity prices is more symptom than cause of problems in grain markets – but this position seems not to take account of the reflexive nature of markets in which factors can be both cause and effect (e.g. see Soros 1988).

Acronyms

AFA	Alliance for Food Aid (US)
CCC	Commodity Credit Corporation (US)
CCP	Committee on Commodity Problems (FAO)
CFA	Committee on Food Aid Policies and Programmes (WFP), replaced IGC in 1976, replaced by EB in 1996
CFB	Combined Food Board
CIDA	Canadian International Development Agency
CS	Cooperating Sponsor
CSD	Subcommittee on Surplus Disposal (FAO CCP; renamed CSSD in 1995)
CSSD	Consultative Subcommittee on Surplus Disposal (FAO CCP; CSD prior to 1995)
D-G	Director-General (FAO)
DAC	Development Assistance Committee (OECD)
DFID	Department for International Development (UK)
DSC	Direct Support Costs (WFP)
EB	Executive Board (WFP), replaced CFA in 1996
EC	European Commission
ECOSOC	United Nations Economic and Social Council
ED	Executive Director (WFP)
EMOPS	Emergency Operations (WFP)
EU	European Union
FAC	Food Aid Convention
FAO	Food and Agriculture Organization of the United Nations
FAS	Foreign Agricultural Service (USDA)
FCR	Full Cost Recovery (WFP)
FD	Fundraising and communications department (WFP)
FFHC	Freedom from Hunger Campaign (FAO)
FFP	Food for Peace (US)
FMIP/ WINGS	Financial Management Improvement Programme/ WFP Information Network Global System (WFP)
FoWFP	Friends of WFP (US)
FY	Fiscal Year (US, October – September)

G8	Group of 8 (states with the world's leading economies)
G20	Group of 20 (states with the world's leading economies)
G77	Group of 77 (developing country UN member-states)
GATT	General Agreement on Tariffs and Trade
GNI	Gross National Income
HIV/AIDS	Human immuno-deficiency virus/Acquired Immune Deficiency Syndrome
HQ	Headquarters
ICCH	International Commodity Clearing House
IEFC	International Emergency Food Council (later Committee)
IEFR	International Emergency Food Reserve
IFAD	International Fund for Agricultural Development
IFAR	International food aid regime
ILO	International Labor Organisation
IGC	Inter-Governmental Committee (governing body of the World Food Programme, replaced by CFA in 1976)
IGO	Intergovernmental Organisation
IR	International Relations
ISC	Indirect Support Costs (WFP)
IIA	International Institute of Agriculture
LTSH	Landside transport, storage and handling (WFP)
MDG	Millennium Development Goal
MOU	Memorandum of Understanding (WFP)
MSF	Medecins sans Frontières (Doctors without Borders)
NAFTA	North American Free Trade Agreement
NGO	Nongovernmental Organisation
NIEO	New International Economic Order
ODA	Official Development Assistance
ODOC	Other Direct Operational Costs (WFP)
OECD	Organisation for Economic Cooperation and Development
OPEC	Organisation of Petroleum Exporting Countries
P5	Permanent Five members of the UN Security Council
PL480	Public Law 480 (US); The Agricultural Trade Development and Assistance Act, 1954
PRRO	Protracted Relief and Recovery Operation (WFP)
PSA	Programme Support and Administration (WFP)
PVO	Private Voluntary Organization (US)
SDDP	Special Dairy Distribution Program (US)

TEFAP	Temporary (later The) Emergency Food Assistance Program (US)
TNC	Transnational corporation
UK	United Kingdom
UN	United Nations
UNDP	United Nations Development Program
UNFPA	United Nations Fund for Population Activities
UNHCR	United Nations High Commissioner for Refugees
UNHRC	United Nations Human Rights Commission
UNICEF	United Nations International Children's Fund
US	United States of America
USAID	United States Agency for International Development
USDA	United States Department of Agriculture
USSR	Union of Soviet Socialist Republics
VAM	Vulnerability Analysis and Mapping (WFP)
WFB	World Food Board
WFP	World Food Programme (Note 'Programme' adopted instead of 'Program' in 1967)

Appendix 1: UN General Assembly Resolution 1714

Text of Resolution 1714 of the XVIth Session, UN General Assembly, 19 December 1961 – World Food Program (Incorporating as Annex 1, Resolution of the FAO Conference, 24 November 1961)

The General Assembly

Recalling its resolution 1496 (XV) of 27 October 1960 and Economic and Social Council resolution 832 (XXXII) of 2 August 1960 on the provision of Food surpluses to food-deficient peoples through the United Nations system,

Having considered the report of the Director-General of the Food and Agriculture Organization of the United Nations entitled *Development through Food – A Strategy for Surplus Utilization*, the report of the Secretary-General entitled "The role of the United Nations and the appropriate specialized agencies in facilitating the best possible use of food surpluses for the economic development of the less developed countries", and the joint proposal by the United Nations and the Food and Agriculture Organization of the United Nations regarding procedures and arrangements for multilateral utilization of surplus food,

Having reviewed the action taken at the eleventh session of the Conference of the Food and Agriculture Organization on the utilization of food surpluses and, specifically, its resolution of 24 November 1961 stating that, subject to the concurrence of the General Assembly of the United Nations, an initial experimental programme for three years, to be known as the World Food Programme should be undertaken, having also noted in particular the reference to safeguards contained in paragraph 13 of the above-mentioned resolution,

Recognizing the existing facilities for consultation provided by the Food and Agriculture Organization through its Consultative Sub-Committee on Surplus Disposals,

Bearing in mind its resolution 1710 (XVI) of 19 December 1961 on the United Nations Development Decade, and in particular the reference in paragraph 4 (*d*) to the elimination of illiteracy, hunger and disease,

I

1. *Approves* the establishment of an experimental World Food Programme to be undertaken jointly by the United Nations and the Food and Agriculture Organization of the United Nations, in co-operation with other interested United Nations agencies and appropriate inter-governmental bodies, bearing in mind that the establishment of such a programme in no way prejudices the bilateral agreements between developed and developing countries, and accepts and endorses the purposes, principles and procedures formulated in the first part of the resolution approved by the Conference of the Food and Agriculture Organization on 24 November 1961, the text of which is annexed to the present resolution, including the safeguards mentioned in that resolution and General Assembly resolution 1496 (XV), especially in paragraph 9 thereof;
2. *Approves* specifically the establishment of a United Nations/FAO Inter-Governmental Committee of twenty States Members of the United Nations and members of the Food and Agriculture Organization to provide guidance on policy, administration and operations, and of a joint United Nations/FAO administrative unit reporting to the Secretary-General of the United Nations and the Director-General of the Food and Agriculture Organization;
3. *Requests* the Economic and Social Council at its resumed thirty-second session to elect, subject to the provisions of paragraph 9 below, ten States Members of the United Nations and members of the Food and Agriculture Organization to the United Nations/FAO Inter-Governmental Committee, taking into account:

   (a) The representation provided by the ten States that were elected to serve on the United Nations/FAO Inter-Governmental Committee by the Council of the Food and Agriculture Organization;

   (b) The need for balanced representation of economically developed and developing countries, and other relevant factors such as the representation of potential participating countries, both contributing and recipient, equitable geographical distribution and the representation of both developed and less

developed countries having commercial interests in international trade in foodstuffs, especially those highly dependent on such trade;

4. *Calls upon* the Economic and Social Council at its thirty-third session, in co-operation with the Council of the Food and Agriculture Organization, to review and to take appropriate action on the procedures and arrangements for the World Food Programme recommended by the United Nations/FAO Inter-Governmental Committee;
5. *Decides* that pilot projects to be undertaken by the joint United Nations/FAO administrative unit, under the guidance of the United Nations/FAO Intergovernmental Committee, involving the use of food as an aid to economic and social development, shall be undertaken in agreement between the Secretary-General, acting on behalf of the United Nations, and the Director-General, acting on behalf of the Food and Agriculture Organization;
6. *Concurs* in the calling of a conference where States Members of the United Nations and members of the Food and Agriculture Organization will be invited to pledge contributions;
7. *Requests* the Secretary-General, in co-operation with the Director-General of the Food and Agriculture Organization, to convene such a conference at United Nations headquarters as soon as feasible after the concurrent sessions of the Economic and Social Council and the Council of the Food and Agriculture Organization;
8. *Urges* States Members of the United Nations and members of the Food and Agriculture Organization, in considering their contributions, to make every effort to assure the early attainment, on a voluntary basis, of the $100 million programme;
9. *Further requests* the Economic and Social Council, in co-operation with the Council of the Food and Agriculture Organization, at its next regular session following the pledging conference, to review the composition of the United Nations/FAO Inter-Governmental Committee and to make, by election for the balance of the three-year programme, any adjustments of membership that might be deemed desirable in the light of the considerations outlined in paragraph 3 above;
10. *Instructs* the United Nations/FAO Inter-Governmental Committee, in preparing recommendation on the conditions and procedures for the establishment and operation of the programme for the review and approval by the Economic and Social Council and the Council of the Food and Agriculture

Organization, to proceed on the basis of the present resolution and the resolution of the Conference of the Food and Agriculture Organization of 24 November 1961, taking into account the joint proposal by the United Nations and the Food and Agriculture Organization regarding procedures and arrangements for the multilateral utilization of surplus food, statements made during the debates in the General Assembly and in the Conference of the Food and Agriculture Organization and such other conditions and procedures as may seem to it appropriate;

11. *Recommends* that Governments requesting assistance under this programme, the United Nations/FAO Inter-Governmental Committee, and the joint United Nations/FAO administrative unit responsible for the administration of the program, keep the resident representatives fully informed about, and, within their field of competence, associated with, activities undertaken under the programme;
12. *Invites* the Secretary-General of the United Nations and the Director-General of the Food and Agriculture Organization to ensure that, in carrying out the programme, the joint United Nations/FAO administrative unit rely to the fullest extent possible on the existing staff and facilities of the United Nations and the Food and Agriculture Organization, as well as other appropriate inter-governmental agencies;
13. *Requests* the United Nations/FAO Inter-Governmental Committee to report annually to the Economic and Social Council and to the Council of the Food and Agriculture Organization on the progress made in the development of the programme and on its administration and operation;
14. *Decides* to undertake, not later than at its nineteenth session, a general review of the programme, taking into account the objectives of its resolution 1496 (XV);

II

Recognizing that the experimental programme outlined above constitutes a step towards the broader objectives outlined in its resolution 1496 (XV),

Recognizing further that the ultimate solution to this problem of food deficiency lies in self-sustaining economic growth of the economies of the less developed countries to the point where they find it possible to meet their food requirements from their food-producing industries or from the proceeds of their expanding export trade,

Recognizing that the effective utilization of available surplus foodstuffs, in ways compatible with the principles of surplus disposal recommended by the Food and Agriculture Organization of the United Nations, provides an important transitional means of relieving the hunger and malnutrition of food-deficient peoples, particularly in the less developed countries, and for assisting these countries in their economic development,

Recognizing further that food aid is not a substitute for other types of assistance, in particular for capital goods,

1. *Recognizes* that food aid to be provided under this programme should take into account other forms of assistance and country plans for economic and social development;
2. *Requests* the Secretary-General of the United Nations, in close co-operation with the Director-General of the Food and Agriculture Organization of the United Nations and with interested groups or agencies, and jointly where appropriate, to undertake, as soon as feasible, expert studies which would aid in the consideration of the future development of multilateral food programmes;
3. *Expresses the hope* that, in the light of these studies and of the experience gained, the progress of the experimental programme will be such as to permit the United Nations and the Food and Agriculture Organization to consider the possibility and advisability of increasing the programme, taking into account the advantages to developing countries, the interests of the contributing States, the interests of the food-exporting countries, the effectiveness of the programme and its contribution to the objectives of General Assembly resolution 1496 (XV);
4. *Endorses again* the Freedom from Hunger Campaign launched by the Food and Agriculture Organization and requests the Secretary-General of the United Nations and the Director-General of the Food and Agriculture Organization, simultaneously with the implementation of the present resolution, to pay particular attention to the necessity of improving and increasing local food production and to include, where appropriate, reference to this subject in the reports mentioned above, and requests the United Nations/FAO Inter-Governmental Committee to consider the possibility of applying to this purpose a reasonable proportion of resources resulting from the World Food Programme.

1084th plenary meeting, 19 December 1961.

Annex

PART I OF THE RESOLUTION ON THE UTILIZATION OF FOOD SURPLUSES ADOPTED BY THE CONFERENCE OF THE FOOD AND AGRICULTURE ORGANIZATION OF THE UNITED NATIONS ON 24 NOVEMBER 1961

The Conference,

...

I

Resolves, subject to the concurrence of the General Assembly of the United Nations, that:

1. An initial experimental programme for three years of approximately $100 million with contributions on a voluntary basis be undertaken jointly by the Food and Agriculture Organization and the United Nations, in co-operation with other United Nations agencies, and appropriate inter-governmental bodies;
2. Contributions to the programme, to be known as the World Food Programme, may be pledged by countries in the form of appropriate commodities, acceptable services, and cash aiming in the aggregate at a cash component of at least one-third of the total contributions, and countries should give due regard to the importance of achieving this over-all objective when determining the cash element in their contribution;
3. An Inter-Governmental Committee of twenty nations which are members of FAO or the United Nations be established to provide guidance on policy, administration and operations, as outlined in paragraphs 11 and 12 of part III of the joint report of the Secretary-General and the Director-General;
4. The Committee be elected half by the FAO Council and half by the United Nations, taking into account the need for balanced representation of economically developed countries and of less developed countries and other relevant factors. In appointing its representative each Government should pay due regard to the complexities of the executive and operational planning required for the proposed programme;

5. The Inter-Governmental Committee meet in Rome early in 1962 to develop detailed procedures and arrangements for the Programme on the basis of this resolution, taking due account of the joint report of the Secretary-General and the Director-General and giving consideration to the views expressed in reports of meetings related to this subject held under the auspices of FAO and the United Nations;
6. The procedures and arrangements drawn up by the Inter-Governmental Committee be reviewed and approved in concurrent sessions of the Council of FAO and the Economic and Social Council in New York in April 1962;
7. A conference for contributing countries to pledge their contributions in accordance with paragraph 2 above be convened by the Secretary-General and the Director-General after the concurrent sessions of the FAO Council and the Economic and Social Council;
8. The FAO Council and the Economic and Social Council, at their next regular meetings following the pledging conference, should make any adjustment of country composition on the Inter-Governmental Committee (of twenty) that might be deemed desirable in view of the considerations mentioned in paragraph 4 above;
9. Subject to the guidance of the Inter-Governmental Committee, the Programme will be carried on by a joint FAO/United Nations administrative unit located at FAO Headquarters in Rome and reporting to both the Director-General and the Secretary-General, with the costs of administration and operation under this resolution to be met from contributions to the programme;
10. In the administration of the Programme attention should be paid to:

(*a*) Establishing adequate and orderly procedures on a world basis for meeting emergency food needs and emergencies inherent in chronic malnutrition (this could include the establishment of food reserves);

(*b*) Assisting in pre-school and school feeding; and

(*c*) Implementing pilot projects, with the multilateral use of food as an aid to economic and social development, particularly when related to labour-intensive projects and rural welfare;

11. Projects should be undertakèn only in response to requests from the recipient country or countries concerned;
12. The administration of the proposed Programme will be require close co-operation, particularly on development projects,

between FAO and the United Nations, as well as with appropriate United Nations agencies, and other appropriate inter-governmental bodies;

13. The Inter-Governmental Committee shall ensure that:

(i) In accordance with the FAO principles of surplus disposal and with the consultative procedures established by the Committee on Commodity Problems, and in conformity with the United Nations General Assembly resolution 1496 (XV), particularly paragraph 9, commercial markets and normal and developing trade are neither interfered with nor disrupted;

(ii) The agricultural economy in recipient countries is adequately safeguarded with respect both to its domestic markets and the effective development of food production;

(iii) Due consideration is given to safeguarding normal commercial practices in respect to acceptable services.

Source: (UN General Assembly 1961, 20-3)

Appendix 2: FAO Principles of Surplus Disposal

Excerpted from FAO Council Resolution No. 2/20, 1954

General Principles

1. The solution to problems of agricultural disposal should be sought, wherever possible, through efforts to increase consumption rather than through measures to restrict supplies.
2. Member Governments which have excess stocks of agricultural products should dispose of such products in an orderly manner so as to avoid any undue pressure resulting in sharp falls of prices on world markets, particularly when prices of agricultural products are generally low.
3. Where surpluses are disposed of under special terms, there should be an undertaking from both importing and exporting countries that such arrangements will be made without harmful interference with the normal patterns of production and international trade.

Source: (FAO 2001, Appendix G, 34).

Appendix 3: Statement by George S. McGovern, 10 April 1961

Statement by the Honourable George S. McGovern, Delegate of the United States of America to FAO Intergovernmental Advisory Committee, Rome, Italy, 10 April 1961.

1. The United States favors a multilateral approach for the use of agricultural commodities as a supplement to bilateral arrangements.
2. We think FAO should have a major role in such a program, in co-operation with other UN organizations.
3. We believe this should be a truly multilateral program with the widest possible contributions by member countries.
4. We recognize that countries are here to advise the FAO Director-General on his report – not to take government positions on subjects covered in his report. Because of the need to move to the consideration of specific action proposals, however, we have been in touch with our Government over the weekend.
5. As a result, we are authorized to propose that an initial program on a multilateral basis might aim at a fund of $100 million in commodities and cash contributions. For its part, the United States would be prepared to offer $40 million in commodities, and the possibility of a supplementary cash contribution will be explored in Washington.
6. The $100 million total would be available for use over a fixed forward period. We are thinking of three years.
7. We recognize the desire of the (FAO) Director-General to make the widest possible use of commodities in alleviating malnutrition. However, we continue to believe that the primary aim of the program in its initial stage should be to meet emergency needs. At the same time, we would support use of the program fund for pilot activities in other fields such as school lunch or labor-intensive projects, in order to develop some diversified experience.

8. Specifics including additional staffing would have to be worked out for consideration by governments. This could be the responsibility of the (FAO) Director-General in informal consultation with individual countries.
9. The purpose of our proposal is to help in launching a multilateral program utilizing food to test approaches. After such experience, we could then examine the question of future additional work.

Source: (FAO 1962, 121-22).

Appendix 4: WFP Mission Statement

'In December 1994, WFP's governing body adopted the WFP Mission Statement, the first for an United Nations organization. The Mission Statement was based on a fundamental review of WFP's policies, objectives and strategies that involved member states of WFP, non-governmental organizations, United Nations and other agencies, academics and staff members. The WFP Mission Statement is to be considered as a living document that will be reviewed periodically.' (WFP 2007e)

The WFP Mission Statement

WFP is the food aid arm of the United Nations system. Food aid is one of the many instruments that can help to promote food security, which is defined as access of all people at all times to the food needed for an active and healthy life.[1] The policies governing the use of World Food Programme food aid must be oriented towards the objective of eradicating hunger and poverty. The ultimate objective of food aid should be the elimination of the need for food aid.

Targeted interventions are needed to help to improve the lives of the poorest people - people who, either permanently or during crisis periods, are unable to produce enough food or do not have the resources to otherwise obtain the food that they and their households require for active and healthy lives.

Consistent with its mandate, which also reflects the principle of universality, WFP will continue to:

- use food aid to support economic and social development;
- meet refugee and other emergency food needs, and the associated logistics support; and
- promote world food security in accordance with the recommendations of the United Nations and FAO.

The core policies and strategies that govern WFP activities are to provide food aid:

- to save lives in refugee and other emergency situations;
- to improve the nutrition and quality of life of the most vulnerable people at critical times in their lives; and
- to help build assets and promote the self-reliance of poor people and communities, particularly through labour-intensive works programmes.

In the first case, food aid is essential for social and humanitarian protection. It will be used in a way that is as developmental as possible, consistent with saving lives. To the extent possible, the provision of relief food aid will be coordinated with the relief assistance provided by other humanitarian organizations. In the second case, food aid is a pre-investment in human resources. In the third, it uses poor people's most abundant resource, their own labour, to create employment and income and to build the infrastructure necessary for sustained development.

WFP is well placed to play a major role in the continuum from emergency relief to development. WFP will give priority to supporting disaster prevention, preparedness and mitigation and post-disaster rehabilitation activities as part of development programmes. Conversely, emergency assistance will be used to the extent possible to serve both relief and development purposes. In both cases the overall aim is to build self-reliance.

In carrying out its mandate, WFP will concentrate on what it is best suited to do with the resources available as cost-effectively as possible. WFP will focus on those aspects of development where food-based interventions are most useful. It will make all necessary efforts to avoid negative effects on local food production, consumption patterns and dependency on food aid. WFP will continue to play a major and significant role in providing transport and logistics expertise and assistance to ensure rapid and efficient delivery of humanitarian aid.

WFP's multilateral character is one of its greatest strengths. WFP will exploit its capability to operate virtually everywhere in the developing world, without regard to the political orientations of governments, and to provide a neutral conduit for assistance in situations where many donor countries could not directly provide assistance. WFP will provide services: advice, good offices, logistic support and information; and support to countries in establishing and managing their own food assistance programmes.

WFP, on request, will provide bilateral services to donors, UN agencies and NGOs on the basis of full cost recovery. These will be administered and accounted for separately. Such services will complement WFP's regular operations to the extent possible.

WFP will concentrate its efforts and resources on the neediest people[2] and countries in accordance with the CFA's decision to provide at least 90 percent of WFP's development assistance to low-income, food-deficit countries and at least 50 percent of its development assistance to the least developed countries by 1997.

WFP will ensure that its assistance programmes are designed and implemented on the basis of broad-based participation. Women in particular are key to change; providing food to women puts it in the hands of those who use it for the benefit of the entire household, especially the children. WFP assistance will aim to strengthen their coping ability and resilience.

To be truly effective, food aid should be fully integrated into the development plans and priorities of recipient countries and coordinated with other forms of assistance. WFP's starting point is the national policies, plans and programmes of developing countries, including their food security plans. WFP will pull together its activities in an integrated way at the country level so that it can respond to urgent needs as they occur while retaining core development objectives. The country strategy note, where this exists, should provide the framework for an integrated response by the United Nations system. In some special cases WFP will adopt a multi-country or regional approach. particularly for the provision of humanitarian assistance.

No single agency has either the resources or the capacity to deal with all the problems of hunger and underdevelopment. Hence the importance WFP attaches to collaboration with other agencies, particularly with its parent bodies, the United Nations and FAO. WFP will continue to work closely with the United Nations Department of Humanitarian Affairs, UNHCR, other relevant agencies and non-governmental organizations (NGOs) in the response to emergencies and humanitarian crises. WFP will also collaborate closely with the Rome-based United Nations food and agriculture agencies, FAO and IFAD, especially in using food aid for achieving household food security. WFP will continue to forge effective partnerships of action with the World Bank and the International Monetary Fund, regional bodies and institutions, bilateral donors and NGOs in support of economic and social development.

WFP will play its part as an active member of the United Nations system to bring the issue of hunger to the centre of the international agenda. In its dialogue with recipient governments and the aid community, WFP will advocate policies, strategies and operations that directly benefit the poor and hungry.

[1] FAO/WHO (1992) International Conference on Nutrition

[2] Normally, poor and hungry people are those who earn less than the equivalent of one dollar a day, or who allocate the majority of their household budget to food.

Source:(WFP 2007e).

Bibliography

Aal, William, Lucy Jarosz and Carol Thompson (2009). "Open Letter to Paul Collier, in response to 'Politics of Hunger'." 22 January 2009. http://www.seattleglobaljustice.org/2009/01/open-letter-to-paul-collier-in-response-to-%E2%80%9Cpolitics-of-hunger%E2%80%9D/ accessed 25 November 2009.

Accardo, G. P. and S. T. O'Neall (2005). *Empire of Shame: A Conversation with Jean Ziegler*, 19 December 2005. http://www.countercurrents.org accessed 18 October 2007.

Adam, D. (2008). "Food Price Rises Threaten Global Security - UN." *The Guardian* (UK), 9 April 2008. http://www.commondreams.org/archive/2008/04/09/8192/ accessed 8 June 2008.

Agexporter (2003). "A Small Agency With a Big Mission: 50 Years of the Foreign Agricultural Service." *AgExporter*, March 2003: 12-15. http://www.fas.usda.gov/info/agexporter/2003/March/pgs12-15.pdf accessed 27 September 2006

Al-Bawaba Reporters (2006a). "Lebanese Singer Assi Helani Sings for the World's Hungry Children." Comtex News Network, Inc., Wire service report, 8 September 2006. http://web.lexis-nexis.com.ezproxy.lib.unimelb.edu.au/universe/document?_m=28ee3a407a306ae37e4aaa534fb1c845&_docnum=79&wchp=dGLbVzWzSkVb&_md5=3dc6388343108bd5337cca09afd3e1ad accessed 14 January 2007.

Al-Bawaba Reporters (2006b). "Saudis step in to support WFP in West Africa." Comtex News Network, Inc., Wire service report, 19 September 2006. http://web.lexis-nexis.com.ezproxy.lib.unimelb.edu.au/universe/document?_m=e662d5c8f87bfd152ec01db8df36f681&_docnum=75&wchp=dGLbVzW-zSkVb&_md5=fc2d1b3fe8b7cf18202b684ed64bec98 accessed 14 January 2007.

Alger, C. F. (2001). "Thinking About the Future of the UN System" in *The Politics of Global Governance: International Organizations in an Interdependent World*. P. F. Diehl (ed). Boulder, Co: Lynne Rienner Publishers: 483-508.

Alliance for Food Aid (2007a). "AFA Comments on GAO Food Aid Review." Washington DC: Alliance for Food Aid. News Release, 13 April 2007. http://www.allianceforfoodaid.com/Default.aspx?tabid=58&metaid=H5ER0043-69a accessed 22 August 2007.

Alliance for Food Aid (2007b). "Twisting the Facts on Food Aid." Washington DC: Alliance for Food Aid. News Release, 17 August 2007.

http://www.allianceforfoodaid.com/Default.aspx?tabid=58&metaid=H9IU5555-d6f accessed 22 August 2007.

Annan, Kofi (2010). "Africa's Breadbaskets: Key to Achieving Food Security." Statement from Chairman: Alliance for a Green Revolution in Africa. http://www.agra-alliance.org/section/news/chairman_speech/ accessed 20 February 2010.

Anon. (2005). Personal communication, *NGO staffer*. Rome, 16 June 2005.

Archer, C. (2001). *International Organizations*. London: Routledge.

Asia Pulse (2006). "Philippines wins seat on World Food Programme Executive Board." Manila: Asia Pulse Pty Limited. Wire service report, 29 November 2006. http://web.lexis-nexis.com.ezproxy.lib.unimelb.edu.au/universe/document?_m=e13d36b2846faeedf8606a8b44ca104f&_docnum=31&wchp=dGLbVzW-zSkVb&md5=7b51408d1ef61286880961d4b732587b accessed 14 January 2007.

Associated Press (2006a). "Food Crisis looms in North, says UN agency." *The Age* (Melbourne), 17 October 2006: 8.

Associated Press (2006b). "Hunger declines 1st time in 6 years. 3 million fewer people struggled to get food in '05, USDA says." 16 November 2006. http://www.msnbc.msn.com/id/15737285/ accessed 16 November 2006.

Associations, Union of International, (ed) (2005). *Yearbook of International Organizations 2004/2005*. Munich: K.G. Saur.

Balaam, D. N. and M. J. Carey (eds) (1981). *Food Politics: The Regional Conflict*. Totowa, NJ: Allanheld, Osmun.

Bailey, Sarah (2010). "Somalia Food Aid Diversion." ODIblog, 15 March 2010. ODI. http://blogs.odi.org.uk/blogs/main/archive/2010/03/15/somalia_food_aid_diversion.aspx accessed 20 August 2010.

Barnett, M. and M. Finnemore, (eds) (2004). *Rules for the World: International Organizations in Global Politics*. Ithaca and London: Cornell University Press.

Barrett, C. B. and D. G. Maxwell (2005). *Food Aid After Fifty Years: Recasting its Role*. London and New York: Routledge.

Baxter, Joan (2010). "Africa's Land and Family Farms - Up for Grabs?" *Seedling*, January 2010: 13-16.

Bello, Walden (2009). *The Food Wars*. London and New York: Verso.

Bennett, A. L. R. and J. K. Oliver (2002). *International Organizations: Principles and Issues*. Upper Saddle River, NJ, Prentice Hall.

Bentley, A. (2002). Islands of Serenity: Gender, Race, and Ordered Meals During World War II. in *Food in the USA: A Reader*. C. M. Counihan. New York and London, Routledge: 171-192.

Bentley, A. L. (1994). "Uneasy Sacrifice: The Politics of United States Famine Relief, 1945-48." *Agriculture and Human Values* **11**(4): 4-18.

Berry, J. M. (1984). *Feeding Hungry People: Rulemaking in the Food Stamp Program*. New Brunswick, NJ, Rutgers University Press.

Bertini, C. (1998). *Annual Report of the Executive Director: 1997 Recovery from Crisis*. Rome, WFP, WFP/EB.A/1998/3-A, 4 May 1998. http://www.wfp.org/eb/docs/1998/wfp001616.pdf accessed 3 September 2007.

Bertini, C. (2005a). HIRC Testimony. 2172 Rayburn House Office Building, Washington DC, US House of Representatives International Relations Committee, 19 May 2005.

Bertini, Catherine (2005b). WFP Executive Director 1992-2002. Interview, Cortland, NY, 26-27 May 2005.

Bertini, Catherine and Dan Glickman (cochairs) (2009). *Renewing American Leadership in the Fight Against Global Hunger and Poverty*. Report issued by an Independent Leaders Group on Global Agricultural Development, Chicago: Chicago Council on Global Affairs.

Bird, G. (2001). "The International Monetary Fund and Developing Countries: A Review of the Evidence and Policy Options" in *The Politics of Global Governance: International Organizations in an Interdependent World*. P. F. Diehl (ed). Boulder, Co: Lynne Rienner Publishers: 277-312.

Bittman, Mark (2008). "Rethinking the Meat-Guzzler." *The New York Times*, 29 January 2008.

Blas, Javier (2009). "Number of Chronically Hungry Tops 1 Billion." *Financial Times* (UK), 27 March 2009.

Blyth, M. M. (2002). Great Transformations: Economic ideas and institutional change in the Twentieth Century. Cambridge: Cambridge University Press.

Boli, J. and G. Thomas (1999). "INGOs and the Organization of World Culture" in *Constructing World Culture: International nongovernmental organizations since 1375*. J. Boli and G. Thomas (eds). Stanford: Stanford University Press: 13-49.

Bolton, J. R. (2008). *Surrender is not an option : defending America at the United Nations and abroad*. New York: Threshold Editions.

Borione, D. and G. Comergnat (1998). *Results of Survey on WFP/NGOs Collaboration at Country Level*. September 1998, Rome: WFP.

Bourn, S. J. (2007). "Special Audit Requested by the Executive Board in Relation to WFP's Activities in the Democratic People's Republic of Korea." WFP/EB.2/2007/5-F, 27 August 2007, Rome: WFP. http://www.wfp.org/eb/docs/2007/wfp137241.pdf accessed 10 September 2007.

Bovard, J. (1993). Box One: "How American Food Aid Keeps the Third World Hungry." in *Why Food Aid?* V. W. Ruttan (ed). Baltimore: The Johns Hopkins University Press: 95-96.

Bovens, M. (1998). The Quest for Responsibility: Accountability and Citizenship in Complex Organisations. Cambridge: Cambridge University Press.

Bowers, D. E., W. D. Rasmussen and G. L. Baker (1985). *History of Agricultural Support and Price-Adjustment Programs 1933-84*. Economic Research Service: USDA. Agriculture Information Bulletin Number 485. http://www.ers.usda.gov/publications/aib485/aib485.pdf accessed 27 July 2007.

Bredholt, Nick (2005). International Cooperation Department, Caritas Internationalis. Interview, Rome, 16&20 June 2005.

Brett, J. (2007). "The Country, the City and the State in the Australian Settlement." *Australian Journal of Political Science* **42**(1): 1-17.

Brown, J. L. and H. F. Pizer (1987). *Living Hungry in America*. New York: Macmillan Publishing Company.

Bryden, Matt, Arnaud Laloum and Jorg Roothooft (2010). *Report of the Monitoring Group on Somalia Pursuant to Security Council Resolution 1853 (2008)*. UN Security Council S/2010/91, 10 March 2010.

http://daccess-dds-ny.un.org/doc/UNDOC/GEN/N10/246/89/PDF/N1024689.pdf?OpenElement accessed 18 March 2010.

Lyers, Emily (2005). *Senior Trade Policy Analyst, Bread for the World.* Interview, Washington DC, 20 May 2005.

Cathie, J. (1982). *The Political Economy of Food Aid.* Aldershot: Gower.

Cerny, P. G. (1995). "Globalization and the changing logic of collective action." *International Organization* **49**(4): 595-625.

Charlton, M. W. (1992). "Innovation and inter-organizational politics: the case of the World Food Programme." *International Journal* **XLVII** (Summer 1992): 630-665.

Charlton, M. W. (1993). *The Making of Canadian Food Aid Policy.* Montreal and Kingston: McGill-Queen's University Press.

Chayes, A. and A. H. Chayes (1998). *The New Sovereignty: Compliance with International Regulatory Agreements.* Cambridge, Mass.: Harvard University Press.

Checkel, J. T. (1997). "International Norms and Domestic Politics: Bridging the Rationalist—Constructivist Divide." *European Journal of International Relations* **3**(4): 473-495.

Checkel, J. T. (1998). "The Constructivist Turn in International Relations Theory." *World Politics* **58**(2): 324-348.

Checkel, J. T. (1999). "Norms, Institutions, and National Identity in Contemporary Europe." *International Studies Quarterly* **43**(1): 83-114.

Chr. Michelsen Institute (1994). *Evaluation of the World Food Programme.* Bergen, Norway: Chr. Michelsen Institute.

Clapp, J. (2004). "WTO agricultural trade battles and food aid." *Third World Quarterly* **25**(8): 1439-1452.

Clapp, J. (2005). "The Political Economy of Food Aid in an Era of Agricultural Biotechnology." *Global Governance* **11**(4): 467-485.

Clark, I. (2005). *Legitimacy in International Society.* Oxford: Oxford University Press.

Clark, I. and C. Reus-Smit (2007). "Preface to Special Issue: Resolving International Crises of Legitimacy." *International Politics* **44**(2/3): 153-156.

Clay, E. J. (2003). "Responding to Change: WFP and the global food aid system." *Development Policy Review* **21**(5): 697-709.

Clay, J. W. and B. K. Holcomb (1986). *Politics and the Ethiopian Famine 1984-1985.* Cambridge Mass.: Cultural Survival, Inc.

Coleman, W., W. Grant and T. Josling (2004). *Agriculture in the New Global Economy.* Cheltenham, UK; Northampton MA, USA: Edward Elgar.

Collier, Paul (2008). "The politics of hunger: how illusion and greed fan the food crisis." *Foreign Affairs* **87**(6): 67-80.

Commonweal (2007). "Standing Up to Mugabe." *Commonweal.* **134**(9), 4 May 2007.

Cortell, A. P. and J. W. Davis (1996). "How do International Institutions Matter? The Domestic Impact of International Rules and Norms." *International Studies Quarterly* **40**(4): 451-478.

Cortell, A. P. and J. W. Davis (2005). "When norms clash: international norms, domestic practices, and Japan's internalisation of the GATT/WTO." *Review of International Studies* **31**(1): 3-25.

Coultan, M. (2006). "Nepotism and bias 'rife' at UN." *The Age* (Melbourne), 16 June 2006: 8.

Counihan, C. M. (2002). "Introduction: Food and the Nation." in *Food in the USA: A Reader*. C. M. Counihan (ed). New York and London: Routledge.

Craig, R. A. and K. J. Phillips (1983). "Agrarian Ideology in Australia and the United States." *Rural Sociology* **48**(3): 409-420.

Dallek, R. (1979). Franklin D. Roosevelt and American foreign policy, 1932-1945. New York: Oxford University Press.

Davis, B. and V. Tarasuk (1994). "Hunger in Canada." *Agriculture and Human Values* **11**(4): 50-57.

Dawe, David (2009). "The Unimportance of 'Low' World Grain Stocks for Recent World Price Increases." ESA Working Paper No. 09-01, Rome: FAO.

de Waal, A. (1997). Famine Crimes: Politics & the Disaster Relief Industry in Africa. Oxford: James Currey.

Demeke, Matt, Guendalina Pangrazio and Materne Maetz (2008). "Country responses to the food security crisis: Nature and preliminary implications of the policies pursued." December 2008, Rome: FAO.

DeParle, Jason (2009). "Hunger in U.S. at a 14-Year High." *The New York Times*, 16 November 2009.

Diehl, P. F., (ed) (2001). *The Politics of Global Governance: International Organizations in an Interdependent World.* Boulder: Lynne Rienner Publishers.

Doyle, Leonard (2007). "US Food Aid is 'Wrecking' Africa, Claims Charity." *The Independent* (UK), 17 August 2007.

Doyle, Leonard (2008). "Starving Haitians Riot As Food Prices Soar." *The Independent* (UK), 10 April 2008.

Drago, Tito (2009). "Food Summit – Concern Yes, Concrete Steps No." Inter Press Service, 27 January 2009. http://www.commondreams.org/headline/2009/01/27-11 accessed 15 February 2009.

Dufwenbergy, M. and M. Lundholmz (1998). *Social norms and moral hazard.* Uppsala University, Department of Economics, Working Paper Series No. 1997:28, Uppsala: Uppsala University,

Dugger, C. (2007). "CARE Turns Down Federal Funds for Food Aid." *The New York Times*, 16 August 2007.

Dutta, P. and R. Radner (1994). "Moral hazard." in *Handbook of Game Theory* (Vol. 2). R. J. Aumann and S. Hart (eds). Amsterdam: Elsevier Science B.V.: 869-903.

Eckersley, R. (2007). "Norms and Interests in US Climate Policy: The Fate of 'Common but Differentiated Responsibilities'." Paper presented at the 4th General ECPR Conference, Pisa, Italy, 6-8 September 2007.

Economist. (2008). "A Screaming Start." *Economist.* **387:** 77-78.

Egeland, J. (2008). A Billion Lives: An Eyewitness Report from the Frontlines of Humanity. New York: Simon and Schuster.

Elliott, L. M. (1994). *International Environmental Politics.* New York: St Martin's Press.

Environmental News Service (2008). "UN: Biofuel Production 'Criminal Path' to Global Food Crisis." 29 April 2008: Environmental News Service. http://www.commondreams.org/archive/2008/04/29/8595/ accessed 8 June 2008.

Esty, D. (2002). "The World Trade Organization's legitimacy crisis." *World Trade Review* **1**(1): 7-22.

European Food Security Group (2005). "European NGO comments on the WFP Strategic Plan 2006-2009." Brussels/The Hague: Concord and Euronaid.

Evans, G. (2006). "The United Nations: Vision, Reality and Reform." *Australian Fabian News* **46**(1): 3-6.

Evans, T. (1996). *US Hegemony and the Project of Universal Human Rights*. Houndmills, Basingstoke and London: Macmillan Press Ltd.

Evans, T. and P. Wilson (1992). "Regime Theory and the English School of International Relations: A Comparison." *Millennium* **21**(3): 329-351.

Farm Bill (2008). *Food Conservation and Energy Act 2008*, HR2419, 110th Congress, 2nd Session. Washington DC: US Congress.

FAO (1955). Uses of Agricultural Surpluses to Finance Economic Development in Under-Developed Countries: A Pilot Study in India. Commodity Policy Studies No. 6, Rome: FAO.

FAO (1956). *Functions of a World Food Reserve. Scope and Limitations*. Commodity Policy Studies No. 10, Rome: FAO.

FAO (1961). " 'Expanded Program of Surplus Food Utilization' - Report by the Expert Group to the Director General of FAO." in *Development Through Food: A Strategy for Surplus Utilization*. FAO, Rome: FAO: 69-117.

FAO (1962) *Development Through Food: A strategy for surplus utilization*. Basic Study (Freedom from Hunger Campaign) No. 2, Revised Edition. Rome: FAO.

FAO (2001). Reporting Procedures and Consultative Obligations Under the FAO Principles of Surplus Disposal: A Guide for Members of the FAO Consultative Subcommittee on Surplus Disposal. Rome: FAO.

FAO (2006a). Food aid in the context of international and domestic markets and the Doha Round. Trade Policy Brief No. 8, Rome: FAO.

FAO (2006b). "Membership of the WFP Executive Board." Agenda Paper, 131st Council Session, Rome, 20-25 November 2006, CL131/4 - Sup.1. September 2006, Rome: FAO.

FAO (2006c). State of Food Insecurity in the World 2006. Rome: FAO.

FAO (2007). The State of Food and Agriculture 2007. Rome: FAO.

FAO (2008). "About 50 million more hungry people in 2007; Hunger on the rise due to soaring food prices." Media Release, 3 July 2008, Rome/Brussels: FAO.

FAO Committee on Commodity Problems (2005). *A Historical Background on Food Aid and Key Milestones*. CCP 05/CRS.6, March 2005, Rome: FAO.

FAO Committee on Commodity Problems (2007). Consultative Subcommittee on Surplus Disposal (CSSD) Forty-First Report to the CCP. CCP 07/14, February 2007, Rome: FAO.

FAO Committee on Commodity Problems (2010). *Impacts of the Financial Crisis on Agricultural Commodity Markets*. CCP 10/02, April 2010, Rome: FAO.

FAO Committee on World Food Security (2007). *Report of the 33rd Session of the Committee on World Food Security, 7-10 May 2007*. CL 132/10, May 2007, Rome: FAO Council.

FAO Consultative Subcommittee on Surplus Disposal (2003). *Thirty-Ninth Report to the Committee on Commodity Problems*. Rome: FAO.

FAO Consultative Subcommittee on Surplus Disposal (2005). *Fortieth Report to the CCP*. CCP 05/15, February 2005, Rome: FAO Committee on Commodity Problems.

Finnemore, M. and K. Sikkink (1998). "International Norm Dynamics and Political Change." *International Organization* **52**(4): 887-917.

Flinn, W. L. and D. E. Johnson (1974). "Agrarianism Among Wisconsin Farmers." *Rural Sociology* **39**(2): 187-204.

Florini, A. (1996). "The evolution of international norms." *International Studies Quarterly* **40**(3): 363-389.

Fogel, R. W. (2004). The Escape from Hunger and Premature Death, 1700-2100: Europe, America and the Third World. Cambridge: Cambridge University Press.

Food Speculation Coalition (2009). "Letter to the Hon Barack Obama, President of the United States." 24 March 2009: Food&Water Watch. http://www.fwwatch.org/press/Food-Speculation-Coalition-Letter-to-President-Obama accessed 25 March 2009.

Fore, H. H. (2007). "Remarks by Henrietta H. Fore, Acting Director of Foreign Assistance & Acting USAID Administrator, World Food Prize Announcement Ceremony, Loy Henderson Auditorium. Department of State, 18 June 2007." Washington DC: USAID.

Friedman, H. (2002). The International Political Economy of Food: A Global Crisis. in *Food in the USA: A Reader*. C. M. Counihan. New York and London, Routledge: 325-346.

Friends of WFP (2007). "About Friends of WFP." Washington DC, Friends of WFP, Inc. http://www.friendsofwfp.org/site/pp.asp?c=7oIJLSOsGpF&b=245184 accessed 5 April 2007.

Friends of WFP Inc. (2006). "IRS Form 990, Year ended December 31, 2005, Public Display Copy." Washington DC, Friends of WFP Inc.

G8 (2009). *Joint Statement on Global Food Security*. The G8 Summit, L'Aquila, 10 July 2009.

G20 (2009). *G20 Final Communique*. The G20 Summit, Pittsburgh, 25 September 2009.

George, S. (1979). *Feeding the Few: Corporate Control of Food*. Washington DC: Institute for Policy Studies.

George, S. (1991). *How the Other Half Dies: The Real Reasons for World Hunger*. Harmondsworth: Penguin.

Gettleman, Jeffrey and Mohamed Ibrahim (2010). "U.N. to End Some Deals for Food to Somalia." *The New York Times*, 11 March 2010.

Gettleman, Jeffrey and Neil MacFarquhar (2010). "Somalia Food Aid Bypasses Needy, U.N. Study Says." *The New York Times*, 9 March 2010.

Giarraputo, J. (moderator) (2006). "Citigroup And WFP Work Together To Combat Hunger." *Global Finance Magazine*, Sponsored Roundtable, October 2006. http://web.lexis-nexis.com.ezproxy.lib.unimelb.edu.au/universe/document?_m=e662d5c8f87bfd152ec01db8df36f681&_docnum=71&wchp=dGLbVzW-zSkVb&_md5=98a2e94a3f8c4908428949200d06d84f accessed 14 January 2007.

Gilpin, R. (1987). *The Political Economy of International Relations*. Princeton, NJ: Princeton University Press.

Glaser, M. P. (2005). *Humanitarian Engagement with non-state armed actors: The parameters of negotiated access*. Network Paper No. 5,June 2005, London: Humanitarian Practice Network, ODI.

Goldstein, Amy (2009). "Sharp rise in Americans going hungry." *The Age* (Melbourne), 18 November 2009, 14.

Gregory, Peter (2009). "Food security in a changing climate." The Selby Fellow Public Lecture, 20 October 2009. Canberra: Australian Academy of Science.

Haas, P. (1992). "Introduction: Epistemic Communities and International Policy Coordination." *International Organization* **46**(Special Issue: Knowledge, Power, and International Coordination, ed. P Haas): 1-35.

Hambidge, G. (1955). *The Story of FAO*. New York, Toronto, London: D. Van Nostrand Company Inc.

Hammink, W. (2007). "Testimony of William Hammink, Director, Office of Food for Peace, USAID." US House of Representatives Committee on Agriculture, Subcommittee on Specialty Crops, Rural Development, and Foreign Agriculture, May 10, 2007. Washington DC: US House of Representatives.

Hancock, G. (1989). *The Lords of Poverty: The free-wheeling lifestyles, power, prestige and corruption of the multi-billion dollar aid business*. London: Macmillan.

Hanrahan, C. E. and C. Canada (2006). *International Food Aid: U.S. and Other Donor Contributions*. CRS Report for Congress, 18 October 2006, Washington DC: Congressional Research Service.

Hansen, J. M. (1991). *Gaining Access: Congress and the Farm Lobby, 1919-1981*. Chicago and London: University of Chicago Press.

Hardin, G. (1974). "Living on a Lifeboat." *Bioscience* **24**(10): 561-568.

Hay, C. (2002). *Political Analysis: A critical introduction*. Houndmills: Palgrave.

Headey, Derek and Shenggen Fan (2008). "Anatomy of a crisis: the causes and consequences of surging food prices." *Agricultural Economics* **39**(s1): 375-391.

Held, D. (2004). "Democratic Accountability and Political Effectiveness from a Cosmopolitan Perspective." *Government and Opposition* **39**(2): 364-391.

Held, D., A. McGrew, D. Goldblatt and J. Perraton (1999). *Global Transformations: Politics, Economics and Culture*. Cambridge: UK, Polity Press.

Henriques, Diana B (2008). "Odd Crop Prices Defy Economics." *The New York Times*, 28 March 2008.

Hindess, B. (1996). *Discourses of Power: From Hobbes to Foucault*. Oxford: Blackwell Publishers.

Hirschman, A. O. (1970). *Exit, voice, and loyalty: responses to decline in firms, organizations, and states*. Cambridge, Mass: Harvard University Press.

Hjertholm, P. and H. White (2000). *Survey of Foreign Aid: History, Trends and Allocation*. Discussion Paper 2000/04, Institute of Economics, University of Copenhagen. http://www.econ.ku.dk/wpa/pink/2000/0004.pdf accessed 6 April 2006

Hobden, S. and R. Wyn Jones (2001). "Marxist Theories of International Relations." in *The Globalisation of World Politics: An Introduction to*

International Relations. J. Baylis and S. Smith (eds). Oxford: Oxford University Press: 200-223.

Hobson, A. (1931). *The International Institute of Agriculture: An Historical and Critical Analysis of its Organization, Activities, and Policies of Administration*. Berkeley, California: University of California Press.

Hobson, A. (1932). "An American Pioneer in International Agriculture." *Journal of Farm Economics* **14**(4): 574-585.

Hodgson, J. G. (1932). "Review - The International Institute of Agriculture: An Historical and Critical Analysis of Its Organization, Activities and Policies of Administration." *The Journal of Political Economy* **40**(3): 405-409.

Hopkins, R. (1977). *Overcoming Hunger: A Global Regime for the Future*. New York and London: McGraw-Hill.

Hopkins, R. F. (1987). "The Evolution of Food Aid: Toward a Development-First Regime." in *Food policy: integrating supply, distribution, and consumption*. J. P. Gittinger, J. Leslie and C. Hoisington (eds). Baltimore and London: Johns Hopkins University Press for the World Bank: 246-259.

Hopkins, R. F. (1990). "International Food Organizations and the United States: Drifting Leadership and Diverging Interests." *The United States and Multilateral Institutions: Patterns of Changing Instrumentality and Influence*. M. P. Karns and K. A. Mingst (eds). Boston: Unwin Hyman: 177-204.

Hopkins, R. F. (1992). "Reform in the International Food Aid Regime: The Role of Consensual Knowledge." *International Organization* **46**(1): 225-264.

Hopkins, R. F. and D. J. Puchala, (eds) (1979). *The Global Political Economy of Food*. Madison and London: University of Wisconsin Press.

Horton, Sue (2009). "The 1974 and 2008 Food Price Crises: Déjà Vu?" in *The Global Food Crisis: Governance Challenges and Opportunities*, Jennifer Clapp and Marc Cohen (eds). Waterloo, ON: Wilfred Laurier University Press: 29-42.

Hotakainen, R. (2007). "Study: Half of Nation's Poor Don't Get Food Stamps." McClatchey Newspapers, 14 August 2007. http://www.commondreams.org /archive/2007/08/14/3150/ accessed 15 August 2007.

Humphrey, Hubert (1974). "Foreword - Selected Materials for the use of the U.S. Congressional Delegation to the World Food Conference - Rome, Italy." Washington DC: Subcommittee on Foreign Agricultural Policy of the Committee on Agriculture and Forestry, U.S. Senate, 30 October 1974

Hutchings, R. (2006). " Empire and the state: a critical theoretical assessment." *Australian Journal of International Affairs* **60**(3): 429-438.

Ikenberry, G. J. and C. A. Kupchan (1990). "Socialization and Hegemonic Power." *International Organization* **44**(3): 283-315.

IMF (2010). "IMF Commodity Prices." 4 February 2010 edition.

Ingram, James (2005a). WFP Executive Director 1982-1992. Interview, Canberra, 23 March 2005.

Ingram, James (2005b). WFP Executive Director 1982-1992. Interview, Canberra, 22 September 2005.

Ingram, J. (2006). *Bread and Stones: Leadership and the Struggle to Reform the United Nations World Food Programme*. North Charleston, SC: BookSurge LLC.

Institute for Agriculture and Trade Policy, Food & Water Watch, Pesticide Action Network North America, Grassroots International, Food First,

Maryknoll Office for Global Concerns, World Hunger Year, Robert F. Kennedy Center for Human Rights, Center of Concern, Partners for the Land & Agricultural Needs of Traditional Peoples (PLANT), The Oakland Institute, Greenpeace USA, Organic Consumers Association, Via Organica (Mexico), Sisters of Notre Dame de Namur Justice and Peace Network, Edmonds Institute, United Church of Christ Justice and Witness Ministries, Washington Biotechnology Action Council, Food Systems Integrity, Inc Agricultural Missions, National Family Farm Coalition, A Well-Fed World and Slow Food USA (2009). "Open Letter to Alonzo L Fulgham, Acting Administrator, US Agency for International Development." 13 November 2009, IATP. http://www.tradeobservatory.org/library.cfm?refid=106962 accessed 14 November 2009.

INTERFAIS/WFP (2005). *2004 Food Aid Flows*. June 2005, Rome:WFP.

INTERFAIS/WFP (2008). *2007 Food Aid Flows*. Rome: WFP. http://www.wfp.org/interfais/index2.htm# accessed 23 August 2008.

International Fund for Agricultural Development (2008). *IFAD at a Glance, 1978-2007, Table 1*. Rome: IFAD. http://www.ifad.org/pub/ar/2007/e/glance.pdf accessed 9 August 2008.

International Grains Council (2007). *About Us - International Grains Agreement*. London: IGC. http://www.igc.org.uk/en/aboutus/default.aspx#fac accessed 9 August 2008.

Interview #4 (2005). Senior WFP official. Interview, Rome 27 June 2005.

Interview #9 (2005). NGO staffer. Interview, Rome, 16 June 2005.

Interview #11 (2005). Senior WFP official. Interview, Rome 23 June 2005.

Interview #12 (2005). Senior WFP official. Interview, Rome 27 June 2005.

Interview #14 (2005). Senior WFP official. Interview, Rome 24 June 2005.

Interview #16 (2005). Senior WFP official. Interview, Rome 20 June 2005.

Interview #17 (2005). WFP official. Interview, Rome, 22 June 2005.

Interview #19 (2005). WFP official. Interview, Rome, 17 & 22 June 2005.

Isenman, P. J. and H. W. Singer (1993). "Food Aid: Disincentive Effects and Their Policy Implications." in *Why Food Aid?* V. W. Ruttan. Baltimore and London: The Johns Hopkins University Press: 99-122.

Jacobson, H. K. (1984). *Networks of Interdependence: International Organizations and the Global Political System*. New York: McGraw-Hill.

Judt, T. (2007). Is the UN Doomed? *The New York Review of Books*. **LIV**(2), 15 February 2007: 45-48.

Kanbur, R. (2003). "The Economics of International Aid." Paper prepared for the Handbook on "The Economics of Giving, Reciprocity and Altruism," edited by Serge Christophe-Kolm and Jean Mercier-Ythier, North-Holland. http://www.arts.cornell.edu/poverty/kanbur/HandbookAid.pdf, accessed 23 April 2005.

Karns, M. P. and K. A. Mingst (1990a). "The United States and Multilateral Institutions: A Framework for Analysis." in *The United States and Multilateral Institutions: Patterns of Changing Instrumentality and Influence*. M.P. Karns and K.A Mingst (eds). Boston: Unwin Hyman: 1-24.

Karns, M. P. and K. A. Mingst (2004). *International Organizations: The Politics and Processes of Global Governance*. Boulder; London: Lynne Rienner Publishers.

Keane, J. (2003). *Global Civil Society?* Cambridge: Cambridge University Press.

Keck, M. E. and K. Sikkink (1998). *Activists Beyond Borders: Advocacy Networks in International Politics*. Ithaca, NY: Cornell University Press.

Kennedy, P. and B. Russett (1995). "Reforming the United Nations." *Foreign Affairs* **74**(5): 56-71.

Keohane, R. O. (1984). *After Hegemony: Cooperation and discord in the world political economy*. Princeton, N J: Princeton University Press.

Keohane, R. O. (2003). "Global Governance and Democratic Accountability." in *Taming Globalization: Frontiers of Governance*. D. Held and M. Koenig-Archibugi (eds). Cambridge: Polity Press: 130-159.

King, R. F. (1999). "Welfare Reform: Block Grants, Expenditure Caps, and the Paradox of the Food Stamp Program." *Political Science Quarterly* **114**(3): 359-385.

Klingebiel, S. (1999). Effectiveness and Reform of the United Nations Development Programme (UNDP). London; Portland Or.: Frank Cass.

Klotz, A. (1995). *Norms in International Relations: The Struggle Against Apartheid*. Ithaca and London: Cornell University Press.

Knight, W. A. (2002). "The Future of the UN Security Council: Questions of legitimacy and representation in multilateral governance." in *Enhancing Global Governance: Towards a new Diplomacy*. A. F. Cooper, J. English and R. Thakur (eds). Tokyo: UN University Press: 19-37.

Kotz, N. (1984). "The Politics of Hunger." *The New Republic*, 30 April 1984.

Krasner, S. D. (1983). "Structural causes and regime consequences: regimes as intervening variables." in *International Regimes*. S. D. Krasner (ed). Ithaca and London: Cornell University Press: 1-21.

Kratochwil, F. and J. G. Ruggie (1986). "International Organization: A state of the art on an art of the state." *International Organization* **40**(4): 753-775.

Kratochwil, F. V. (1989). *Rules, Norms, and Decisions: On the conditions of practical and legal reasoning in international relations and domestic affairs*. Cambridge: Cambridge University Press.

Krugman, P. (2007). *The Conscience of a Liberal*. New York and London: W W Norton & Company.

La Via Campesina (2010). "Say 'No!' to Corporate Control of Agriculture and Food! 17 April 2010 - Join the International Day of Peasant Struggle." Media Release, 23 February 2010, La Via Campesina. http://www.commondreams.org/view/2010/02/23-6 accessed 26 February 2010.

Landis, Lauren (2005). Director, Office of Food for Peace, USAID. Interview, Washington DC, 17 May 2005.

Lappé, Frances Moore, Joseph Collins and Cary Fowler (1977). *Food first : beyond the myth of scarcity*. Boston: Houghton-Mifflin.

Lappé, Frances Moore, Joseph Collins, Peter Rosset and with Luis Esparza (1998). *World Hunger: Twelve Myths*. 2nd, Edition, Fully Revised and Updated edition. New York: Grove Press/Institute for Food and Development Policy.

Lawson, S. (2002). "After the Fall: International Theory and the State." in *The New Agenda for International Relations: From Polarization to Globalization in World Politics?* S. Lawson (ed). Cambridge, UK: Polity: 205-222.

Leach, R. (2005). Executive Director, Friends of WFP. Interview, Washington DC, 20 May 2005.

Leahy, S. (2007). "Biofuels - Great Green Hope or Swindle." Brooklin, Canada, Inter Press Service, 20 October 2007. http://www.commondreams.org/archive/2007/10/20/4700/ accessed 22 October 2007.

Lederer, E. M. (2006). "American diplomat Josette Sheeran selected to head U.N. World Food Program, U.N. announces." Associated Press, Wire service report, 8 November 2006. http://global.factiva.com.ezproxy.lib.uni.melb.edu.au/ha/default.aspx accessed 20 January 2007.

Levenstein, H. (2003). *Paradox of Plenty: A Social History of Eating in Modern America*. Berkely, Los Angeles, London: University of California Press.

Levinson, E. (2007). "Written Testimony of Ellen S. Levinson, President, Levinson & Associates and Executive Director, The Alliance for Food Aid." Committee on Agriculture, SubCommittee on Specialty Crops, Rural Development and Foreign Agriculture Programs, US House of Representatives, 10 May 2007, Washington DC: US House of Representatives.

Lipschutz, R.D. (1992). "Reconstructing World Politics: The emergence of global civil society." *Millennium* **21**(3): 389-420.

Luttrell, Clifton B. (1973). "The Russian Wheat Deal: Hindsight vs. Foresight." *The Federal Reserve Bank of St. Louis Review*, October 1973: 2-9. http://research.stlouisfed.org/publications/review/73/10/Russian_Oct1973.pdf accessed 4 September 2010.

Lynch, C. (2006). "State Department Official Picked to Run U.N. Food Program." *The Washington Post*, 8 November 2006: A13.

Mallaby, S. (2004). "NGOs: Fighting Poverty, Hurting the Poor." *Foreign Policy* **144**: 50-58.

Malone, D. M. (2007). *The International Struggle over Iraq: Politics in the UN Security Council 1980-2005*. Oxford: Oxford University Press.

Malthus, T. R. (1992). *An Essay on the Principle of Population, or, A view of its past and present effects on human happiness : with an inquiry into our prospects respecting the future removal or mitigation of the evils which it occasions*. New York, NY, USA; Cambridge, UK: Cambridge University Press.

Maren, M. (1993). "The Food-Aid Racket." *Harper's Magazine*, August 1993.

Maren, M. (1997). *The Road to Hell: The Ravaging Effects of Foreign Aid and International Charity*. New York: The Free Press.

Marshall, T. H. (1965). *Class, citizenship, and social development*. Garden City, NY: Doubleday.

McConnell, K. (2006). "State Dept: State's Sheeran Named New Head of U.N. World Food Program." Wire service report, 7 November 2006, Washington: HT Media Ltd./US Fed News. http://web.lexis-nexis.com.ezproxy.lib.unimelb.edu.au/universe/document?_m=e13d36b2846faeedf8606a8b44ca104f&_docnum=46&wchp=dGLbVzW-zSkVb&_md5=72294b56f1bbaf6b78efe63d2a552cfa accessed 14 January 2007.

McGovern, G. (2001). *The Third Freedom: Ending Hunger in Our Time*. New York: Simon and Schuster.

McHenry, D. F. and K. Bird (1977). "Food Bungle in Bangladesh." *Foreign Policy* **27**: 72-88.

Meadows, D. H., D. L. Meadows, J. Randers and W. W. I. Behrens (1972). *The Limits to Growth*. New York: Club of Rome/Universe Books.

Meredith, M. (2005). *The State of Africa*. London, New York, Sydney, Toronto: The Free Press.

Mittal, Anuradha (2009). "What Will the G8 Summit Accomplish: Feed the Hungry or Fuel Hunger?" 8 July 2009, CommonDreams.org. http://www.commondreams.org/view/2009/07/08-1 accessed 23 July 2009.

Moravcsik, A. (2004). "Is there a 'Democratic Deficit' in World Politics? A Framework for Analysis." *Government and Opposition* **39**(2): 336-363.

Morgenthau, H. J. (1973). *Politics among nations : the struggle for power and peace*. New York: Knopf.

Morris, J. T. (2006). "Still Dying of Hunger: More Can Be Done to Ease the Toll on Children and Countries." *The Washington Post*, 25 May 2006: A29.

Mousseau, Frederic (2010). *The High Food Price Challenge: A review of responses to combat hunger*. Oakland, CA: Oakland Institute and the UK Hunger Alliance.

Murphy, C. N. (2001). "What the Third World Wants: An Interpretation of the Development and Meaning of the New International Economic Order Ideology." in *The Politics of Global Governance: International Organizations in an Interdependent World*. P. F. Diehl (ed). Boulder: Lynne Rienner Publishers: 261-276.

Murphy, C. N. (2006). *The United Nations Development Programme: A Better Way?* Cambridge: Cambridge University Press.

Murphy, S. and S. Suppan (2008). *The 2008 Farm Bill and the Doha Agenda*. Commentary Report, 25 June 2008, Minneapolis, Minnesota: IATP. http://www.iatp.org/iatp/commentaries.cfm?refID=103103 accessed 21 July 2008.

Mustard, A. (2003). "An Unauthorized History of FAS." *Foreign Service Journal* **80**(5): 36-43.

Natsios, A. S. (2001). "NGOs and the UN System in Complex Humanitarian Emergencies: Conflict or Cooperation?" in *The Politics of Global Governance: International Organizations in an Interdependent World*. P. F. Diehl (ed). Boulder, Co: Lynne Rienner Publishers: 388-405.

Nestle, M. (2002). "Hunger in the United States: Policy Implications." in *Food in the USA: A Reader*. C. M. Counihan (ed). New York and London: Routledge: 385-399.

Newman, E., R. Thakur and J. Tirman (2006). *Multilateralism Under Challenge?* Research Brief Number 1, Tokyo: United Nations University Press.

Noland, M. (2003). *Famine and Reform in North Korea*. Institute for International Economics, IIE WP 03/5, July 2003. http://www.iie.com/publications/wp/03-5.pdf accessed 28 August 2008.

Nye, J. S. (2003). *The "democracy deficit" in the global economy: enhancing the legitimacy and accountability of global institutions*. A report to the Trilateral Commission. Triangle Papers: No. 57, Washington DC: Trilateral Commission.

Obasanjo, His Excellency Chief Olusegun. (2005). "Keynote Address to the Annual Session of the Executive Board of the World Food Programme." 10 June 2005, Rome: WFP.

OECD (2006). *The Development Effectiveness of Food Aid: Does Tying Matter?* Paris: OECD Development Assistance Committee.

O'Grada, Cormac (2009). *Famine: A Short History*. Princeton University Press: Princeton and Oxford.

Ostrom, E. (2003). "How Types of Goods and Property Rights Jointly Affect Collective Action" *Journal of Theoretical Politics* **15**(3): 239-270.

Oxfam International (2008). "Double-Edged Prices: Lessons from the food price crisis; ten actions developing countries should take." Oxfam Briefing Paper 121, October 2008: Oxfam International.

Ozer, K. (2008). "The Irony of a Bush Farm Bill Veto." CommonDreams.org, 22 May 2008. http://www.commondreams.org/archive/2008/05/22/9124/ accessed 8 June 2008.

Patel, R. (2007). *Stuffed & Starved: Markets, Power & the Hidden Battle for the World Food System.* Melbourne: Black Inc.

Pauchari, R. (2007). "The Climate Crisis for Humanity." *The Age* (Melbourne), 15 October 2007: 13.

Pierson, P. (2000). "Increasing Returns, Path Dependence, and the Study of Politics." *American Political Science Review* **94**(2): 251-267.

Pisik, B. (2006). "Sheeran will lead U.N. food program; She's a former editor at The Times." *The Washington Times*, 7 November 2006: 1.

Pogge, T. (2007). Speech at Book Launch for 'Freedom from Poverty as a Human Right: Who owes what to the very poor?' University of Melbourne, 5 November 2007.

Poppendieck, J. (1986). *Breadlines Knee-Deep in Wheat: Food Assistance in the Great Depression*. New Brunswick, NJ: Rutgers University Press.

Poppendieck, J. (1997). "The USA: Hunger in the Land of Plenty." in *First World Hunger: Food Security and Welfare Politics*. G. Riches (ed). Houndmills, Basingstoke: Macmillans Press: 134-164.

Poppendieck, J. (1998). *Sweet Charity? Emergency Food and the End of Entitlement*. New York: Viking Penguin.

Puchala, D. J. and R. F. Hopkins (1983). "International Regimes: lessons from inductive analysis." in *International Regimes*. S. D. Krasner (ed). Ithaca and London: Cornell University Press: 61-91.

Ravallion, M. (2004). "How are the World's Poor Faring in the Current Era of Globalization?" 2nd Annual Max Corden Lecture, University of Melbourne, 4 March 2004.

Reus-Smit, C. (2001). "Constructivism." in *Theories of International Relations*. S. Burchill, R. Devetak, A. Linklater, M. Paterson, C. Reus-Smit and J. True (eds). Basingstoke, UK: Palgrave: 209-230.

Reus-Smit, C. (2004). *American Power and World Order*. Cambridge, UK and Malden, Mass.: Polity.

Reus-Smit, C. (2007). "International Crises of Legitimacy." *International Politics* **44**(2/3): 157-174.

Riches, G. (ed) (1997a). *First World Hunger: Food Security and Welfare Politics*. Houndmills, Basingstoke: Macmillans Press.

Riches, G. (1997b). "Hunger in Canada: Abandoning the Right to Food." *First World Hunger: Food Security and Welfare Politics*. G. Riches (ed). Houndmills, Basingstoke: Macmillans Press: 46-77.

Risse, T. (1999). "International Norms and Domestic Change: Arguing and Communicative Behavior in the Human Rights Area." *Politics and Society* **27**(4): 529-559.

Ritchie, M. and K. Ristau (1987). *Crisis by Design: A Brief Review of U.S. Farm Policy.* Minneapolis: League of Rural Voters Education Project. http://www.iatp.org/iatp/publications.cfm?accountID=258&refID=48644 accessed 27 July 2007.

Robinson, M. (2002). "The Right to Food: Achievements and Challenges." Speech to World Food Summit: Five Years Later, Rome, June 2002. http://www.unhchr.ch/Huridocda/Huridoca.nsf/TestFrame/12e96b2a62529a4cc1256cc30039f942?Opendocument accessed 12 September 2006.

Rosenau, J. N. (2002). "Ageing Agendas and Ambiguous Anomalies: Tensions and Contradictions of an Emergent Epoch." in *The New Agenda for International Relations: From Polarization to Globalization in World Politics?* S. Lawson (ed). Cambridge, UK: Polity: 19-34.

Ross, Sandy. (2000). "Citizenship Accountability: A Framework for Addressing the Problem of Accountability in Liberal Democracy." MA Thesis, Dept of Political Science, University of Melbourne.

Ross, Sandy (2007). "The World Food Programme: a case of benign US policy?" *Australian Journal of International Affairs* **61**(2): 267-281.

Rothschild, E. (1993). "Is it Time to End Food for Peace?" in *Why Food Aid?* V. W. Ruttan (ed). Baltimore: The Johns Hopkins University Press: 84-94.

Ruggie, J. G. (1975). "International Responses to Technology: concepts and trends." *International Organization* **29**(3): 557-583.

Ruggie, J. G. (1998). *Constructing the World Polity: Essays on international institutionalization.* London and New York: Routledge.

Ruggie, J. G. (2003). "Taking Embedded Liberalism Global: the Corporate Connection." in *Taming Globalization: frontiers of governance.* D. Held and M. Koenig-Archibugi (eds). Cambridge: Polity Press: 93-129.

Russo, L., A.-C. Luzot, A. Martella and L. Wilhelm (2005). *Joint Evaluation of Effectiveness and Impact of the Enabling Development Policy of the World Food Programme (WFP): Synthesis Report, Volume 1.* February 2005, Bonn, Germany: Steering Committee for the Evaluation of EPD [Canadian International Development Agency (CIDA); Danish International Development Assistance (DANIDA); Royal Danish Ministry of Foreign Affairs; Department of International Development Cooperation, Ministry of Foreign Affairs, Finland; Directorate General for International Cooperation and Development, Ministry of Foreign Affairs, France; Federal Ministry for Economic Cooperation and Development, Germany (BMZ); Directorate General for Development Cooperation, Ministry of Foreign Affairs, Italy (DGCS); United States Agency for International Development (USAID)].

Ruttan, V. W. (1993a). "The Politics of U.S. Food Aid Policy: A Historical Review." in *Why Food Aid?* V. W. Ruttan (ed). Baltimore and London: The Johns Hopkins University Press: 2-38; (+endnotes pp229-238).

Ruttan, V. W., (ed) (1993b). *Why Food Aid?* Baltimore and London: The Johns Hopkins University Press.

Saouma, E. (1993). *FAO in the front line of development.* Rome: FAO.

Scharpf, F. W. (1999). *Governing in Europe: Effective and Democratic?* Oxford: Oxford University Press.

Schenkenberg, Ed (2005). Coordinator, International Council of Voluntary Agencies. Interview, Geneva, 13 June 2005.

Schmidt, Vivien A (2010). "Taking ideas and discourse seriously: explaining change through discursive institutionalism as the fourth 'new institutionalism'." *European Political Science Review* **2**(1): 1-25.

Schultz, T. W. (1993). "Value of U.S. Farm Surpluses to Underdeveloped Countries." in *Why Food Aid?* V. W. Ruttan (ed). Baltimore and London: John Hopkins University Press: 53-63.

Sen, A. (1981). *Poverty and Famines: An Essay on Entitlement and Deprivation.* Oxford: Oxford University Press.

Sen, A. (1999). "Democracy as a Universal Value." *Journal of Democracy* **10**(3): 3-17.

Sennett, R. (2003). *Respect in a World of Inequality.* New York and London: W W Norton & Company.

Shaw, D. J. (2001). *The UN World Food Programme and the Development of Food Aid.* Hampshire: Palgrave.

Shaw, J. and E. Clay, Eds. (1993). *World Food Aid: Experiences of Recipients and Donors.* Rome/London/Portsmouth(NH): World Food Programme in Association with James Currey (UK) and Heinemann (USA).

Shaw, R. W. and C. McKay (2006). *An Analysis of PL 480 Title II Monetization Data (2001-2005): Impacts on Domestic Production, Local Marketing and Global Trade.* Food Security Network, 9 February 2006. http://www.foodsecuritynetwork.org/resources/food_aid/monetization.html accessed 27 August 2007.

Singer, H. W. (2001). "Foreword." in *The UN World Food Programme and the Development of Food Aid.* D. J. Shaw. Basingstoke, Hampshire and New York, NY: Palgrave: ix-xi.

Singer, P. (1993). "Reconsidering the Famine Relief Argument." in *Why Food Aid?* V. W. Ruttan (ed). Baltimore: The Johns Hopkins University Press: 68-83.

Slaughter, A.-M. (2004a). *A New World Order.* Princeton: Princeton University Press.

Slaughter, A.-M. (2004b). "Sovereignty and Power in a Networked World Order." *Stanford Journal of International Law* **40**(Summer 2004): 283-327.

Smiles, S. (2008). "UN bid to mend fences with Canberra." *The* Age (Melbourne), 17 March 2008: 8.

Soros, George (1988). *The Alchemy of Finance: Reading the mind of the market.* Simon & Schuster: New York.

Squires, Nick (2009). "UN Food Summit 'Fails Before It Begins': A UN food summit aimed at helping the one billion people worldwide suffering from hunger has been declared a failure a week before it has even begun." *The Telegraph* (UK), 12 November 2009.

Steffek, J. (2003). "The Legitimation of International Governance: A Discourse Approach." *European Journal of International Relations* **9**(2): 249-275.

Stein, A. A. (1983). "Coordination and Collaboration: regimes in an anarchical world." in *International Regimes.* S. D. Krasner (ed). Ithaca and London: Cornell University Press: 115-140.

Stiglitz, J. E. (2003). *The Roaring Nineties: A New History of the World's Most Prosperous Decade.* New York and London: W W Norton & Company.

Strange, S. (1983). "*Cave! hic dragones* : a critique of regime analysis." in *International Regimes.* S. D. Krasner (ed). Ithaca and London: Cornell University Press: 337-354.

Sui, C. (2006). "China world's third largest food donor; most aid to N Korea." Wire service report, 20 July 2006, Beijing: Agence France Presse. http://web.lexis-nexis.com.ezproxy.lib.unimelb.edu.au/universe/document?_m=8255575932de0f0b4294e1e17578260e&_docnum=124&wchp=dGLbVzW-zSkVb&_md5=07e74b84ac16eb6cf938c13ede38dfa4 accessed 14 January 2007.

Suppan, S. (2002). *Food Sovereignty in the Era of Trade Liberalization: Are Multilateral Means Toward Food Sovereignty Feasible?* Briefing paper prepared for the NGO Forum on Food Sovereignty and the NGO Regional Consultation Process for the World Food Summit+6, 15 January 2002: IATP. http://www.tradeobservatory.org/library.cfm?RefID=25383 accessed 27 July 2007.

Swanson, R. (2003). "The History of the Foreign Agricultural Service: Helping U.S. Producers Feed, Clothe and House the World." *AgExporter*, March 2003: 4-11.

Talbot, R. B. (1990). *The Four World Food Agencies in Rome: FAO, WFP; WFC; IFAD*. Ames: Iowa State University Press.

Telegraph (2006). Hans Singer Obituary. *The Age* (Melbourne), 15 March 2006, News: 15.

Terry, F. (2000). "Condemned to Repeat?: The Paradoxes of Humanitarian Action." PhD Thesis, Department of International Relations, Research School of Pacific and Asian Studies, ANU, Canberra.

Thakur, R. (2001). "Human Rights: Amnesty International and the United Nations." in *The Politics of Global Governance: International Organizations in an Interdependent World*. P. F. Diehl (ed). Boulder, Co: Lynne Rienner Publishers: 365-387.

The Food Research and Action Center (2008). "Food Stamp Participation in September 2008 Tops 31.5 Million." FRAC news webpage. http://www.frac.org/html/news/fsp/2008.09_FSP.htm accessed 1 January 2009.

Thompson, S. B. (1981). "International Organizations and the Improbability of a Global Food Regime." in *Food Politics: The Regional Conflict*. D. N. Balaam and M. J. Carey (eds). Totowa, NJ: Allanheld, Osmun: 191-206.

Townsend, J. G. and A. R. Townsend (2004). "Accountability, Motivation and Practice: NGOs North and South." *Social and Cultural Geography* 5(2): 271-284.

Toy, M.-A. (2006). "UN restarts food aid to Pyongyang." *The Age* (Melbourne), 12 May 2006: 13.

Traub, J. (2006). *The Best Intentions: Kofi Annan and the UN in the Era of American Power*. London: Bloomsbury.

Turner, M. (2006). "Top job for US official raises UN reform fear." *Financial Times*, 20 January 2007.

Turse, Nick (2009). "Younger and Hungrier in America: The Struggle to Feed America's Nouveau Needy." 9 March 2009, TomDispatch.com. http://www.commondreams.org/view/2009/03/09-2. accessed 12 March 2009.

UN (2000). *Millennium Development Goals*. New York: UN.

UN (2006). "Organization Chart of the United Nations." DPI/2431. New York: UN Department of Public Information. http://www.un.org/aboutun/chartlg.html accessed 14 June 2007.

UN Commission on Human Rights (1997). "The Right to Food." Resolution 1997/8, 36th Meeting, 3 April 1997. Geneva: Office of the United Nations High Commissioner for Human Rights,.

UN Commission on Human Rights (2000). "The Right to Food." Resolution 2000/10, 52nd Meeting, 17 April 2000. Geneva: Office of the United Nations High Commissioner for Human Rights.

UN Economic and Social Council (2005). "Elections, nominations, confirmations and appointments to subsidiary and related bodies of the Economic and Social Council." 2005-201C, 27 April 2005. Resolutions File, New York: UN. http://www.un.org/docs/ecosoc/documents/2005/decisions/edec2005-201C.pdf accessed 20 January 2007.

UN General Assembly (1961). "World Food Program." Resolution 1714 (XVI), 19 December 1961. New York: UN.

UN General Assembly (1973). "World Food Conference." Resolution 3180 (XXVIII) 28th Session, 2204th Plenary meeting, 17 December 1973. New York: UN.

UN General Assembly (1974). "World Food Conference." Resolution 3348 (XXIX), 29th Session, 2323rd Plenary, 17 December 1974. New York: UN.

UN General Assembly (1993). "Further measures for the restructuring and revitalization of the United Nations in the economic, social and related fields." Resolution No. 48/162, 20 December 1993. New York: UN.

UN General Assembly (2000). "United Nations Millennium Declaration." Resolution A/RES/55/2, 18 September 2000. New York: UN.

UN General Assembly (2001). "The Right to Food." Resolution 56/155, 19 December 2001. Geneva: UN Commission on Human Rights.

Urquhart, B. (2006). "The UN Oil-for-Food Program: Who Is Guilty?" *The New York Review of Books*. **LIII**(2), 9 February 2006: 45-50.

USAID (2006). *U.S. International Food Assistance Report 2006*. December 2006. Washington DC: US Congress

USAID Office of Food for Peace (2005). *Strategic Plan for 2006-2010*. May 2005. Washington DC: USAID

Usborne, D. (2008). "USA 2008: The Great Depression" *The Independent* (UK), 1 April 2008.

USDA Foreign Agricultural Service (2001). *Report to Congress on Food Aid and Monetization*. 10 August 2001. Washington DC: US Congress.

Uvin, P. (1992). "Regime, Surplus, and self-Interest: The International Politics of Food Aid." *International Studies Quarterly* **36**(3): 293-312.

Uvin, P. (1994). *The International Organization of Hunger*. London and New York: Keegan Paul International.

Vogler, J. (2003). "Taking Institutions Seriously: How Regime Analysis can be Relevant to Multilevel Environmental Governance." *Global Environmental Politics* **3**(2): 25-39.

Wagenhofer, E. (2005). *We Feed the World*. (film, 96 mins). Austria: Films Transit International.

Wallerstein, M. B. (1980). *Food for War - Food for Peace: United States Food Aid in a Global Context*. Cambridge, Mass: MIT Press.

Wapner, P. (1995). "Politics beyond the state: environmental activism and world civic politics." *World Politics* **47**(3): 311-341.

Webb, P. (2003). *Food as Aid: Trends, Need and Challenges in the 21st Century*. WFP Occasional Papers No. 14. Rome: WFP.

Weber, M. (1976). *The Protestant Ethic and the Spirit of Capitalism*. London: Allen & Unwin.

Weiner, M. (2002). "Consumer Culture and Participatory Democracy: The Story of Coca-Cola During World War II." in *Food in the USA: A Reader*. C. M. Counihan (ed). New York and London: Routledge: 123-141.

Wendt, A. (1999). *Social Theory of International Politics*. Cambridge: Cambridge University Press.

Westendorf, Egon (2006). Former NGO staffer. Interview, Melbourne, 1 August 2006.

WFP (1994). *Review of WFP Policies, Objectives and Strategies*. CFA: 37/P/7, 7 April 1994. Rome: WFP.

WFP (1996). *Annual Report of the Executive Director:1995 - Ending the Inheritance of Hunger*. WFP/EB.A/96/4, 10 May 1996. Rome: WFP.

WFP (1998). *From Crisis to Recovery*. WFP/EB.A/98/4-A, 1 August 1998. Rome: WFP.

WFP (1999). *Enabling Development*. Draft policy for EB Agenda, WFP/EB.A/99/4-A, 17 May 1999. Rome: WFP.

WFP (2000). *A Resource Mobilization Strategy for the World Food Programme*. WFP/EB.3/2000/3-B, 4 September 2000. Rome: WFP.

WFP (2001a). *Local Purchases of Food and Non-Food Items*. WFP/EB.A/98/8-B, 22 November 2001. Rome: WFP.

WFP (2001b). *WFP Working with NGOs: A Framework for Partnership*. WFP/EB.A/2--1/4-B, 17 April 2001. Rome: WFP.

WFP (2002). *A Decade of Change: Renewal and Transformation of the World Food Programme, 1992-2002*. WFP/EB.1/2002/9, 29 January 2002. Rome: WFP.

WFP (2003a). *Comparison Study of WFP and Non-Governmental Organizations*. WFP/EB.1/2003/4-D, 7 January 2003. Rome: WFP.

WFP (2003b). *WFP Annual Report - 2002*. Rome: WFP.

WFP (2004a). *General Regulations; General Rules; Financial Regulations; Rules of Procedure of the Executive Board*. Rome: WFP.

WFP (2004b). *Information Note on Geographical and Gender Distribution of International and Locally Recruited Staff*. WFP/EB.A/2004/INF/7, 12 May 2004. Rome: WFP.

WFP (2004c). *New Partnerships to Meet Rising Needs - Expanding the WFP Donor Base*. WFP/EB.3/2004/4-C, 14 September 2004. Rome: WFP.

WFP (2004d). *Note for the Record*. WFP Global Meeting, Dublin, 7-10 June 2004. Rome: WFP.

WFP (2004e). *WFP Policy on Staff Recruitment and Geographical Representation of Member States*. WFP/EB.1/2004/4-B/Rev.1, 23 February 2004. Rome: WFP.

WFP (2005). *Decisions and Recommendations of the Annual Session of the Executive Board, 2005*. WFP/EB.A/2005/15, 10 June 2005. Rome: WFP.

WFP (2006a). *Comprehensive Human Resources Review*. WFP/EB.2/2006/13-B, 24 October 2007. Rome: WFP.

WFP (2006b). *Comprehensive Human Resources Review Corrigendum*. WFP/EB.2/2006/13-B/Corr.1, 2 November 2006. Rome: WFP.

WFP (2006c). *Consolidated Framework of WFP Policies*. WFP/EB.2/2006/4-E, 12 October 2006. Rome: WFP.

WFP (2006d). "Facts and Figures." http://www.wfp.org/aboutwfp/facts/2004/index.asp?section=1&sub_section=5 accessed 4 July 2006.

WFP (2006e). *Food Procurement in Developing Countries*. WFP/EB.1/2006/5-C, 30 January 2006. Rome: WFP.

WFP (2006f). *Progress Report on the Ethiopia Drought Insurance Pilot Project*. WFP/EB.A/2006/10-A/Rev.1, 8 June 2006. Rome: WFP.

WFP (2006g). *World Hunger - Korea (DPR)*. http://www.wfp.org/country_brief brief/indexcountry.asp?country=408 accessed 4 August 2006.

WFP (2006h). "Africa: WFP Welcomes China's Growing Role as a Major Food Donor." Wire service report, AllAfrica Inc., 2 November 2006. http://web.lexis-nexis.com.ezproxy.lib.unimelb.edu.au/universe/document?_m=e662d5c8f87bfd152ec01db8df36f681&_docnum=51&wchp=dGLbVzW-zSkVb&_md5=f5b665b202e8a70dc76efc8e416d4aae accessed 14 January 2007.

WFP (2007a). *Statistical Report on WFP International Professional staff and Higher Categories at 31 December 2006*. WFP/EB.A/2007/12-B, 28 May 2007. Rome: WFP.

WFP (2007b). *Tackle Hunger webpage*. http://www.wfp.org/english/?n=665 accessed 18 September 2007.

WFP (2007c). *Update on the WFP Management Plan (2006-2007)*. 11 January 2007. Rome: WFP.

WFP (2007d). *WFP in Statistics - 2006*. June 2007. Rome: WFP. http://www.wfp.org/aboutwfp/facts/2006/pdf/WFP_Statistics_complete_06.pdf?section=1&sub_section=5 accessed 15 November 2007.

WFP (2007e). *WFP Mission Statement*. Rome: WFP. http://www.wfp.org/policies/Introduction/mission/index.asp?section=6&sub_section=1 accessed 25 September 2007.

WFP (2008). *WFP Strategic Plan 2008-2011*. Rome: WFP.

WFP (2009). 2009 *Annual Report*. Rome: WFP.

WFP (2010a). *Update on the WFP Biennial Management Plan (2010-2011)*. Rome: WFP.

WFP (2010b) *Update on WFP Food Procurement*. WFP/EB.A/2010/13-C, 29 April 2010. Rome: WFP.

WFP Governance Group (2005). *Final Report on the Governance Project*. WFP/EB.2/2005/4-C/Rev.1, 9 November 2005. Rome: WFP.

Whiteford, S. and A. E. Ferguson (1991). "Social Dimensions of Food Security and Hunger: An Overview." in *Harvest of Want: Hunger and Food Security in Central America and Mexico*. S. Whiteford and A. E. Ferguson (eds). Boulder, Co; San Francisco; Oxford: Westview Press: 1-21.

Wise, T. A. (2005). *Identifying the Real Winners from U.S. Agricultural Policies*. Working Paper No. 05-07, December 2005. Medford, Mass: Global Development and Environment Institute, Tufts University.

Woods, N. (2006). *The Globalizers: The IMF, the World Bank, and their Borrowers*. Ithaca, NY: Cornell University Press.

Woolley, J. and G. Peters (nd). *Annual Message to Congress, 6 January 1941, Franklin D Roosevelt*. Santa Barbara, Ca, The American Presidency Project [online]. University of California (hosted), Gerhard Peters (database). http://www.presidency.ucsb.edu/ws/?pid=16092 accessed 12 July 2007.

World Summit on Food Security (2009). *Declaration of the World Summit on Food Security*. Rome: World Summit on Food Security.

Xinhua General News Service (2006). "Zambia elected to WFP executive board." Wire service report, 1 December 2006: Xinhua News Agency. http://web.lexis-nexis.com.ezproxy.lib.unimelb.edu.au/universe/document?_m=e13d36b2846faeedf8606a8b44ca104f&_docnum=26&wchp=dGLbVzW-zSkVb&_md5=6c6ea2ec46dd406b3dcadf67065a638c accessed 14 January 2007.

Zafar, A. (2007). "The Growing Relationship between China and sub-Saharan Africa: macroeconomic, trade, investment, and aid links." *World Bank research observer* **22**(1): 103-130.

Zeigler, Margaret (2005). Deputy Director, Congressional Hunger Center. Interview, Washington DC, 18 May 2005.

Zieger, R. H. (1976). "Herbert Hoover: A Reinterpretation." *American Historical Review* **81**(4): 800-810.

Ziegler, J. (2005). *Empire of Shame*, Paris: Editions Faya

Index

About the Book

How has the World Food Programme come to be so well-regarded—even in the US—despite being part of the much-maligned UN system? What are the political and institutional conditions that have enabled it to accrue legitimacy as an international organization? And how much substance lies behind the perceptions of its effectiveness?

Finding the answers to these questions in his analysis of the institutional politics of the WFP, Sandy Ross illustrates important larger issues about international institutions and global governance. He also shows that the very terms of its success limit the WFP's capacity to change the systemic problems that generate large-scale global hunger.

Sandy Ross is research fellow in the School of Social and Political Sciences, University of Melbourne.